AF600707

Egil, the Viking Poet

NEW APPROACHES TO *EGIL'S SAGA*

Egil, the Viking Poet

NEW APPROACHES TO *EGIL'S SAGA*

Edited by Laurence de Looze, Jón Karl Helgason, Russell Poole, and Torfi H. Tulinius

UNIVERSITY OF TORONTO PRESS
Toronto Buffalo London

© University of Toronto Press 2015
Toronto Buffalo London
www.utppublishing.com

ISBN 978-1-4426-4969-9

Library and Archives Canada Cataloguing in Publication

Egil, the viking poet : new approaches to Egil's saga / edited by Laurence De Looze, Jón Karl Helgason, Russell Poole, Torfi Tulinius.

(Toronto Old Norse and Icelandic Series ; 9)
Includes bibliographical references and index.
ISBN 978-1-4426-4969-9 (bound)

1. Snorri Sturluson, 1179?–1241. – Egils saga. 2. Sagas – History and criticism. I. Poole, Russell Gilbert, editor II. De Looze, Laurence, author, editor III. Jón Karl Helgason, 1965–, author, editor IV. Torfi H. Tulinius, 1958–, author, editor

PT7269.E4E45 2015 839'.61 C2015-902372-6

University of Toronto Press gratefully acknowledges the financial assistance of the Centre for Medieval Studies, University of Toronto in the publication of this book.

University of Toronto Press gratefully acknowledges the financial assistance of the Centre for Research in the Humanities, University of Iceland in the publication of this book.

University of Toronto Press acknowledges the financial assistance to its publishing program of the Canada Council for the Arts and the Ontario Arts Council, an agency of the Government of Ontario.

Canada Council for the Arts Conseil des Arts du Canada

Funded by the Government of Canada Financé par le gouvernement du Canada

Contents

Reception

Egil, the Viking Poet

1 Introduction Egil, the Viking Poet: New Approaches to *Egil's Saga*

RUSSELL POOLE

What was there not to be seen and conquered? Where would he go? Where would he not go? For the spirit of Odin the Goer, the spirit which has sent his children round the world, was strong within him.

(Kingsley 1891, 31)

One of the children that Charles Kingsley's Odin the Goer propels into the wide world could be Egil, the hero of our saga. His first experience of travel comes when his father excludes him from a family visit to his grandfather. Not deterred, the truculent three-year-old finds his own way. The saga narrative explains how the little boy, scarcely of a height to see over scrub and hillocks, can track the main party:

> So Skallagrim mounted his horse and rode away, leaving Egil behind disgruntled. Egil went out of the farmyard and found one of Skallagrim's pack-horses, mounted it and rode after them. He had trouble negotiating the marshland because he was unfamiliar with the way, but he could often see where Skallagrim and the others were riding when the view was not obscured by knolls or trees. His journey ended late in the evening when he arrived at Alftaness. Everyone was sitting around drinking when he entered the room. (55)[1]

> [Steig þá Skalla-Grímr á hest sinn ok reið í brott, en Egill unði illa við sinn hlut. Hann gekk ór garði ok hitti eykhest einn, er Skalla-Grímr átti, fór á bak ok reið eptir þeim Skalla-Grími; honum varð ógreiðfœrt um mýrarnar, því at hann kunni enga leið, en hann sá þó mjǫk opt reið þeira Skalla-Gríms, þá er eigi bar fyrir holt eða skóga. Er þat at segja frá hans ferð, at síð um kveldit kom hann á Álptanes, þá er menn sátu þar at drykkju; gekk hann inn í stofu. (81)]

At the house of his kindly maternal grandfather, he recites a little poem in an intricate skaldic verse-form, receives a whimsical reward, and follows it up with a second poem. In a schema where the child is father of the man, the episode aptly foreshadows the adult Egil's bravura as a poet – and a socially and geographically mobile poet at that.

Egil's potential as a Viking is also recognized in his youth:

My mother said
I would be bought
a boat with fine oars,
set off with Vikings,
stand up in the prow,
command the precious craft,
then enter port,
kill a man and another. (68)

[Þat mælti mín móðir,
at mér skyldi kaupa
fley ok fagrar árar,
fara á brott með víkingum,
standa upp í stafni,
stýra dýrum knerri,
halda svá til hafnar,
hǫggva mann ok annan.] (100–1)

Once again, the child is the father of the man, and the man will be a doughty warrior. Given that Egil kills two older males by age twelve, it is clear that childhood was constructed differently in those days.

Hence the first half of the title of this volume: "Egil, The Viking Poet." Although we will mostly be discussing the Egil of the saga, the same descriptor would probably hold true of the historical Egil, as best we can infer from the extant poems most likely to be by him. The hero of the saga seeks adventure and treasure in true Viking style, ranging across Norway, Denmark, and England, and is richly rewarded. His raid on Lund is a classic example of Viking strategy, as described in chronicles written by victims of the Vikings, in later medieval sagas, and in modern media: a target of predation (in this case a market town) is identified and its assets are efficiently appropriated. All this occurs without repercussions for the Viking. But Egil's life contains fewer triumphs and more tribulations than that of the stereotypical Viking. Consider in this regard his quest for a wife. Evidently he has harboured feelings for Asgerd, the foster-child who grew up alongside him in the family home at Borg. These feelings are sternly repressed, although we note that he cannot bear to see his elder brother Thorolf sail away from Iceland with Asgerd and pleads sickness to avoid attending their wedding feast in Norway. But then Thorolf falls in battle in England. Egil returns to Norway with alacrity – though not without first collecting due rewards and compensation from King Athelstan – and marries the young widow. While the marriage proves good and prosperous, a problem remains: Egil expected an inheritance to accompany it, and that is precluded by the hostility of the Norwegian king, Eirik Blood-axe. Conflict escalates between king and Icelander, as Egil seeks reinstatement of what he sees as his legal rights, culminating in his murder of the king's son. Subsequently, on a stormy voyage from Iceland to England, Egil is shipwrecked in the Humber estuary. This highly inopportune landfall puts him fair and square at the mercy of Eirik, who, having fled Norway, now sits as a newly minted king in Northumbria. But Egil disdains escape and disguise, instead seeking out and facing up to the aggrieved king:

> I have travelled on the sea-god's steed
> a long and turbulent wave-path
> to visit the one who sits
> in command of the English land.
> In great boldness, the shaker
> of the wound-flaming sword
> has met the mainstay
> of King Harald's line. (114–15)

> [Kominn emk á jó Ívu
> angrbeittan veg langan
> ǫldu enskrar foldar
> atsitjanda at vitja;
> nú hefr sískelfir sjalfan
> snarþátt Haralds áttar
> við ofrhuga yfrinn
> undar bliks of fundinn.] (180)

The show of bravado in this verse notwithstanding, Egil's head is in jeopardy. He cannot salvage the situation through his own "might and main." Fortunately, he has a true friend in Arinbjorn, a Norwegian magnate, who in turn is a trusted friend of the king. Risking Eirik's displeasure, Arinbjorn arranges for Egil to honour the king with a poetic eulogy. The resulting poem, an inventive and virtuosic effusion known to us as *Hǫfuðlausn* ("Head-ransom"), celebrates the king's martial triumphs, throws in a few of his more peaceable activities, and ignores his penchant for fratricide. Looked at closely, it is admittedly somewhat vague on details and perhaps more fulsome than sincere. Nonetheless, the king grudgingly grants its author clemency. The whole fraught episode is commemorated by our hero some years later in *Arinbjarnarkviða* ("Poem for Arinbjorn"). Characteristically, while lavishing due praise on his friend, he reserves his greatest inventiveness for the description of his own unregenerately ugly head.[2]

We might fancy that by now Egil would be weary of heroic journeys and royal vendettas and grateful to sink into settler existence in Iceland. Instead we find him once again on his travels in Norway, protecting the interests of Arinbjorn's nephew Thorstein. That brings him into antagonism with Eirik's successor, King Hakon the Good, whose men lure him into a trap:

> On their way to Eid, it snowed so much one night that it was impossible to make out where the trails were. The next day they made slow progress, because they kept sinking into the snowdrifts whenever they left the trail. In the course of the day they paused to rest their horses near a wooded ridge. "The trail forks here," they told Egil. "The farmer who lives beneath the ridge is named Arnald and he's a friend of ours. We will go and stay with him, and you should go up on the ridge. When you get there you'll soon see a big farm where you are sure of a place to stay. A very wealthy man called Armod Beard lives there. We will meet up again early tomorrow morning and go to Eideskog in the evening. A farmer lives there, a good man called Thorfinn." Then they parted. Egil and his men went up on the ridge. As for the king's men, as soon as they were out of Egil's sight, they put on skis they had brought with them, then went back as fast as they could. … Egil and his companions crossed the ridge that evening and lost their way at once in the heavy snows. Their horses repeatedly sank down into the drifts and had to be pulled out. There were rocky slopes and brushwood which were difficult to negotiate. The horses caused them a long delay, and it was extremely hard going on foot too. Exhausted, they made their way down from the ridge at last, saw a big farm and headed for it. … They spoke at length about their tough journey that night, and the people who lived there were astonished that they had made it at all, saying that the ridge could not be crossed even when it was free of snow. (153–4)

> [Ok er þeir sóttu austr til Eiða, þá var þat á einni nótt, at fell snjór mikill, svá at ógǫrla sá vegana; fórsk þeim þá seint um daginn eptir, því at kafhlaup váru, þegar af fór veginum. Ok er á leið daginn, dvǫlðusk þeir ok áðu hestum sínum; þar var nær skógarháls einn. Þá mæltu þeir við Egil: "Nú skiljask hér vegar, en hér fram undan hálsinum býr bóndi sá, er heitir Arnaldr, vinr várr; munu vér fǫrunautar fara

> þangat til gistingar, en þér skuluð fara hér upp á hálsinn, ok þá er þér komið þar, mun brátt verða fyrir yðr bœr mikill, ok er yðr þar vís gisting; þar býr stórauðugr maðr, er heitir Ármóðr skegg. En á morgin árdegis skulu vér hittask ok fara annat kveld til Eiðaskógs, þar býr góðr bóndi, er Þorfinnr heitir." Síðan skiljask þeir; fara þeir Egill upp á hálsinn, en frá konungsmǫnnum er þat at segja, at þegar er sýn fal í milli þeira Egils, þá tóku þeir skíð sín, er þeir hǫfðu haft, ok stigu þar á. ... Egill ok fǫrunautar hans fóru um kveldit yfir hálsinn; var þat þar skjótast af at segja, at þeir fóru þegar af veginum; var snjórinn mikill; lágu hestarnir á kafi annat skeið, svá at draga varð upp. Þar váru kleifar ok kjarrskógar nǫkkurir, en um kjǫrrin ok kleifarnar var alltorsótt; var þeim þá seinkan mikil at hestunum, en mannfœrðin var in þyngsta. Mœddusk þeir þá mjǫk, en þó komusk þeir af hálsinum ok sá þá fyrir sér bœ mikinn ok sóttu þangat til. Þeir rœddu mart um, hversu erfilliga þeir hǫfðu farit um kveldit, en heimamǫnnum þótti mikit undr, er þeir hǫfðu fram komisk, ok sǫgðu, at þar væri engum manni fœrt, þó at snjólaust væri. (222–4)]

Here is one occasion where Egil fails to smoke out his enemies. He and his party have been led into a truly tight spot. The only conceivable outcome is death – or so the king's men believe. But with true Viking resourcefulness Egil's party finds the way and triumphs over all adversities: topographical, climatic, and social. Nor does he desist from this final expedition into foreign lands until he has gained the tribute he was seeking. "Wean ahsode," it is said of Hygelac in the old English epic *Beowulf* (line 1206b) – "he asked for trouble" – and in this respect, as also in his large dimensions and insatiable rapacity, Egil could give his Geatish counterpart a fair run for his money.

But back to Iceland he eventually comes, and there life rapidly proceeds downhill for him. Grieving at the death of two of his sons, Egil is encouraged by his daughter to find solace in composing a lament. The resulting poem, *Sonatorrek* ("Hard Loss of Sons"), indeed finds its difficult way from raw grief to defiant consolation. The aged poet has not forsaken his Viking values: motifs of theft and plunder are prominent in the imagery. When poetry itself is referred to via the kenning "Odin's theft" ("Viðurs þýfi"), at play is no mere rhymester's formula but a linking of Egil's poetic efforts with the god Odin's theft of the "mead of poetry." In the myth, as recounted by Snorri Sturluson in the *Edda*, Odin made his tortuous way into the mountain fastness of the giants to purloin this commodity, from which stems all subsequent poetry. Correspondingly Egil retrieves poetry from the "hiding-place of thought" ("ór fylgsni hugar"), meaning the breast, where it is being hoarded by the giants of sorrow and despair. All the powers of this stolen commodity are needed to assuage the pain inflicted by Rán ("Theft"), goddess of the sea, when she robbed Egil of one of his sons.

If the period of Egil's old age proves disappointing and disillusioning to him, it is in part demography that is the enemy. By this time Iceland has largely ceased to be a Viking society, except insofar as it continues to contribute men to the retinues of kings on the Scandinavian mainland. Egil's surviving son Thorstein is one of those to embrace the now dominant settler values. In this he resembles Egil's father Skallagrim, but he has nothing of Skallagrim's brutal effectiveness. Old age and decrepitude have not cost Egil his tenacity and he summons up all his old legal wizardry to protect Thorstein's interests when Thorstein himself proves incapable. Altruism, however, never goes very far with Egil: he keeps his own two great chests of treasure in a jealous grasp that could be compared, if unflatteringly, to that of the dragon in *Beowulf* or the undead father-figure in several Sagas of Icelanders. Although greatly enfeebled and virtually blind, he manages to hide his English bullion in a location that defied detection then and continues to do so today:

> One evening when everyone was going to bed at Mosfell, Egil called in two of Grim's slaves. He told them to fetch him a horse, "because I want to go to bathe in the pool." When he was ready he went out, taking his chests of silver with him. He mounted the horse, crossed the hayfields to the slope that begins there and disappeared. In the morning, when all the people got up, they saw Egil wandering around on the hill east of the farm, leading the horse behind him. They went over to him and brought him home. But neither the slaves nor the chests of treasure ever returned, and there are many theories about where Egil hid his treasure. East of the farm is a gully leading down from the mountain. It has been noticed that English coins have been found in the gully when the river recedes after floods caused by sudden thaws. Some people believe Egil must have hidden his treasure there. Then there are large and exceptionally deep marshes below the hayfields at Mosfell, and it is claimed that Egil threw his treasure into them. On the south side of the river are hot springs with big pits nearby, where some people believe Egil must have hidden his treasure, because a will-o'-the-wisp is often seen there. Egil himself said he had killed Grim's slaves and hidden his treasure somewhere, but he never told a single person where it was. (203)

> [Þat var eitt kveld, þá er menn bjuggusk til rekkna at Mosfelli, at Egill kallaði til sín þræla tvá, er Grímr átti; hann bað þá taka sér hest – "vil ek fara til laugar." Ok er Egill var búinn, gekk hann út ok hafði með sér silfrkistur sínar; hann steig á hest, fór síðan ofan eptir túninu fyrir brekku þá, er þar verðr, er menn sá síðast. En um morguninn, er menn risu upp, þá sá þeir, at Egill hvarflaði á holtinu fyrir austan garð ok leiddi eptir sér hestinn; fara þeir þá til hans ok fluttu hann heim. En hvárki kom aptr síðan þrælarnir né kisturnar, ok eru þar margar gátur á, hvar Egill

> hafi fólgit fé sitt. Fyrir austan garð at Mosfelli gengr gil ofan ór fjalli; en þat hefir orðit þar til merkja, at í bráðaþeyjum er þar vatnfall mikit, en eptir þat er vǫtnin hafa fram fallit, hafa fundisk í gilinu enskir penningar; geta sumir menn þess, at Egill muni þar fét hafa fólgit. Fyrir neðan tún at Mosfelli eru fen stór ok furðuliga djúp; hafa þat margir fyrir satt, at Egill muni þar hafa kastat í fé sínu. Fyrir sunnan ána eru laugar ok þar skammt frá jarðholur stórar, ok geta þess sumir, at Egill mundi þar hafa fólgit fé sitt, því at þangat er optliga sénn haugaeldr. Egill sagði, at hann hefði drepit þræla Gríms, ok svá þat, at hann hafði fé sitt fólgit, en þat sagði hann engum manni, hvar hann hefði fólgit. (297–8)]

Taking these logistic and verbal feats together, we may fairly speak of Egil's "Odinic" character. He takes after the great god as a poet, a warrior, and a finder of ways. Complementarily, he resembles the not-so-great god Loki in his native cunning and a tendency to mischief that can be as defeating to self as it is destructive to others. Beyond the Norse pantheon, he merits comparison with those gods and heroes of the classical world, including Zeus himself, who display *mētis* – a Greek concept that encompasses intelligence, wisdom, forethought, subtlety, cunning, flair, deceptiveness, resourcefulness, vigilance, and opportunism.[3]

Egil is not our only Viking adventurer: the saga presents an array of seekers and finders that spans two generations. Kveldulf's elder son, Thorolf, is an accomplished expeditionary in his own right. He seeks a place in the following of King Harald Fair-hair, mulcting tribute on the king's behalf from far-flung tribes. Sadly, his ambition proves to be his undoing. Jealous of Thorolf's success, the king listens to the slander of his detractors, and Thorolf is forced into rebellion, revealing almost Odinic capacities of concealment and surprise:

> When the wind was favourable, Thorolf sailed the ship south, hugging the shore, then when he reached Byrda they headed out to sea beyond all the islands, sometimes so far that they could only see the top half of the mountains. They continued south and did not hear any news of anybody until they arrived in Vik. There they were told that the king was in Vik and would be going to Oppland in the summer. No one on land knew of Thorolf's whereabouts. With a favourable wind in his sails, he headed for Denmark, and from there into the Baltic. … In the autumn he headed back to Denmark, around the time that the big Norwegian fleet pulled out from Oyr, after being stationed there as usual during the summer. Thorolf let them all sail past without being noticed, then sailed to Mostrarsund one evening. A large knorr had called there on its way from Oyr, skippered by Thorir Thruma, one of King Harald's agents. He was in charge of the king's land at Thruma, a large estate where the king spent much time when he was in Vik. Since a lot of provisions

were needed for that estate, Thorir had gone to Oyrar to buy cargo, malt and flour and honey, and spent a great amount of the king's money on it. Thorolf and his men attacked the ship and gave Thorir's crew the option of defending it, but, lacking the manpower to keep such a large force at bay, Thorir surrendered. (31)

[En er byr gaf, helt Þórólfr skipinu suðr með landi, ok þegar er hann kom suðr um Byrðu, þá heldu þeir útleið fyrir útan eyjar allar, en stundum svá, at sjór var í miðjum hlíðum, létu svá ganga suðr fyrir landit, hǫfðu ekki tíðendi af mǫnnum, fyrr en þeir kómu austr í Vík; þá spurðu þeir, at Haraldr konungr var í Víkinni ok hann ætlaði um sumarit at fara til Upplanda. Ekki vissu landsmenn til um ferð Þórólfs; honum byrjaði vel, ok helt hann suðr til Danmerkr ok þaðan í Austrveg. … Um haustit helt hann til Danmerkr í þann tíma, er leystisk Eyrarfloti; þar hafði verit um sumarit, sem vant var, fjǫlði skipa af Nóregi. Þórólfr lét þat lið sigla allt fyrir ok gerði ekki vart við sik; hann sigldi einn dag at kveldi til Mostrarsunds; þar var fyrir í hǫfninni knǫrr einn mikill, kominn af Eyri. Þórir þruma hét maðr sá, er stýrði; hann var ármaðr Haralds konungs; hann réð fyrir búi hans í Þrumu; þat var mikit bú, sat konungr þar lǫngum, þá er hann var í Víkinni; þurfti þar stór fǫng til bús þess. Hafði Þórir farit fyrir þá sǫk til Eyrar at kaupa þar þunga, malt ok hveiti ok hunang, ok varit þar til fé miklu, er konungr átti. Þeir lǫgðu at knerrinum ok buðu þeim Þóri kost á at verjask, en fyrir því at þeir Þórir hǫfðu engan liðskost til varnar móti fjǫlmenni því, er Þórólfr hafði, gáfusk þeir upp. (46–7)]

The Viking skill of identifying a suitably remunerative (and provocative) target and hitting it in a focused and effective fashion is clearly something Thorolf possesses. Unfortunately, his skills do not run to smoking out his enemies and checking slanderers. Convinced that Thorolf seeks not just a place but the king's own place, Harald orders his death. Meanwhile the king's mission to subjugate the petty kingdoms of Norway has left many magnates feeling aggrieved and threatened. They abandon Norway,[4] Kveldulf and his family among them, and seek new land in Iceland. Kveldulf dies during the voyage, but that does not prevent him posthumously making landfall,[5] tacitly confirming that his son's slightly different landfall is propitious:

"I have not been prone to illness," he said, "but if it happens, as I think it probably will, that I die, make a coffin for me and put me overboard. Things will not turn out as I imagined, if I do not reach Iceland and settle there. Give my greetings to my son Grim, when you see him, and tell him too that if he reaches Iceland and, unlikely as it seems, I am there already, to make himself a home as close as possible to the place I have come ashore." Shortly afterwards Kveldulf died. The crew did as he had told them, put him in a coffin and cast it overboard. … Grim the Halogalander's crew sailed along Borgarfjord beyond the skerries, then cast anchor until the storm died down and the weather brightened up. Then they waited for the tide to come in, and floated their ship into the estuary of the river called Gufua (Steam river). After pulling the ship as far upstream as they could, they unloaded their cargo and spent their first winter there. They explored the land along the coast, both up the mountains and towards the sea, and after travelling a short distance they found a bay where Kveldulf's coffin had been washed ashore. They carried the coffin out to the headland, laid it down and piled rocks over it. Skallagrim reached land where a huge peninsula juts out into the sea, with a narrow spit below it. He and his men unloaded their cargo there and called the site Knarrarnes (Knorr ness). Then Skallagrim explored the land, which stretched a long way from the shore to the mountains and had a great marshland and wide woods, and plenty of seals to hunt and good fishing. When he and his men explored the shore to the south they came to a great fjord, and they skirted it without stopping until they found their companions, Grim the Halogalander and his companions. It was a joyful reunion. They told Skallagrim about his father's death and that Kveldulf's body had come ashore and they had buried it, then accompanied him to the place, which Skallagrim felt was not far from a good site to build a farm. (49)

["Hefi ek," sagði hann, "ekki kvellisjúkr verit, en ef svá ferr, sem mér þykkir nú líkligast, at ek ǫndumk, þá gerið mér kistu ok látið mik fara fyrir borð, ok verðr þetta annan veg en ek hugða, at vera myndi, ef ek skal eigi koma til Íslands ok nema þar land. Þér skuluð bera kveðju mína Grími syni mínum, þá er þér finnizk, ok segið honum þat með, ef svá verðr, at hann kemr til Íslands, ok beri svá at, þótt þat muni ólíkligt þykkja, at ek sjá þar fyrir, þá taki hann sér þar bústað sem næst því, er ek hefi at landi komit." Litlu síðar andaðisk Kveld-Úlfr; gerðu skipverjar hans svá sem hann hafði fyrir mælt, at þeir lǫgðu hann í kistu ok skutu síðan fyrir borð. … Sigldu þeir inn eptir Borgarfirði, til þess er þraut sker ǫll; kǫstuðu þá akkerum, til þess er veðr lægði ok ljóst gerði; þá biðu þeir flœðar; síðan fluttu þeir skipit upp í árós nokkurn; sú er kǫlluð Gufuá. Leiddu þar skipit upp eptir ánni, svá sem gekk; báru síðan farm af skipinu ok bjuggusk þar um inn fyrsta vetr. Þeir kǫnnuðu landit með sæ, bæði upp ok út; en er þeir hǫfðu skammt farit, þá fundu þeir í vík einni, hvar upp var rekin kista Kveld-Úlfs; fluttu þeir kistuna á nes þat, er þar varð, settu hana þar niðr ok hlóðu at grjóti. Skalla-Grímr kom þar at landi, er nes mikit gekk í sæ út, ok eið mjótt fyrir ofan nesit, ok báru þar farm af; þat kǫlluðu þeir Knarrarnes. Síðan kannaði Skalla-Grímr landit, ok var þar mýrlendi mikit ok skógar víðir, langt í milli fjalls ok fjǫru, selveiðar nógar ok fiskifang mikit. En er þeir kǫnnuðu landit suðr með sjónum, ok varð þar fyrir þeim fjǫrðr mikill, en er þeir fóru inn með firði þeim, þá léttu þeir eigi fyrr ferðinni en þeir fundu fǫrunauta sína, Grím hinn háleyska ok þá fǫrunauta; varð þar fagnafundr. Sǫgðu þeir Skalla-Grími, at Kveld-Úlfr var þar til lands kominn ok þeir hǫfðu hann jarðat; síðan fylgðu þeir Skalla-Grími þar til, ok sýndisk honum svá, sem þaðan myndi skammt á brott, þar er bólstaðargerð góð myndi vera. (71–3)]

With such an auspicious entry to *terra nova*, Skallagrim never has reason to return to his native land. As we have seen, he is an early adopter of settler values, using his wide range of practical skills tirelessly and fruitfully on his estate.

In the next generation a second Thorolf, nephew of the first and Skallagrim's elder son, reverses the trend by leaving the estate to seek opportunities back in Norway. Ignoring the cautionary example of his senior namesake, he seeks a place among the following of Eirik Blood-axe, the son of King Harald, and joins him on an expedition. In contrast to the rest of his family, however, he is left none the worse for wear by his contact with Norwegian royalty. His adventurous spirit leads him onward to Denmark, Friesland, and England, where (as we have seen) he meets his end supporting the cause of King Athelstan.

Initiative, inventiveness, resourcefulness, tenacity, audacity, and temerity: these qualities loom large in the saga and, putting them together, we can propose one type of meaning produced by the text. Imagine the saga as heard or read by its Icelandic audience down through the ages and the messages they might have inferred from it. What gave their forebears the capacity to make landfall in the new land and later generations the capacity to survive and prosper in a daunting physical environment? In such a context the Icelandic voyage of Kveldulf and Skallagrim has archetypal significance. We can consider it from two perspectives, first from outside the culture and second from within.

Viewed from the generalizing perspective of population geography, their voyage follows a typical Viking pattern of a large, abrupt, and audacious move, often across a sea barrier of some kind, followed by a series of shorter consolidatory moves within the new territory. The Vikings were of course powerfully helped in making the great leaps by their marine technology, centring on advances in keel, mast, and sail, and the short hops by their equestrian proficiency. First Skallagrim makes his grand journey across the dangerous ocean and gains landfall in the new territory; then he allows himself to be guided a short distance to a propitious location by Grim the Halogalander, who is acting by proxy for the deceased Kveldulf; finally, he makes an additional short move on his own initiative to reach what he sees as the most desirable location for an estate. A comparable pattern is seen in the advent of the great Viking army to England in the 860s. Having suddenly made a large and audacious leap into English territory from overseas, the expeditionary force then takes a series of shorter skips and hops, from East Anglia across the Humber to York in Northumbria in one year, from York to Nottingham in Mercia the next, and from Nottingham back to Thetford in East Anglia in the third year. Such is the account in the *Anglo-Saxon Chronicle*. Alcuin, reacting to an earlier Viking incursion in 793, records how unexpected it was that such an inroad could be made from the sea.[6]

Mathematically speaking, a pattern consisting of long leaps (technically termed "saltations") to a new area, followed by short hops within it, conforms to a model termed "Lévy flight." Lévy flights are the optimum way of foraging for food in the natural world, reducing the probability of an energy-wasting return to places that have already been depleted of resources. Many animals have evolved so as to favour this pattern.[7] If you have observed the behaviour of rabbits in your yard, as they leap in from a neighbour's lot or an adjoining park and then make a series of short hops, consuming your flowers and shrubs as they go, you will recognize it. The executors of Lévy flight typically have a degree of "free will" in their choice of movements, even while they are subject to physical and biological constraints on their behaviour.[8] In the case of the Vikings, when we seek to locate the agency of this "free will" we are helped by Colin Renfrew's model of "élite dominance," where the word "élite" implies small groups of immigrants based on kindreds and other social networks.[9] The model posits that each such group looked to certain key personages for counsel and resources. These need not have been long-established dynastic leaders of high status such as kings and earls. Indeed, a good deal of the literary evidence, including *Egil's Saga*, points away from them and in the direction of more localized land-holders, such as Skallagrim and Grim the Halogalander. Men (and sometimes women) of this kind represented nodal points in a social network centred on islands offshore from Norway or on stretches of coastline on the Norwegian mainland.[10]

The merit of mathematical and sociological models like the ones briefly outlined above lies in graphing broad patterns of movement from the perspective of a scientific observer standing outside the culture. What needs to be added is some appreciation of how these Lévy flights were perceived within the culture and how the leadership was situated ideologically in making them. The belief systems and ideologies that enabled the flights emerge saliently from *Egil's Saga*. In part it is a matter of belief in one's own "might and main," as seen in the tirelessness of Skallagrim and the at times almost animal ferocity of Egil. But equally if not even more formative, as we would expect from all we have heard about him so far, is a belief in empowerment lent by Odin, the finder of the way to the poetic mead. This is an ideology that can be richly paralleled in other texts, noteworthy among them the genealogical poem *Háleygjatal* ("List of the Men of Halogaland"). Composed in the tenth century by the Norwegian magnate Eyvindr skáldaspillir ("plunderer of the poets"), *Háleygjatal* presents Odin as a "travel-strengthener" ("farmǫgnuðr").[11] The second element in this telling compound is cognate with an Old Norse word *megin*, signifying "(supernatural) power, strength." Travel that is thus empowered is naturally of a bold saltatory kind, not a mere incremental creep: Odin is conceived of as an expansionist deity, who takes his people on long journeys or migrations. According to the Prologue to Snorri's *Edda* he leads his people from Asia to the far North to found Scandinavia. In *The Saga of the Volsungs* (*Vǫlsunga saga*) he gives similar guidance to a man named Sigi, who is said to be his son. In a primal scene reminiscent of the Cain and Abel story, Sigi culpably murders a slave and is declared "a wolf in the sacred places" ("vargr í véum"). Odin ensures his survival by conducting him safely "for such a long way that it was extraordinary" ("svá langa leið at stóru bar").[12] Thanks to Odin's guidance, Sigi achieves victory in his raids, makes a prosperous marriage, becomes king of the land of the Huns, and founds a dynasty. Like the story of Kveldulf and Skallagrim's landfall, these two stories represent a mythic rendering of the saltatory type of travel or migration practised by the Vikings. *The Book of Settlements* (*Landnámabók*), *The Saga of the People of Eyri* (*Eyrbyggja saga*), and some other texts offer further analogues, though there guidance is ascribed to the god Thor.[13]

In sum, Egil, as a pre-eminent finder of ways, holds true to the special Odinic skill of his kindred from his earliest youth until his final senescence. Along with his kinsfolk, he embodies the myths that enabled the founding and perpetuation of viable human livelihoods in the *terra nova* of Iceland,[14] as well as the continuance of access to the mother-land and the lands of the Viking diaspora. Although this element in *Egil's Saga* is largely subliminal for a modern reader, and may already have been so for its contemporary audience, it is precisely at the subliminal level that the ideological content of myth has its profoundest effect. Similar content regarding the finding of ways occurs in other Sagas of Icelanders, notably the sagas of Grettir and of Hrafnkel, where the theme is handled more explicitly, demonstrating that confidence and an assured skill in negotiating hazardous terrain at home and in hostile territory abroad were the traits that distinguished the most celebrated Icelanders.

At the same time, the above discussion of *Egil's Saga* exemplifies just one possible avenue to interpretation among numerous others that can be taken.

Represented in this collective volume is a wide range of further possible lines of enquiry, hence the second half of its title, "New Approaches to *Egil's Saga*." The first two essays focus upon aspects of composition. Taking a formalistic approach, Torfi H. Tulinius looks into the structure of the saga, in a quest for significant moments accented by significant naming. He points in particular to the role of the recurrent name Ketil in subtly demarcating episodes and phases of the narration. In his analysis, features of this kind are not purely prosopographical or genealogical accretions but also have a literary function. On them Tulinius bases his thesis that the design of the saga, rather than collapsing as the narrative proceeds, possesses some of the elegance, tightness, and aesthetic cohesion exhibited by skaldic poetry, not least the verses ascribed to Egil himself. Guðrún Nordal starts her essay with the observation that the saga contains a veritable treasury of such verses, quoted in the course of the narration. Even if we allow for the likelihood that some major poems were not quoted in full in the earliest state of the saga, it is apparent that the writing of *Egil's Saga* reflects a cultural milieu that greatly prized skaldic verse, in particular poetry attached to Egil's name, probably held much of it in memory, and stood possessed of a kind of skaldic literacy. The stanzas, Nordal shows, far from being mere citations, enrich the total composition, investing it with an aesthetic generated by special features of metre, alliteration, and rhyme.

The second group of essays engages with aspects of identity. Using recent literary theory, notably that of Paul Ricoeur, Laurence de Looze analyses the sense of the protagonist's self projected by the saga narrative. He notes that the enigmatic, ambiguous self that we call Egil eludes any broad schema of characterization in the Sagas of Icelanders and shows that the saga's construction of Egil's self rests upon a tension between predictability and surprise. Egil is both "himself" and "not himself," in a culture which regards deviation from a set of long-established personality traits as deeply threatening. As a specific manifestation of the construction of the protagonist's self, the striking penchant for self-description in poetry connected with Egil's name is investigated by Margaret Clunies Ross. In particular, the descriptions of the protagonist's head and facial features, while arising naturally from the fact that he must ransom his head if he is not to undergo death at the hands of Eirik Blood-axe, are dilated into a kind of comic excess and extravagance. The effect is in part owed to the remarkable, self-confessed ugliness of those features, with their more than passing resemblance to those of the wolf. Clunies Ross goes on to argue for a relationship between these self-descriptions and the speaker's gift of poetic composition.

The third group of essays focuses on aspects of emotions and affiliations that manifest themselves in the saga. Focusing on the hero's youth, and adopting a psychological approach, Ármann Jakobsson looks into the dynamics of Skallagrim's dysfunctional family, showing how the father and his younger son are locked in conflict. As Jakobsson points out, the result is extreme violence on both sides, as the father brutally kills Egil's foster mother and the son, taking vengeance, just as brutally kills Skallagrim's favourite servant. Jakobsson identifies such traumatic events as formative for the developing Egil and suggests that this saga is one of several of the Sagas of Icelanders (notable among them the *Saga of Grettir*) to shine an intense light upon family relationships in almost a modern sense. Less explicitly, in the midst of this trauma, the saga throws up an instance of profoundly contrasting behaviour: the exemplary kindness shown to Egil by his older brother Thorolf. Focusing on the tribulations of the hero's old age, Alison Finlay notes the centrality of *Sonatorrek* to the narrative and demonstrates how knowledge of this poem on the part of the saga's author may have prompted the compilation of the anecdotes about Egil's final years that form such a distinctive conclusion to the saga. Her discussion shows that the stylization of the aging process and the predicament of a helpless old man that we find in *Egil's Saga* run deep in literary tradition, with analogues in *Beowulf*. The effect of her analysis is also to take us into the workshop that created the saga and to hint at the dynamism of the process. Focusing on the hero's middle years, Oren Falk takes his departure from a remarkable absence: the fact that Egil, despite his penchant for including a personal element in his poetry, is nowhere credited with any poem commemorating his deceased wife. Falk enquires into possible systematic reasons why the composition of a poem on such a topic would scarcely have been thinkable within the prevailing social and cultural dynamic. In addition, he considers an aspect of the saga so fleetingly covered in the narration that it has largely eluded scholarly attention, namely the protagonist's role first as a lover and then as a widower. Finally in this group, and taking the hero's entire life-span into his analysis, Timothy R. Tangherlini investigates the labyrinth of *dramatis personae* in the saga, a notorious puzzle for any first-time reader. Until recently translators and adaptors often masked this element by relegating genealogical and other prosopographical information to footnotes. More constructively, with recourse to the rapidly developing methodology of Social Network Analysis, Tangherlini reveals the potential of such information to define and articulate the intricate social and causal relationships and affiliations of the saga personages. Using a series of graphs, complemented by prose exposition, he shows how these relationships can be assessed in terms of their status as an asset or a liability to the protagonist and other key personages.

The final group of essays engages with questions of reception. Svanhildur Óskarsdóttir explores the dynamism of oral and scribal transmission by analysing the various versions of the saga. Even in the Middle Ages significant deviations can be detected between the main realizations of the story materials, although the core narrative remains essentially the same. More spectacularly, however, Óskarsdóttir unearths a little-known but strikingly innovative early modern re-working, the so-called silly saga of Egil (*vitlausa Eigla*), and shows that while it may have appeared silly to some eminent nineteenth- and twentieth-century literary scholars, it nonetheless held appeal for at least some members of the seventeenth-century élite. A corollary of her argument is that modern literary taste where sagas in their various instantiations are concerned is possibly far removed from that of an audience contemporary with their production. Focusing on modern-day reception, Jón Karl Helgason enquires into a notorious yet seldom discussed feature of *Egil's Saga* – its ability to evoke disgust and revulsion on the part of the reader. In a series of scenes and episodes, actions involving gross bodily harm and other barbaric, even animalistic, behaviour inflicted by Egil on his opponents, and sometimes vice versa, are elaborately described. Common foodstuffs such as curds and ale are invested with powerfully aversive connotations. Helgason adduces Julia Kristeva, with her key concept of the "abject," alongside other twentieth-century thinkers, in an attempt to define the essence of these repugnant elements in the saga and gauge their effects. Finally, in their bibliographic essay, Katelin Parsons, Álfdís Þorleifsdóttir, and Jane Appleton reveal the riches of the scholarly and critical reception of *Egil's Saga* through the last one hundred years and more.

To assist the reader and to confer a certain unity upon the essays, the edition by Sigurður Nordal[15] and the translation by Bernard Scudder[16] have been used as the basis for references virtually throughout this volume; in each case only the page numbers are given in the in-line references. The personages of the saga are referred to by the names given them in Scudder's translation, thus "Egil" not "Egill" and "Asgerd" not "Ásgerðr." Place-names are likewise as in Scudder, thus "Borgarfjord" not "Borgarfjǫrðr." The saga itself is referred to as *Egil's Saga* not *Egils saga Skallagrímssonar*.

These unities of style and presentation do not extend to the content of our essays. Rather, we have encouraged productive dissent and searching critique. We have not, for instance, sought to establish a "party line" on the authenticity of the skaldic stanzas or on the conjecture that the great chieftain and poet Snorri Sturluson was the author of the saga.[17] Ultimately our hope in compiling this volume of essays is to contribute to the recognition of *Egil's Saga* as one of the great works of world literature, whoever may have composed it – a work that stands on its own and is *sui generis*, like the entire array of Sagas of Icelanders among which it is numbered.

NOTES

The editors gratefully acknowledge financial support towards publication from the Centre for Research in the Humanities of the University of Iceland, the Rosslyn Kelly Swanson Humanities Fund, Faculty of Arts and Humanities, The University of Western Ontario, and the Centre for Medieval Studies, University of Toronto. We are indebted to the Social Sciences and Humanities Research Council Canada, as also to our respective universities, for funding towards some of the research embodied in this volume. We also thank Alexandra Dawson, PhD student in Classical Studies at The University of Western Ontario, for her assistance with copy-editing.

1 Translations are taken, with occasional modifications, from Scudder 2005.
2 As will be seen in the essays by Guðrún Nordal, Margaret Clunies Ross, and Svanhildur Óskarsdóttir, the manuscripts of the saga do not uniformly include these two poems or *Sonatorrek*, to be mentioned shortly. It is possible that the oldest redactions of the saga did not include them. This is most likely because they were part of the communal *memoria* and therefore in no need of transcription, unlike the apparently carefully compiled prose narration of the saga and perhaps also some of the inset "loose verses" (*lausavísur*), which do not necessarily originate with Egil. The assumption therefore is that the audience of the saga knew these three poems and that they were, at the very least, an implicit part of the story of Egil.
3 Wanner 2009, 211–12, citing Detienne and Vernant 1978.
4 See Hines 1992, 17–20 for a fuller discussion of this process.
5 On Kveldulf's maintenance of leadership of the expedition after his death, see Wellendorf 2010, 10–11.
6 Alcuin, Letter to Ethelred, King of Northumbria, quoted in Loyn 1977, 55–6 from Dümmler 1895, 42 (no. 16).
7 For a discussion of the mathematical and biological aspects of this phenomenon see Viswanathan et al. 2002, 209.
8 Ibid.
9 Renfrew 1987, 131–3. See also the essay by Timothy R. Tangherlini in this volume.
10 Cf. Gaskins 2005 on the use of network logic to explain how in early Iceland social institutions could have evolved, without any explicit plan, from the common needs of immigrants.
11 Poole 2012, 197–8.
12 Text and translation are from Finch 1965, 1–2.
13 For a broader study of myths of settlement and colonisation, see the chapter of that name in Clunies Ross 1998.

14 For the term *terra nova*, see Schier 1975.
15 Nordal 1933.
16 Scudder 2005.
17 For a discussion of this conjecture, see Cormack 2001 and references there given.

BIBLIOGRAPHY

Clunies Ross, Margaret. 1998. *Prolonged Echoes. Old Norse Myths in Medieval Northern Society,* vol. 2: *The Reception of Norse Myths in Medieval Iceland.* Viking Collection: Studies in Northern Civilization 10. Odense: Odense University Press.

Cormack, Margaret. 2001. "*Egils Saga, Heimskringla,* and the Daughter of Eiríkr blóðøx." *Alvíssmál* 10: 61–8.

Detienne, Marcel, and Jean-Pierre Vernant. 1978. *Cunning Intelligence in Greek Culture and Society*, translated by Janet Lloyd. Hassocks, UK: Harvester Press. Translated from the original *Les ruses d'intelligence: La mètis des grecs* (Paris: Flammarion, 1974).

Dümmler, Ernst, ed. 1895. *Epistolae Karolini Aevi II.* MGH Epist. 4. Berlin: Weidmanns.

Finch, Rowland George, ed. and trans. 1965. *Vǫlsunga saga. The Saga of the Volsungs*. London: Nelson.

Gaskins, Richard. 2005. "Network Dynamics in Saga and Society." *Scandinavian Studies* 77: 201–16.

Hines, John. 1992. "Kingship in *Egils Saga.*" In *Introductory Essays on Egils Saga and Njáls Saga*, edited by John Hines and Desmond Slay, 15–32. London: Viking Society for Northern Research.

Kingsley, Charles. 1891. *Hereward, the Last of the English.* New York: Macmillan.

Loyn, Henry Royston. 1977. *The Vikings in Britain.* London: Batsford.

Nordal, Sigurður, ed. 1933. *Egils saga Skallagrímssonar*. Íslenzk fornrit 2. Reykjavík: Hið Íslenzka Fornritafélag.

Poole, Russell, ed. 2012. "Eyvindr skáldaspillir, *Háleygjatal*." In *Skaldic Poetry of the Scandinavian Middle Ages* I: *Poetry from the Kings' Sagas* 1: *From Mythical Times to c. 1035*, edited by Diana Whaley, 195–213. Brepols: Turnhout.

Renfrew, Colin. 1987. *Archaeology and Language: The Puzzle of Indo-European Origins.* New York: Cambridge University Press.

Schier, Kurt. 1975. "Iceland and the Rise of Literature in 'terra nova': Some Comparative Reflections." *Gripla* 1: 168–81.

Scudder, Bernard, trans. 2005. *Egil's Saga.* London: Penguin.

Viswanathan, G.M., F. Bartumeus, Sergey V. Buldyrev, J. Catalan, U.L. Fulco, Shlomo Havlin, M.G.E. da Luz, M.L. Lyra, E.P. Raposo, and H. Eugene Stanley.

2002. "Lévy Flight Random Searches in Biological Phenomena." *Physica* A 314: 208–13.

Wanner, Kevin. 2009. "Cunning Intelligence in Norse Myth: Loki, Óðinn, and the Limits of Sovereignty." *History of Religions* 48: 211–46.

Wellendorf, Jonas. 2010. "The Interplay of Pagan and Christian Traditions in Icelandic Settlement Myths." *Journal of English and Germanic Philology* 109: 1–21.

Composition

2 The Construction of *Egil's Saga*

TORFI H. TULINIUS

There is no doubt that whoever wrote *Egil's Saga* appreciated skaldic poetry and knew it well, whether or not he composed himself any of the poetry the saga attributes to the tenth century warrior and poet.[1] In this essay, I will discuss some aspects of the way the saga is constructed and consider whether its author had skaldic forms in mind when he shaped his narrative.[2] Expanding a chapter of my 2004 book in Icelandic on the saga, I will further show that the saga is consciously planned, especially its second and main part, the one devoted to the life of Egil.[3] Most critics have considered the saga's depiction of Egil's life to be a collection of sundry tales, more or less derived from oral tradition. A close reading of this part of the saga shows on the contrary that it is structured to give coherence to his story. Observations will be made on the ordering of the episodes, on the repetition of key elements at structurally important points in the narrative, as well as on the use of multiples of the number three. While some of these features need not be the result of conscious design, there is reason to believe that whoever composed the saga had a keen sense of form and shaped his narrative in order to highlight aspects of its meaning. Moreover, this part of the saga seems to be constructed in a similar way to a formal skaldic praise-poem (*drápa*), which suggests that the narrative is no less governed by formal considerations than the poetry it frames.[4]

The first part of *Egil's Saga* is set in Norway and is the political tragedy of Thorolf Kveldulfsson, which ends with his surviving family being forced to flee the country and settle in Iceland. The second is double the length and tells the life story of Egil. While the first part is fairly clearly demarcated in time, spanning several years in the life of Thorolf and entirely focused on the plot that culminates in his fall and the flight of his family, the second part spans over ninety years and seems somewhat disjointed. On first impression there appears to be little to link the disparate episodes that make up the story of

Egil's life, with most of the incidents described in the saga occurring outside Iceland during journeys he undertakes for a variety of reasons.

The apparent contrast between the two parts has led to disagreement among scholars about how well the saga is constructed. There is, however, a consensus that whoever compiled the tale of Thorolf Kveldulfsson (3–57: 3–38) knew how to construct a narrative.[5] No element is extraneous, each is carefully placed to create the maximum effect, and nowhere is there any slackening in the dramatic tension that climaxes with the hero's death. Conversely, it has been claimed that the second part of the saga lacks coherence and that its author fails to display the same command of his material. In the opinion of the eminent saga scholar Theodore M. Andersson, the section of the saga concerned with Egil suffers from the fact that the material is heterogeneous, the plot is stretched out over too long a time-span, and the geographical settings are too scattered, with the result that the narrative lacks a single focus, or climax, to give it form.[6]

Andersson was not the first scholar to come to this conclusion. At the beginning of the last century W.H. Vogt wrote a brief study on the structure of *Egil's Saga* in which he claimed that the two parts could not be by the same author. He maintained that they reflected two different stages in the development of Icelandic narrative. The first part must have been by an author who had learnt the art of storytelling from books, since he knew how to construct a two-stranded (*zweisträngig*) narrative, whereas the second was by an author who was still at the cultural stage characterized by the oral transmission of stories, being content to arrange his material in a simple, linear, one-stranded (*einsträngig*) narrative (Vogt 1909, 58). Vogt inferred from this that Thorolf's tale was probably the invention of an author capable of shaping his story according to artistic requirements, while the continuation of the story was dependent on oral tradition. Andersson agreed with Vogt to the extent that he thought the author who compiled the saga probably had at his disposal an excess of information about Egil, on which he was unable to impose a suitable form.[7]

If these two commentators are correct in their assessment of the second part of *Egil's Saga*, it would support the contentions of scholars like Sigurður Nordal, who believed that the author had based his work primarily on oral traditions that had been handed down by the descendants of Skallagrim, but also on Egil's poems and skaldic verses, which were still preserved in people's memories when the saga came to be written down in the first half of the thirteenth century.[8]

However, not everybody agrees that the saga's construction is particularly loose after the demise of Thorolf Kveldulfsson. In recent decades other scholars have pointed out that considerable thought seems to underlie the organization of the material in the second part of the saga. In their books on *Egil's*

Saga, both Bjarni Einarsson (1975) and Baldur Hafstað (1995) have highlighted parallels and recurring motifs which indicate that the person who compiled the saga was in far better control of his material than either Vogt or Andersson gave him credit for. Indeed, Einarsson makes a strong case for the saga's having been based only to a minor degree on independent oral sources about Egil. He argues that it is actually governed to a far greater extent by the laws of literature, in which the repeated interplay of parallels, oppositions, and variations on themes invariably has an important role.[9]

Since *Egil's Saga* is the story of a family, it seems natural for a new section to begin at the point where the focus of the narrative shifts to a new generation. After the account of the dealings of Kveldulf and his sons with Harald Finehair and their emigration to Iceland, there comes an obvious break in the saga following the description of Skallagrim's settlement. His sons now take centre stage, although there is actually a brief interlude before the new generation assumes the main roles in the saga, as the narrative turns to Bjorn Brynjolfsson and the circumstances that lead to his daughter's growing up at Borg. Soon, however, Thorolf Skallagrimsson assumes the mantle of protagonist, though not for long. When Thorolf returns from his first trip abroad, the focus shifts to Egil and stays on him for the rest of the story. Although he vanishes briefly from view during the account of his son Thorstein's feud with his neighbour Steinar, he participates in its resolution in memorable style, reverting to the centre of the action for the final chapters.

While Egil is little in evidence in the accounts of Bjorn Brynjolfsson or of Thorolf Skallagrimsson's first trip to Norway, he is clearly intended as protagonist from the outset. Among all of Skallagrim's children by far the most space is devoted to the introduction of Egil, and the second part of the saga opens with an account of how the three-year-old Egil goes to a feast that his father has forbidden him to attend. It is no coincidence that the saga as a whole ends with his death. One can therefore say that the first part is a lengthy introduction to the second, main one, of which Egil is clearly the protagonist.[10] Although the work uses the basic structure of the dynastic history or family saga, covering four generations of the same lineage of settlers, it is in its essence the portrait of an individual. Other structural features support this conclusion.

The division of the saga into two parts represents only the simplest level of its organization. It is also important to consider how its smaller units are arranged. One of the features that Andersson draws attention to is the fashion in which the settlement episodes have been fitted into the second part of the saga. Every now and then the arrival of some settler in Iceland is announced with a description of his land-taking, and Andersson criticizes such information as clumsily inserted and detracting from the tension and consequently from the reader's interest.[11] Here again, I disagree with Andersson, because these settlement episodes can in fact be shown to play a highly significant role in the structure of the saga.

Bjarni Einarsson addressed the problem of these stories in his book on *Egil's Saga*, concluding that the author did not hesitate to diverge from his sources in order to achieve aims that can be categorized as literary rather than historical (Einarsson 1975, 66–7).[12] One of the points to which Einarsson draws attention is the similarity between the story of Ketil Haeng's settlement in Iceland (58–60: 39–40) and the much later account of Ketil Gufa's arrival in Iceland and his search for a place for himself and his followers (240–1: 167–8). Einarsson argues convincingly that the author made various modifications to the story of Ketil Gufa, inventing details to enhance the similarity between the stories. This becomes apparent when the saga's account of Ketil Gufa is compared to the accounts in those versions of *The Book of Settlements* (*Landnámabók*) that are independent of *Egil's Saga*. Einarsson concludes that the author included these stories for a purpose and that they constituted an indispensable part of his overall design (Einarsson 1975, 66).[13]

The story of yet another settler, Ketil Blund (97–8: 66–7), arguably belongs to the same category. Einarsson points out that all the other versions of *Landnámabók* that record his settlement clearly derive their knowledge from *Egil's Saga*. However, he omits to mention a discrepancy between these and another version of the same story, preserved in the manuscript known as Þórðarbók, which contains a version of *Landnámabók* that is independent of *Egil's Saga*. There Blund-Ketil is said to be the grandson of one Ornolf, not of Ketil Blund as is claimed in *Egil's Saga*. On this evidence it would seem that the author of the saga invented Ketil Blund in order to introduce yet another settler of this name into the story (Einarsson 1975, 49).[14] Whether or not this is true, the significant point is that among the host of settlers who came to Iceland and claimed land in proximity to Skallagrim, all the men of whom there are special accounts in *Egil's Saga* are named Ketil and have a cognomen.

Significantly, these three settlement stories are all placed at clear breaks in the narrative. Ketil Haeng and his journey to Iceland are described immediately after the fall of Thorolf Kveldulfsson and before Skallagrim assumes the central role in the saga. The interpolation functions as a kind of dramatic respite: the story of Thorolf ends with his tragic death and we pause for a moment before embarking on the new escalation of tension that will reach its climax in the vengeance exacted by Skallagrim and Kveldulf and their subsequent flight to Iceland (Einarsson 1975, 86).

The same kind of break occurs at the point where the arrival of Ketil Blund is described. It is interpolated after the account of Thorolf Skallagrimsson's journey to Norway, during which he manages to befriend Eirik Blood-axe, son of Harald Fine-hair, despite the earlier animosity between their two families. Thorolf's return to Iceland is described, along with his plans to make a second trip abroad. At this point the saga suddenly reverts back several years, reporting Ketil Blund's arrival in Iceland, followed by two episodes from Egil's childhood: his first killing, committed when he was only seven years old, and a wrestling match during which his father comes close to murdering him, although he is a boy of no more than twelve at the time (101: 68–9). After the account of Ketil Blund's settlement in Iceland, Egil becomes the central character in the saga and remains so more or less until the story of his son Thorstein begins (276: 187).

Ketil Gufa's settlement story marks a similarly clear turning point in the saga.[15] When Egil returns home from his final overseas journey, the narrator leaves him for a while in order to describe Ketil's arrival in Iceland and the dreadful events that ensue when his runaway slaves rob and burn Thord Lambason's farm (241: 167). The narrative then moves on to the marriages of Egil's daughter and stepdaughter, followed by the occasion of his greatest grief, the drowning of his son Bodvar, after which the saga exhibits a marked change in tone. The chapters about Ketil Blundr and Ketil Gufa could thus be likened to staging posts in Egil's life, marking the beginning and end of his travels abroad.

On closer inspection, the three settlement stories about the men called Ketil turn out to have more in common than merely the name of the settler and the marking of a pivotal point in the overall structure of the saga. For example, each is placed immediately prior to a dramatic climax. The story of Ketil Haeng is related shortly before Kveldulf and Skallagrim kill Hallvard Hardfari and Sigtrygg Snarfari and drown the young sons of the Norwegian aristocrat Guttormr, a close relative of King Harald (68–9: 46–7). Ketil Blund enters the story just before Egil jeopardizes his brother's life by cutting the moorings of his ship in a southwesterly gale that is raging in Borgarfjord (103: 69–70). Ketil Gufa appears in the saga shortly before Bodvar Egilsson drowns in a southerly storm on the same fjord (243: 169). It is striking that all three cases involve deadly danger to young men, all of whom are the sons of important men.

Further, it is worth noting that in close proximity to each of the stories of the three men named Ketil there is direct or indirect reference to the killing of slaves. Indeed, Ketil Haeng's slaying of the sons of Hildirid in the first part of the saga could be interpreted as a kind of slave killing. They were deprived of their birthright on the grounds that their mother had been taken by force. As a result it was their fate to be seen as *þýbornir* ("born of a slave-woman"), to use a term that occurs later in the saga (156: 109). The second episode from Egil's childhood involves the killing of two slaves, Thorgerd Brak and

Skallagrim's foreman, while later in the saga Lambi Thordarson kills the slaves of Ketil Gufa in revenge for his father.

Finally, in each case there is reference to weddings in close proximity to the settlements of the three Ketils. The last thing to be reported before the episode of Harald Fine-hair's attack on Thorolf Kveldulfsson is the marriage of Skallagrim, while the account of Ketil Haeng follows directly from Thorolf's fall. That account ends with the king ordering Eyvind Lamb to marry Thorolf's widow (50, 56: 33, 38). The same pattern occurs in relation to the story of Ketil Gufa, directly after which we are told of the marriage of Thordis Thorolfsdottir and subsequently that of Thorgerd Egilsdottir (242: 168). In the case of Ketil Blund's settlement, it seems at first glance as if only one marriage is reported, the wedding of his son to Skallagrim's daughter, but another wedding is already in the offing: Thorolf has informed his father that he intends to travel to Norway with Asgerd, Bjorn Brynjolfsson's daughter, who was raised at Borg, and in due course it emerges that he intends to ask for her hand in marriage.

Some notion of an overall design thus clearly governs the organization of the narrative elements of the saga. Whether conscious or not, there must have been an intention behind the arrangement of all the afore-mentioned features around three characters named Ketil, who otherwise play only a minor role in the action.

As it happens, one other Ketil takes part in the saga, in a minor role similar to the other three.[16] This Ketil has the cognomen Hod (Icelandic *Hǫðr*; rendered as "Ketil the Slayer" in the English translation) and may also be an invention, since he turns up nowhere else in saga literature. He is said to be the kinsman and helmsman of King Eirik, to whom he bears a close resemblance. He is hit with a spear by Egil when Egil's ship passes that of the king in the half-light of early morning (161: 112), and the saga hints strongly that Egil had in fact intended to kill the king, which is doubtless why the resemblance between Ketil and the king is stressed and the incident set in conditions of poor visibility.

Ketil the Slayer is portrayed with more care than his role justifies, given that he is introduced barely a page before his death, and various details are supplied about him that are of little consequence for the development of the narrative. However, if we look more closely, it turns out that many incidents similar to those found in relation to the other Ketil stories have also been arranged around Ketil the Slayer. For example, there is a dramatic climax at this point in the saga when Egil's dispute with Berg-Onund over their father-in-law's legacy escalates into an all-out conflict between Egil and the king (153–60: 106–9). We have here a rebellion against a figure of authority and we do not have to wait long before a young boy, the son of a powerful man, drowns; in this instance it is Rognvald, the son of Eirik Blood-axe and Queen Gunnhild (170:

Figure 1

Settlers' Stories
Ketil + cognomen
Killing of slaves
Dramatic climax
Chieftain's son in mortal danger
Wedding(s)

118). He is described as a promising boy of ten or twelve years, a description which coincides almost exactly with the descriptions of Guttorm's sons and of Bodvar Egilsson. No slaves are executed in proximity to the description of Ketil the Slayer, but the slave motif is still present. Asgerd, Egil's wife, is referred to as "born of a slave-woman" (109: *þýborin*, 156), and accordingly regarded as having the same legal status as a slave, which would mean she had no right to her inheritance, as in the case of Hildirid's sons mentioned earlier.

We also do not have to look far to find two weddings, since the chapter about Egil's marriage is the last but one before the account of his dispute with Berg-Onund, and we have just been told that Berg-Onund had received the hand in marriage of Gunnhild, Asgerd's half-sister (148: 103). A third marriage is also reported on this occasion, that of Egil's follower Thorfinn to his sister Saeunn.

The repeated pattern discernible in relation to characters all named Ketil with a cognomen can hardly be dismissed as mere coincidence. It is tempting to conjecture that it is linked to some overall meaning that the saga is intended to convey. The four characters named Ketil apparently serve the purpose of drawing attention to a recurring pattern, which we could sum up as follows: there is a rebellion against an authority figure, generally in relation to an inheritance claim; this occurs in close proximity to a wedding, followed more often than not by the death of one or more young men shortly afterwards. Whether or not these repetitions have a meaning is not my concern here; it is rather to point out that the stories of the four men named Ketil create a definite infrastructure for the construction of the saga. The colonist Ketil Haeng divides the first part into two narratives of differing length, each with a dramatic climax. The settlement stories of Ketil Blund and Ketil Gufa bracket the section of Egil's life story that tells of his adventures abroad, with his killing of Ketil the Slayer occurring in the middle. Furthermore, the section of the second part of the saga that precedes the account of Ketil Blund is more or less the same length as the section that follows the account of Ketil Gufa. This structural pattern enhances still further the artistic equilibrium that the Ketil stories confer on *Egil's Saga*.

Figure 2

Structural Patterns in *Egil's Saga*[17]

Part One
Thorolf Kveldulfsson (ch. 1 to 22)
KETIL HAENG (ch. 23)
Skallagrim (ch. 24 to 30)

Part Two
Thorolf Skallagrimsson (ch. 32 to 38)
KETIL BLUND (ch. 39)
EGIL'S OVERSEAS JOURNEYS
Egil (ch. 40 to 57)
KETIL THE SLAYER (ch. 57)
Egil (ch. 58 to 77)
EGIL RETIRES FROM TRAVELLING
KETIL GUFA (ch. 78)
Thorstein and Egil (ch. 80 to 90)

Other repetitions of names serve to accentuate the structure of the saga still further. The famous account of Egil's trip to his grandfather's feast against Skallagrim's will is the first incident described in Egil's life and gives him a leading role in the action from the very outset of part two. The reader's attention is therefore bound to be attracted by a strikingly similar event towards the end of the saga, just before Egil's death. Again he is keen to go to a social gathering and again a man named Grim forbids it, only in this case it is Grim of Mosfell, husband of Egil's niece Thordis Thorolfsdottir, with whom he has chosen to live in his old age.

The stories appear to echo one another deliberately, drawing attention to the fact that Egil's strong character remains unchanged from his early childhood to the end of his long life.[18] A degree of manipulation was evidently required to place this incident right at the end of the saga, as it would have made more sense chronologically to include accounts of Egil's extreme decrepitude after this particular episode, in which he still has the strength to kill two slaves (298: 203).[19]

Some may find the correlation between journeys to an assembly and a feast less than self-evident, yet these journeys have much in common. First, they move the protagonist away from home and family to an outside social setting. Second, feasts and assemblies both require the differentiation of people according to rank. The importance of status is stressed in both accounts: Egil is accorded a seat of honour beside the master of the house when he arrives at his grandfather's farm as a wet and weary three year old. However, when, as an old man, Egil asks Grim of Mosfell's permission to ride with him to the assembly, Grim asks Thordis to see if she can find out what is behind his wish. In the seventeenth-century copies of *Egil's Saga*, which seem to preserve a more complete text than Möðruvallabók, the conversation between Thordis and Egil makes explicit how important it is for Egil to lead his party at the assembly. Thordis points out that he would not be accorded the seat of honour that was his due, presumably because his blindness would render him incapable of fulfilling his former role as a chieftain (cf. Einarsson 1993).[20]

These two stories of Egil, at age three and ninety respectively, mark the beginning and end of the section devoted to his story. It is thus striking that between his earlier two and later two overseas journeys we find a chapter in which the same elements are repeated (173–4: 120). I am here referring to the account of the last conversation between Skallagrim and Egil, and the death of the former after he has sunk a chest of silver and a copper cauldron in Krumskelda bog.[21] This chapter is comparable with the others in that it reports the dealings between a man named Grim and Egil, one of whom is going to a social event and the other of whom is not. In this case, as in the first story, the event is a feast at the home of Egil's maternal family at Alftanes. All three episodes involve arguments between a man named Grim and Egil. In the latter two stories the argument is about what is to become of the silver that King Athelstan of England intended for Skallagrim in recompense for his son Thorolf. Significantly, Thorolf's name also crops up in the first episode, when Egil insists on going to the feast because his brother is invited.

It is hardly coincidental that these three stories punctuate the saga at such regular intervals. They constitute a kind of variation on a theme, their distribution bestowing a strong overall character on the section of the saga that centres on Egil. And just as there are three men named Ketil in the second part of *Egil's Saga* and only one in the first, so we can also find a single instance of the motif just described in the first part of the saga. In the account of Thorolf Kveldulfsson's decision to become King Harald's liegeman against his father's will (14: 9–10), a father is again shown trying to dissuade his son from attending a large gathering: here the court can be considered analogous to feasts and assemblies in the sense that it too involves leaving the family to go to a place where social rituals are performed, and where, moreover, social hierarchy is of fundamental importance.[22] All that is lacking from this episode, in comparison to the others, is mention of an inheritance or a brother. Yet, like the others, it centres on a confrontation between paternal authority and a son's wishes, as is clearly revealed by contrast when Skallagrim remarks that he would rather

Figure 3

Motifs Repeated at Key Points

Part One
Thorolf Kveldulfsson goes to Harald's court against the advice of his father Kveldulf.

Part Two
Egil goes to a feast against the orders of his father Skallagrim.
Egil's two overseas journeys
Egil goes to a feast after a quarrel with his father Skallagrim.
Egil's two overseas journeys.
Egil is forbidden to attend the assembly by Grim of Mosfell.

obey his father than the new monarch. The brothers Skallagrim and Thorolf are opposites in this respect, for one obeys his father while the other does not.

This analysis of the construction of *Egil's Saga* has revealed that several components of the narrative seem to play a key role in its organization. On the one hand, there are the cases involving a clash of wills between a father and son.[23] On the other, there are the interpolations about men named Ketil with a cognomen, and around these stories cluster other narrative elements that cannot have been chosen at random. In the first part of the saga (chapters 1 to 30 in the English translation) each type occurs only once, whereas in the second (chapters 31 to 90) each occurs three times. These two structural elements do not merely govern the internal organization of each part, they also serve to bind the saga together, providing it with thematic cohesion. The second part, however, is more complex than the first, because the hero's relations with royal authority, the main theme of the first part, are complicated in the second by the hero's relations with his father and brother.

This discussion would not be complete without pointing out that some editions of *Egil's Saga* divide it into ninety chapters, which is a multiple of three, a number whose prominence in the external structure we have already noted. As it happens, the chapter division is only partly the work of editors. The Möðruvallabók text, on which all editions of the saga are based, is itself divided into chapters but unfortunately there are two lacunae in the manuscript. Most editors fill these using a text from another manuscript, the Wolfenbüttel book, which contains no chapter divisions. However, it has been possible to compensate for this thanks to Bjarni Einarsson's (1993) study of seventeenth-century copies of Möðruvallabók, made before the pages were lost. Similarly, recent editors have assumed that the accounts of the circumstances behind Egil's composition of his major poems, *Sonatorrek* and *Arinbjarnarkviða*, must have formed separate chapters. They have thus introduced a chapter break at the point where the account of Einar skala-glamm begins. Their underlying assumption is that the saga must have contained a total of ninety chapters, and while we cannot state for certain that the saga was organized in this way when it was first written down, it must be considered plausible.[24]

If it was so, it would fit in nicely with the fact that the saga preserves sixty skaldic verses by Egil and three major poems, as well as references to three others. Furthermore, Egil is three years old when he enters the story and ninety when he dies. If the number three and its multiples have influenced the way the work was constructed, it would be perfectly in keeping with the aesthetics of his times. In the Middle Ages, the structure of poems and other works of art was often based on numbers, especially the number three, symbolic of the Holy Trinity. This was consistent with people's understanding of Scripture, since number symbolism was considered an important aid to its interpretation. One of the most celebrated works of medieval literature is Dante Alighieri's *Divine Comedy*, composed more than half a century after *Egil's Saga*.[25] Dante's work consists of one hundred cantos, one forming an introduction, the rest divided into three parts, each containing thirty-three cantos. Dante almost certainly had the Holy Trinity in mind when choosing this form for his work.[26] Icelandic poets of the first half of the thirteenth century often composed with such numbers in mind, an obvious example being Snorri Sturluson's *Hattatal*, which consists of one hundred and two stanzas, again a multiple of three. If the last two stanzas, which form a kind of epilogue, are subtracted, we are left with one hundred stanzas, and indeed the poet emphasizes in the hundredth stanza that "so ten tens are told" (Sturluson 1987, 220, "svá er tírætt hundrað talit": Sturluson 1999, 39).

Due to the circumstances in which *Egil's Saga* has been preserved, we will never be able to state with absolute certainty that the saga's structure is based on a numerical scheme (cf. Fichtner 1982, 355–66). But the way the number three governs the organization of the plot elements in part two of the saga does suggest that this was the intention. This possibility is made a bit more probable by a set of allusions to Scripture that have been woven into the narrative and give the story of Egil a Christian meaning that readers or listeners of the thirteenth century would have clearly perceived (Tulinius 2004, 53–116).

Finally, it is interesting to note how many parallels the overall structure of the second part of the saga, which centres on Egil, has with the structure of the poem *Hǫfuðlausn*. The poem consists of twenty stanzas, divided into three parts. First comes the *upphaf,* or beginning section of five stanzas, then comes the *stefjabálkr*, a set of ten verses including four half stanzas forming a refrain,

Figure 4

Comparison between the structure of *Hǫfuðlausn* and part two of *Egil's Saga*

Structure of *Hǫfuðlausn*	Structure of part two of *Egil's Saga*
Upphaf (vv. 1–5)	Presentation of Egil and his siblings (1 ch.).
	Thorolf Skallagrimsson (7 chs.)
Stefjabálkr (vv. 6–15)	Egil Skallagrimsson (11 chs.)
Refrain	Ketil Blund
2 stanzas	Egil's 1st and 2nd overseas journeys
Refrain	Ketil the Slayer
2 stanzas	Egil's 3rd and 4th overseas journeys
Refrain	Ketil Gufa
2 stanzas	(40 chs. in all)
Refrain	
Slæmr (vv. 16–20)	Thorstein and Egil (11 chs.)
Coda (v. 21)	Egil's death (2 chs.)

and finally comes the so-called *slœmr,* or third and last division of five stanzas and no refrain, and right at the end, the twenty-first stanza, a half stanza that forms a sort of coda.[27]

If we re-examine the structure of the second part of the saga, we could compare the stories of the men named Ketil to a refrain, and the accounts of Egil's childhood adventure and Thorolf at the beginning as the *upphaf* of a *drápa.* The stories of Thorstein and finally Egil can be seen as comparable to the *slœmr* sections. One could also compare Egil's four overseas journeys to the stanzas interposed between the refrains.

The parallel is not exact, but the similarities between the construction of the saga and that of the *drápa* are nevertheless striking.[28] They can be taken as yet another indication that the organization of episodes was dictated by a sense of form rather than the haphazard nature of historical events.

As has already been mentioned, the preserved manuscripts of *Egil's Saga* are probably quite different from the version that was first recorded on vellum, presumably in the first half of the thirteenth century. Because of the length and complexity of the second part of the saga, its elaborate structure has escaped most scholars of *Egil's Saga*. However, as the present study shows, there is considerable evidence that this structure is the result of conscious design, possibly to underline the saga's deeper meaning. Although some of these structural regularities may also have been shaped by tradition, or an author's unconscious, they show that whoever composed the saga had a sense of form that was remarkably akin to that of the skaldic poet.

NOTES

1 For a strong statement about little of the poetry in the saga being authentically by Egil, see Einarsson 1992.
2 This is an addition to my previous work on the saga, especially my contribution to the collective volume *Skaldsagas*, in which I attempt to show the parallels between skaldic poetics and the way meaning is generated in *Egil's Saga* (Tulinius 2000).
3 Tulinius 2004. A revised version of the book in English translation has been accepted for publication by Cornell University Press under the title *The Enigma of Egill: The Saga, the Viking Poet, and Snorri Sturluson.*
4 For further discussion of the relationship between the saga prose and the inset poetry, see Guðrún Nordal's essay in this volume.
5 The reader is advised to keep an edition of *Egil's Saga* handy for reference during the following discussion.
6 See Andersson 1967, 107 on the structure of *Egil's Saga* (the emphasis is mine): "the matter seems more *diversified and less of a piece than elsewhere*. Both the temporal and local framework is dilated much beyond the norm. ... There is *no genuine or inherent focus*. ... Even the central part of the saga concerned with Egil's conflict with Erik is diluted and made bland by *a quantity of episodic scatterings about the Norwegian court*, the *colonization of Iceland*, and Viking raids abroad. In fact *Egil's conflict is handled with less address and considerably less dramatic intensity than Thorolf's*. It lacks any true climax such as the depiction of Þórólfr's monumental fall three strides from his royal antagonist." See also de Vries's similar remarks on the construction of the saga (1967, 350).
7 "In this case it is of course curious that Thorolf's story is brought off so well while Egil's story is dull and long-winded in comparison. A possible explanation of the paradox is that the author was handicapped by too much information in his treatment of Egil and was unable to absorb it into his inheritance conflict. Even as the saga stands, it is clear that he could not integrate Sonatorrek, Arinbjarnarkviða, the friendship with Einarr skálaglamm, and the mission to Värmland" (Andersson 1967, 108). This attitude resurfaces in Vésteinn Ólason's comments on the saga in *Íslensk bókmenntasaga*: "Eftir Jórvíkurför Egils heldur saga hans áfram án þess

að um nokkra eiginlega söguflettu sé að ræða, og er hún þó auðug af atvikum" (1993, 90; After Egil's trip to York, his story continues without any real plot, although it is rich in incident.)

8 Cf., for example, the first sentences of Sigurður Nordal's foreword to his edition of the saga: "Heimildir Egils sögu eru þrenns konar. Meginefni hennar er sótt í munnlegar frásögur, sem gengið höfðu frá kynslóð til kynslóðar ..." (Nordal 1933, v: "*Egil's Saga* is based on three types of source. The bulk of its content derives from stories that had been passed down orally from generation to generation ...").

9 Baldur Hafstað's research supports Einarsson's point of view, reinforcing it with many more arguments (1995, 135–48).

10 This type of bipartite structure was not uncommon in medieval European literature during the lifetime of the *Egil's Saga* author, as Carol Clover, among others, has pointed out (1982, 46). Examples of stories that are similarly divided between two generations include *Cligès* by the twelfth-century French author Chrétien de Troyes, and the translated chivalric romance *Tristrams saga*, which was probably circulating in Norway and perhaps in Iceland at the time *Egil's Saga* was composed. It may be even more apposite to compare the latter work with *Egil's Saga*, since its second part is also the life story of the central character, while the first part is like a prologue that sets the stage for his life and creates the context which lends it meaning. It could be said to play a similar role to the prelude to a piece of music, in which the main themes are introduced before being amplified and interwoven in the main body of the composition, a description that would fit both *Tristrams saga* and *Egil's Saga* equally well.

11 See note 6.

12 Cf. also the section in which he puts forward various arguments in favour of the author's having taken liberties with his sources for artistic reasons (Einarsson 1975, 73–85; his conclusions are summarised at 76–9).

13 "Til trods for disse episoders uafhængighed af sagaens hovedhandling, er de hver for sig knyttet til sagaens hovedpersoner og begivenheder. Det er rimeligt at antage at de er anbragt her i overensstemmelse med forfatterens bevidste plan, – at de er en integrerende del of den helhedsstruktur han havde for øje." ("Although these episodes are independent of the saga's main plot, each of them is linked to the main characters and events of the saga. It is reasonable to suppose they are used here in accordance with a deliberate plan on the part of the author – that they form an integral part of the overall structure he had in mind.")

14 See also Jakob Benediktsson (1968, 84, note 4), as well as Benediktsson's discussion in the introduction about the internal relationship between the various versions of *Landnámabók*.

15 Ibid.

16 Actually, reference is made to two others, though only in genealogies. They are Ketil Haeng, a cousin of Kveldulf and ancestor of the settler Ketil Haeng (ch. 1), and Ketil Keel-farer, grandfather of Grim the Halogalander who steered Kveldulf's ship.

17 The chapter numbers given here are those of the English translation.

18 On this topic of the protagonist's identity, see further the essay by Laurence de Looze in this volume.

19 A further indication that whoever composed the saga is making highly creative use of his sources here is the strikingly similar story preserved in *Landnámabók* of an aged Viking, Ketilbjorn the Old of Mosfell, who is blind and kills the slaves who help him bury some silver that he does not want to fall into the hands of his heirs. This story was probably the origin of the episode in *Egil's Saga*. See Benediktsson 1968, 384–6.

20 The manuscript copies describe the conversation between Thordis and Egil, and include the following about Thordis: "enn er hün fann ad Eigill giordiz mäl-rætenn þä spurde hün so, er þad nockud med alhuga ad þü vilier rÿda i sumar til alþïngs, Þikir mier þad undarlegt ad þü | vilier rÿda til þings so ad þü räder ei firer flocke ad <eg> ætla sÿdan þü varst tvÿtugur, ad þü hafer alldri so til alþïngs ridid ad ei værer þü flockstiöre. Enn ef þü villt nü fara og veita Grÿme filgd þïna og fóruneite, þä mun þikia skilld naudsin til bera umm fór þïna" ("and when she discovered that Egil was in a mood to talk, she asked, 'are you certain you want to ride to the Althing this summer. I find it odd that you should wish to ride to the assembly when you are not in charge of the party, since I imagine that ever since you were twenty you have never ridden to the Althing without being the leader of your party. But if you want to go now, accompanying Grímr, it seems you must have a very urgent reason for your journey'.") See Einarsson 2001, p. 181.

21 Einarsson (1975, 79–80) discusses the links between this chapter and the narratives of Ketil Haeng and Ketil Gufa, drawing attention to the way it is placed between Egil's second and third trips abroad

22 Banquets were important in the Middle Ages, among other reasons because they provided an opportunity for society to place itself on stage. The prevailing social hierarchy was revealed partly by where people were seated. There are countless examples of this theme in early writings. Suffice it to mention the account in *Brennu-Njáls saga* of the quarrel between Bergthor and Hallgerd over the latter's placing during a feast at Bergthorshvall.

23 Grim of Mosfell could also symbolise a father figure, given that he not only bears the same name as Skallagrim but is also master of the household where Egil lives as an old man, and thus has power over him, like a father does over a son.

24 Nordal's edition divides the saga into 88 chapters. Scudder (2005) translates the chapter division of the 1986 Svart á hvítu edition, with which I agree.

25 Vincent Foster Hopper's *Medieval Number Symbolism* provides an invaluable guide to the subject and the justification for it provided by St Augustine, among others, and includes an exploration of the *Divine Comedy*'s roots in this tradition. For Augustine's views, see Hopper 1938, 78f. There is another useful discussion of the influence of numerology on medieval literature in Curtius 1948, 493–500.

26 For Dante and number symbolism, see Hopper 1938.

27 The most recent discussion of the poem is that of Kries and Krömmelbein (2002), who examine the discrepancies between the extant versions of the poem and argue that the poem originally took the form I have described.

28 Judith Jesch (2000, 7–8) briefly discusses structural parallels between saga narrative and longer skaldic poems, but comes to the conclusion that the similarity is "very superficial."

BIBLIOGRAPHY

Andersson, Theodore M. 1967. *The Icelandic Family Saga: An Analytic Reading*, Cambridge, MA: Harvard University Press.

Benediktsson, Jakob, ed. 1986. *Íslendingabók. Landnámabók*. Íslenzk fornrit 1. Reykjavík: Hið íslenzka fornritafélag.

Clover, Carol J. 1982. *The Medieval Saga*. Ithaca, NY: Cornell University Press.

Curtius, Ernest Robert. 1948. *Europäische Literatur und lateinsiches Mittelalter*. Bern: A. Francke AG Verlag.

Einarsson, Bjarni. 1975. *Litterære forudsætninger for Egils saga*. Reykjavík: Stofnun Árna Magnússonar á Íslandi.

– 1992. "Skáldið í Reykjaholti." In *Eyvindarbók. Festskrift til Eyvind Fjeld Halvorsen, 4. mai 1992*, 34–40. Oslo: Universitetet i Oslo.

– 1993. "Um Eglutexta Möðruvallabókar í 17du aldar eftirritum." *Gripla* 8: 7–54.

– Ed. 2001. *Egils saga Skallagrímssonar.* Vol. 1, A-Redaktionen. Editiones Arnamagnæanæ, Series A, vol. 19. Copenhagen: Reitzel.

Fichtner, Edward G. 1982. "The Narrative Structure of Egils Saga." In *Les Sagas de Chevaliers (Riddarasögur). Actes de la Ve Conférence Internationale sur les Sagas, Toulon*, 355–66.. Paris: Presses de l'Université de Paris-Sorbonne.

Hafstað, Baldur. 1995. *Die Egils saga und ihr Verhältnis zu anderen Werken des nordischen Mittelalters*. Reykjavík: Rannsóknarstofnun Kennaraháskóla Íslands.

Hopper, Vincent Foster. 1938. *Medieval Number Symbolism: Its Sources, Meaning, and Influence on Thought and Expression*. New York: Columbia University Press.

Jesch, Judith. 2000. "Sagas and Skaldic Poetry." In *Artikler. Udgivet i anledning af Preben Meulengracht Sørensens 60 års fødselsdag 1. marts 2000*, 7–18. Århus: Norrønt forum..

Kries, Susanne, and Thomas Krömmelbein. 2002. "'From the Hull of Laughter': Egill Skalla-Grímsson's 'Hǫfuðlausn' and Its Epodium in Context." *Scandinavian Studies* 74:2: 111–36.

Nordal, Sigurður, ed. 1933. *Egils saga Skalla-Grímssonar*. Íslenzk fornrit 2. Reykjavík: Hið íslenzka fornritafélag.

Ólason, Vésteinn. 1993. "Íslendingasögur og þættir." In *Íslensk bókmenntasaga* 2. Ed. Halldór Guðmundsson, 25–163. Reykjavík: Mál og menning.

Scudder, Bernard, trans. 2004. *Egil's Saga*. Ed. Svanhildur Óskarsdóttir. London: Penguin.

Sturluson, Snorri. 1987. *Edda*. Trans. Anthony Faulkes. Everyman. London: Dent.

– 1999. *Edda. Háttatal*. Ed. A. Faulkes. London: Viking Society for Northern Research.

Tulinius, Torfi H. 2000. "The Prosimetrum Form 2: Verses as an Influence in Saga Composition and Interpretation." In *Skaldsagas. Text, Vocation and Desire in the Icelandic Sagas of Poets:* Ed. Russell Poole, 191–217. Ergänzungsbände zum Reallexikon der germanischen Altertumskunde 27. Berlin: De Gruyter,

– 2004. *Skáldið í skriftinni. Snorri Sturluson og Egils saga*. Reykjavík: Hið íslenska bókmenntafélag.

Vogt, W.H. 1909. *Zur Komposition der Egils Saga, KPP. I–LXVI.* Görlitz: Hoffmann & Reiber.

de Vries, Jan. 1967. *Altnordische Literaturgeschichte* II. Berlin: W. De Gruyter.

3 *Ars metrica* and the Composition of *Egil's Saga*

GUÐRÚN NORDAL

1

The verses incorporated into the Sagas of Icelanders bring with them a baggage of skaldic theory, taken not only from *Snorra Edda* but also, no less important, from the grammatical treatises. Skaldic theory was practised at an advanced level at the time when the first of the Sagas of Icelanders, such as *Egil's Saga*, were being written in the thirteenth century. Three grammatical treatises can be dated to the twelfth and thirteenth centuries: the *First*, *Second*, and *Third*, all of which are associated with skaldic verse-making and preserved in conjunction with *Snorra Edda* in the manuscripts. All three are preserved in Codex Wormianus; the *Second* also in Codex Upsaliensis as an introduction to *Háttatal*, Snorri Sturluson's *ars metrica*; and the *Third*, by Óláfr Þórðarson, in the *A* and *B* manuscripts of *Snorra Edda*'s *Skáldskaparmál* (cf. Nordal 2001, 77–87). The close association of *Snorra Edda* with the study of *grammatica* throws into relief the theoretical foundation on which the study of skaldic poetry was based in the thirteenth century, and how considerations of phonetics, syntax, metrics, and imagery were all brought to bear upon this corpus of poetry.

The analytical methodology to which the verse was subjected in the grammatical culture must be taken into account when we interpret not only the poetry embedded in the sagas but also the accompanying prose text. In the following essay I shall present a few examples to demonstrate this point in relation to selected verses attributed to Egil Skallagrimsson and their accompanying prose narrative in *Egil's Saga*. The original text of the saga is as elusive as that of many of the Sagas of Icelanders. Typically, these sagas are preserved in a great variety of manuscripts over a long period of time. Since their conception they have undergone a variety of changes. Moreover, the manuscripts often embody distinct redactions whose rationale has to be inferred from their companion texts. *Egil's Saga* for its part is preserved in three main versions, Möðruvallabók (written c. 1320–50), the Wolfenbüttel manuscript (written c. 1350), and Ketilsbók (Ketill Jörundsson's seventeenth-century transcription), as well as in many fragments from the thirteenth century onwards (cf. Helgason 1956, 1969).

When the text of *Egil's Saga* in Möðruvallabók is compared to the earliest (mid-thirteenth century) fragment of the saga, known as θ (theta), it is clear that not only has the text been thoroughly revised, abridged, and polished but also that the three verses that appear in θ are better preserved there than in Möðruvallabók.[1] It should further be noted that Egil's verses in the Möðruvallabók redaction are commonly written by a hand other than that which wrote the prose, perhaps implying that some of them were not in the scribe's copy. If we look at other Sagas of Icelanders in this same manuscript, it is noteworthy that there is a tendency to preserve less verse than we find in other manuscripts from the same period.[2]

Outside the boundaries of his saga, Egil's verse is known from *Skáldskaparmál* (the second section of *Snorra Edda*) and *The Third Grammatical Treatise*, and the methods used there to analyse the verse and the context in which the verse is placed may have the potential to shed light on how the verses are used in *Egil's Saga*. Both works were written by the Sturlungs, who probably also had something to do with the writing of *Egil's Saga*. Snorri Sturluson's selection of poetry for citation in *Skáldskaparmál* is mostly confined to poets known from the kings' sagas or listed in *Skáldatal*. These were the "major poets" (*hǫfuðskáld*), that is to say the cadre of skaldic poets who enjoyed official recognition in the written culture. As Bjarne Fidjestøl observed, there is virtually no overlap between the skaldic corpus in the kings' sagas and *Snorra Edda* on the one hand, and that incorporated into the Sagas of Icelanders on the other (1985, 323). Even though we find verses by the same poets, they are not typically drawn from the same poetic corpus. This is an important point when we assess the use of poetry in the Sagas of Icelanders, which does not belong to the poetic corpus most firmly associated with historical writing (Nordal 2001, 120–30; Nordal 2007, 219–37).

Hallfred, Kormak, and Egil are interesting cases in point. All three were recognized court poets, and Hallfred and Kormak receive mention in the kings' sagas. All three are listed in *Skáldatal* and cited in *Skáldskaparmál*, and therefore qualify as *hǫfuðskáld*.[3] They are also cited in the Sagas of Icelanders. However, the verses by Kormak and Hallfred cited in *Skáldskaparmál* and the kings' sagas belong to their court poetry; there is almost no overlap with the corpus of verses embedded in their respective sagas, which accordingly we might infer to be not as historically reliable. The case of Egil Skallagrimsson is yet more difficult: he is, as we have seen, a known court poet listed in *Skáldatal*, and yet his verse is nowhere cited in the kings' sagas. *Egil's Saga* is, generically speaking, a special case, on the borderline between the kings' sagas and the Sagas of Icelanders. The amount of overlap in citation between *Egil's Saga* and the poetological texts is also a complex question: Egil's poetry is cited nine times in *Snorra Edda* (Codex Regius version), but in seven of these nine instances the source is one of Egil's longer poems, *Arinbjarnarkviða*, *Sonatorrek*, or *Hǫfuðlausn*, which may or may not have belonged to the written saga originally.

Each manuscript of *Skáldskaparmál* presents a different redaction of the text. The case of Codex Upsaliensis is particularly instructive: the manuscript was written c. 1300 and can with some likelihood be linked to the Sturlung family (Nordal 2001, 53–5; Pálsson 2012, xxxii–xxxiii). Arinbjorn's patronage of Egil's poetry is among the additions in a special redaction of *Skáldatal* preserved in this manuscript. The Kringla version of *Skáldatal* does not include this reference, nor does it mention Egil's association with King Athelstan or with Thorstein Thora's son, Arinbjorn's nephew (cf. Nordal 2001, 120–30). Why is Egil's official output enlarged in the Upsaliensis redaction of *Skáldatal*? Is it because of the presence of *Egil's Saga* and the need to give the stamp of authenticity to the poetry purportedly by Egil included in the saga as it existed at this time?

Finally, one further indirect reference to Egil outside his saga occurs in Snorri Sturluson's *Háttatal*, a *clavis metrica* and once again a work associated with the Sturlungs. *Háttatal* is accompanied by a prose commentary elucidating the stylistic and prosodic devices specific to the various types of skaldic metres. About halfway through *Háttatal* Snorri discusses five types of verse that he attributes to early poets who occupy a position on the borderline between history and myth: Ragnar Shaggy-breeches, Turf-Einar, Flein, Bragi Boddason, and Egil Skallagrimsson. To Egil is ascribed a form termed *Egilsháttr*, "Egil's verse-form," and it is exemplified in stanza 56 of *Háttatal*. The common feature of these five types is a certain formal looseness, insofar as most if not all of the constituent lines contain no internal rhyme (*hendingar*), contrary to the situation in later, regular *dróttkvætt,* the classic skaldic verse-form. Snorri works on the assumption that *dróttkvætt* was less advanced in the ninth century and that greater regularity was achieved with time.[4] He warns young poets against emulating these five early poets: "this ought not to be imitated though it is not considered a fault in early poems" (Sturluson 1987, 200: "ok má eigi yrkja eptir [því] þó at þat þykki eigi spilla í fornkvæðum," Sturluson 1991, 26).[5] Features of *Egilsháttr* are found in poetry attributed to Egil in his saga and in the metrical treatises, although never consistently through an entire verse (cf. Sturluson 1991, 63).

In sum, we see a considerable interest in analysing Egil's verse in the textual culture. To Snorri Sturluson and Óláfr Þórðarson, the two best-known scholars of skaldic poetics, metrics were no less important than skaldic imagery; the two, form and content, are always intertwined. The question now to be considered is whether the citation and use of Egil's verse in *Egil's Saga* in any way reflects this analysis. I shall focus on four crucial scenes in the saga: Egil's visit to his grandfather Yngvar; his first feast in Norway; the verbal exchange at the Gulathing regarding Asgerd's inheritance; and Egil's contretemps with his son, Thorstein.

2

Egil's Saga speaks to an audience interested in poetry, and could even be said to revolve around poetry. An abundance of verses is included and, additionally, the saga makes numerous references to verse-making, to the poets of Harald Fair-hair, and to four well-known poets of the West of Iceland, Bjorn Champion of the Hitardal people, Gunnlaug Serpent-tongue, Skuli Thorsteinsson, and Einar Skalaglamm, Egil's protégé. The hero of the saga is undoubtedly a formidable poet. His work is admired in Iceland and England, although he is not accepted within the realms of courtly life in Norway and is never shown presenting his verse to a Norwegian king in the manner of court poets such as Hallfred and Sigvat.[6] *Hǫfuðlausn*, though presented to the outlawed king in York, is hardly comparable to the praise poems presented by a respected court poet to a Norwegian king.

In the context of the saga author's careful creation of the poet's *persona*, Egil's famous entrance to the saga one third of the way through the work is of particular significance. Yngvar, Egil's maternal grandfather, had invited his daughter Bera to a feast along with Skallagrim and Thorolf, but Egil is not invited by name. He wants to come along, but Skallagrim orders his son to stay at home as "you don't know how to behave where there's heavy drinking. You're enough trouble when you are sober" (81: "því at þú kannt ekki fyrir þér at vera í fjǫlmenni þar er drykkjur eru miklar, er þú þykkir ekki góðr viðskiptis, at þú sér ódrukkinn," 54).[7] This is an unexpected statement in light of Egil's age. The three-year-old disobeys his father, takes a horse, rides to Alftanes, and turns up at the feast to be welcomed with open arms by his grandfather.[8] Yngvar, playing to Egil's vanity, which is not known to the saga audience at this early stage in Egil's life, treats him as an honoured guest at the feast and places him at his side opposite to his father and his brother Thorolf. The humorous representation of Egil in this scene foreshadows his portrayal later in the work. His seating at the feast furthermore foreshadows his ambiguous relationship with his immediate paternal kinsmen in the saga. He is alone, shown closer to his mother and to the maternal side of his family.

Egil delivers two verses in this episode and they are both in regular *dróttkvætt*, except for the first line in the second verse. It is quite common in Egil's poetry in the saga to find full rhyme (*aðalhending*) instead of half rhyme (*skothending*) in the first line. This feature occurs here, and the rhyme underlines the contrasts inherent in Yngvar's gift of three shells and a duck's egg: "Síþǫgla gaf sǫglum / sárgagls þría Agli" (82: "gave eloquent / Egil … three shells / that rear up ever-silent in the surf," 55). Egil's visit to his maternal grandfather clearly introduces themes that will be developed in the saga, the careful *mise en scène* at feasting and the poet's relationship with his patron. The story of the boy and his grandfather is an example of the ideal reciprocal relationship between the court poet and his patron, which will *not* be acted out in Egil's relations with the Norwegian king. It is comic, yet tragic; it is the story of a person who, though only three years old, succeeds in behaving impeccably at a feast – not a common occurrence in the saga of the grown-up Egil. He will never have this type of relationship with the Norwegian king.

Egil's visit to Bard at Atley turns out very differently from his visit to Yngvar. This is the first test of his manners in the company of the king. Egil has just arrived in Norway, and the feast held by Bard gives him an unexpected opportunity to present himself to the royal couple, Eirik Blood-axe and his consort Gunnhild, but the meeting does not work out to his advantage. He immediately exhibits his tendency to antisocial behaviour in their company, and it becomes apparent that his dispute with the royal family will have Gunnhild as its focus more than Eirik. This episode is punctuated by three verses, each a variant of *dróttkvætt* verse-form.

The first stanza is composed in regular *dróttkvætt*, and it carries an undisguised piece of verbal abuse (*níð*). Bard responds in a robust manner and joins the queen in an attempt to poison Egil. Egil for his part perceives the threat, cuts runes on the poison-filled horn, and composes a stanza, intended, it would seem, for the servant woman who has brought him the horn:

I carve runes on this horn,
redden words with my blood,
I choose words for the trees
of the wild beast's ear-roots;
drink as we wish this mead

brought by merry serving maids,
let us find out how we fare
from the ale that Bard blessed. (74)

[Rístum rún á horni,
rjóðum spjǫll í dreyra,
þau velk orð til eyrna
óðs dýrs viðar róta;
drekkum veig sem viljum
vel glýjaðra þýja,
vitum, hvé oss of eiri
ǫl, þats Bárøðr signdi.] (109)

This verse differs from the previous one, which, as noted, was composed in regular *dróttkvætt*, in being almost a perfect *háttleysa*, i.e., composed without regular internal rhyme. True to *Egilsháttr*, however, there is full internal rhyme (*aðalhending*) in line 6, "vel glýjaðra þýja," where Egil pays homage to the friendly serving-women. The verse-form is a cue; it carries an implicit signal to the audience. In all, the saga contains five occurrences of *háttleysa*, and I suggest that these instances are thematically linked.

The first verse of this kind is Egil's comment on words spoken by his mother, and he evidently makes it in her presence: "Þat mælti mín móðir" (100: "My mother said," 68). The next example is the verse discussed in the previous paragraph, apparently addressed to the serving woman. The following two are also spoken in the presence of women, one being addressed to the daughter of the earl (121: 84) and the other to Helga Thorfinnsdottir. Helga's health is threatened by a runic message, and there are clear verbal echoes between the first line of that stanza and the one at Bard's feast: "Skalat maðr rúnir rísta" (230: "No man should carve runes," 159). *Háttleysa* is used a final time in a verse spoken to Einar Skalaglamm (268: 184), where Egil boasts of his battles in Norway.

In sum, four of these five verses have women in or as their audience and the fifth is addressed to a young apprentice skald. This may not be a coincidence. The poet steps out of the court verse-form (*dróttkvætt*) to talk to those who are not part of the courtly milieu: the women (aside from Gunnhild in the Atley episode) and the young, inexperienced poet. The irony here, as in so many scenes in the saga, is that Egil himself, like his addressees, is an outsider to the court.

The third verse contained in the Atley episode is composed when Egil's companion, Olvir, has almost sunk into unconsciousness from heavy drinking. It is a metrical and poetic tour de force:

so Egil got up and led him over to the door. He swung his cloak over his shoulder and gripped his sword underneath it. When they reached the door, Bard went after them with a full horn and asked Olvir to drink a farewell toast. Egil stood in the doorway and spoke this verse:

I'm feeling drunk, and the ale
has left Olvir pale in the gills,
I let the spray of ox-spears
foam over my beard.
Your wits have gone, inviter
of showers on to shields;
now the rain of the high god
starts pouring upon you.

Egil tossed away the horn, grabbed hold of his sword and drew it. It was dark in the doorway; he thrust the sword so deep into Bard's stomach that the point came out through his back. Bard fell down dead, blood pouring from the wound. Then Olvir dropped to the floor, spewing vomit. Egil ran out of the room. It was pitch dark outside. (74–5)

[stóð þá Egill upp ok leiddi Ǫlvi útar til duranna ok helt á sverði sínu. En er þeir koma at durunum, þá kom Bárðr eptir þeim ok bað Ǫlvi drekka brautfararminni sitt. Egill tók við ok drakk ok kvað vísu:

Ǫlvar mik, þvít Ǫlvi
ǫl gervir nú fǫlvan,
atgeira lætk ýrar
ýring of grǫn skýra;
ǫllungis kannt illa,
oddskýs, fyr þér nýsa,
rigna getr at regni,
regnbjóðr, Hávars þegna.

Egill kastar horninu, en greip sverðit ok brá; myrkt var í forstofunni; hann lagði sverðinu á Bárði miðjum, svá at blóðrefillinn hljóp út um bakit; fell hann dauðr niðr, en blóð hljóp ór undinni. Þá fell Ǫlvir, ok gaus spýja ór honum. Egill hljóp þá út ór stofunni; þá var niðamyrkr úti. (109–10)]

The pace has quickened, and the imagery in this verse recalls that of the prose. Of particular interest in this verse is the style. Egil uses *dunhent*, "echoing rhyme," where the last word of the line is partially repeated at the beginning of the next – Ǫlvi / ǫl; ýrar / ýring; regni / regn- – throughout the verse, except for lines 5 and 6. This echo device is one of those features of prosody analysed in metrical and grammatical treatises contemporaneous with the writing of the saga. Snorri illustrates it in stanza 24 in *Háttatal* (Sturluson 1931, 227) and Óláfr Þórðarson alludes to similar poetic repetition in *The Third Grammatical Treatise* when he uses Hallfred's famous sword-verse, which includes the word *sverð* ("sword") in seven of its eight lines, to exemplify the figure *polintethon*.[9] Óláfr notes that this figure requires a play of word forms as well as the echo in sound, which is just what we find in this verse by Egil. This technique of linking the odd line to the even is also found in early Irish poetry.[10] In the first half-verse (*helmingr*) there is a remarkable description of how the ale flows across Olvir's cheeks. He is soaked in ale. The *dunhent* or echoic verse-form adds to the impact of the description: the continuity between the lines suggests how the liquid falls in a continuous downpour. Harmony is achieved between form and content.

A liquid of a different colour appears in the second half-verse. The verbal echo is ignored in the "dry" lines 5 and 6 when the clouds are darkening, but is heard again when the rain flows: "rigna getr at regni, / regnbjóðr, Hávars þegna." Here the kenning "regn Hávars þegna" (literally: "rain of the retainers of Odin") is a cleverly devised double entendre. The poet refers to both the mead of poetry and the blood that will flow when Egil drops the horn and flings his sword. The two halves of the verse echo the sequence of events in the hall: Olvir falls unconscious in the vomited liquor and Bard dies amidst the blood spouting from his wound. The image is violent, yet powerful. The two bodily liquids are depicted through a reference to the rain of the heavens, and thus a cosmological allusion is realized.[11]

Egil Skallagrimsson, or should we say the poet of *Egil's Saga*, is particularly fond of both the echo device and the placing of full internal rhyme in odd lines – as in line 1 of the Olvir stanza. Three further examples occur in the saga. Just as the technique of *háttleysa* links five stanzas, and thus five episodes in the saga, the four *dunhent* stanzas connect key scenes in Egil's life: his first encounter with Gunnhild and King Eirik in Atley, Egil's litigation at the Gulathing, and his final confrontation with his son Þorsteinn.

Egil openly provokes King Eirik and Gunnhild by pursuing Asgerd's inheritance in Norway against their will. In the episode at the Gulathing, where Egil litigates regarding Asgerd's inheritance, there are two significant verses which bring out the essence of the lawsuit in a brilliant way. One of his verses, addressed to King Eirik, expresses the skald's distress at the proposition that his wife Asgerd is born a slave-woman:

This man pinned with thorns claims
that my wife, who bears my drinking horn,
is born of a slave-woman;
Selfish Onund looks after himself. (109)

[Þýborna kveðr þorna
þorn reið áar horna,
sýslir hann of sína
síngirnð Ǫnundr, mína.] (156)

The thorns are biting, as is the accusation that Asgerd is of low birth, and in the following lines Onund's avarice in seizing Asgerd's inheritance is underlined. The *dunhenda* technique serves to bring Egil's point home, and reminds the saga audience of the Atley episode where Egil had crossed the royal couple for the first time. The first word, *þý-* ("slave"), furthermore recalls Egil's description of the merry maids at Bard's feast and signals that Egil is seriously offended. Resentment cannot be avoided and Egil leaves the assembly cursing his enemies.

The second verse is composed on board Egil's ship, and there the first two lines and the last two lines are connected through verbal repetition.

Thorn-foot's false heir ruined
my claim to the inheritance.
...
We disputed great fields
That serpents slumber on: gold. (111)

[Erfingi réð arfi
arfljúgr fyr mér svarfa,
...
vér deildum fjǫl foldar
foldværingja, goldin.] (159)

Those echoing words distil the reasons for the dispute, respectively inheritance (*arfi*) in the first lines and land (*fold*), the estate of Asgerd's father, at the heart of the dispute in the last lines; *arfi*/*arfljúgr*, and *foldar*/*foldværingja*.

The third scene is linked to the Gulathing stanza, and again strong feelings in relation to inheritance are evoked. In the stanza Egil describes Thorstein, the only son that survived him. Thorstein is more like Egil's brother Thorolf and his mother's first husband than his own father. Thorolf Skallagrimsson had been "popular with everyone and his father and mother were very fond of him" (54: "vinsæll af alþýðu; unni honum ok vel faðir ok móðir," 80), while Egil was ugly and difficult to deal with. Egil's zealous nature is revealed in his animosity towards Thorstein, who to Egil's irritation was Asgerd's favourite. The rivalry between the brothers Egil and Thorolf is thus echoed at the very end of *Egil's Saga*, underlying the importance of this relationship. Thorstein Egilsson was

> a very handsome man when he grew up, with fair hair and a fair complexion. He was tall and strong, although not on his father's scale. Thorstein was a wise and peaceful man, a model of modesty and self-control. Egil was not very fond of him. Thorstein, in turn, did not show his father much affection, but Asgerd and Thorstein were very close. (186)
>
> [allra manna fríðastr sýnum, hvítr á hár ok bjartr álitum; hann var mikill ok sterkr, ok þó ekki eptir því sem faðir hans. Þorsteinn var vitr maðr ok kyrrlátr, hógværr, stilltr manna bezt; Egill unni honum lítit; Þorsteinn var ok ekki við hann ástúðigr, en þau Ásgerðr ok Þorsteinn unnusk mikit. (274)]

Asgerd and Thorstein come up with the idea that Thorstein should wear Egil's silk scarves to the assembly. These scarves were a gift from Egil's cherished friend and patron Arinbjorn hersir (as already noted, Egil is listed as Arinbjorn's court poet in the version of *Skáldatal* found in Codex Upsaliensis) and Egil keeps them under lock and key in a chest, along with his other treasures. The scarves are dirtied at the assembly, but Asgerd washes them and puts them back in the chest. However, Egil notices that they have been touched, whereupon Asgerd tells him the truth. He then composes a verse, remarkable for the harsh criticism it directs against Thorstein.

> I had little need of an heir
> to use my inheritance.
> My son has betrayed me
> in my lifetime, I call that treachery. (186–7)
>
> [Áttkak erfinytja
> arfa mér til þarfan,
> mik hefr sonr of svikvinn,
> svik telk í því, kvikvan.] (274)

This verse clearly echoes Egil's earlier verse in *dunhent* about Asgerd's inheritance. The first two internal rhymes in the first two lines play on the same consonant clusters: *erfi/arfa/þarfan*. The sorrowful father of *Sonatorrek* is distant, and here we may remind ourselves that the complete text of *Sonatorrek* appears in the narrative only in Ketilsbók, not in Möðruvallabók or in the Wolfenbüttel manuscript. The words in the stanza are chosen with ice-cold precision. Egil says that he has got an heir while he is still alive; Thorstein has seized his inheritance prematurely. By using the echoing device in lines 3 and 4 he draws out the main message: *mik/svikvinn, svik/kvikvan*. His favourite ploy of employing full rhyme instead of half rhyme is used in line 3, bringing home the true message of the verse, and perhaps even of the saga. It is a story of betrayal and distrust. After Asgerd's death, which is noted immediately after this episode, Egil takes leave of his inherited estate at Borg, where Thorstein lives with his family, and moves to Mosfell, to spend the last years of his life with Thordis, the daughter of Asgerd and Thorolf, and her husband Grim. Nevertheless it was his unfavoured son, Thorstein, who carried his family forward, as forefather of the Sturlungs.

3

The saga is written in a cultural milieu passionate about skaldic verse. Moreover, the treatises on skaldic poetics, *Snorra Edda* and *The Third Grammatical Treatise*, and the manuscripts associated with the Sturlungs (such as Codex Upsaliensis), bear witness to a particular fondness for the poet Egil. One of the most striking features of *Egil's Saga* is the sophisticated use of Egil's poetry with its constituent stylistic devices woven right through the work. In this essay we have noted how two distinctive variations of *dróttkvætt*, *háttleysa* and *dunhent*, are used strategically to link key episodes in the saga. On the one hand we see a master poet at ease in the company of women and a young poet, but when the plot thickens and sensitive issues of inheritance and birthright are at stake, he delivers his message with technical virtuosity and panache. Of these two devices *dunhent* is the most arresting – stylistically, aesthetically, and thematically.

The use of non-standard verse-forms, variations of the traditional *dróttkvætt*, emerges as an important characteristic of the poetry spoken by Egil in the saga and alerts the reader and listener to underlying themes in the saga itself. In showing such a high degree of sophistication in its use of verse the saga reveals itself as a worthy counterpart of the poetological and grammatical treatises.

NOTES

1 See a comparison of the texts in Nordal 1933: lxxxiii–lxxxv; see also a transcription of the fragment in the editions of the saga by Finnur Jónsson (1886–8: 335–44) and Bjarni Einarsson (2001).

2 E.g., the text of *Brennu-Njáls saga* and *Bandamanna saga* (Nordal 2007: 228–35).

3 Peter Foote (1984, 222) divided the skaldic canon into three parts on the basis of the sources: kings' sagas; treatises on poetry and grammar; and Sagas of Icelanders. He dismissed the verse in the Sagas of Icelanders as historically unreliable, unless "compelling cases can be made for specific exemptions from this dismissive rule – as can certainly be done for verse by Egil Skallagrimsson, for example ... but otherwise the material must be ignored until we can achieve a more accurate chronology for it" (223). This is an important distinction to make when we discuss the verse in the Sagas of Icelanders.

4 Kuhn (1983, 87–9), under the influence of Snorri Sturluson, comes to pretty much the same conclusion.

5 Spelling is normalized.

6 On Egil's *persona* as a poet, see Clunies Ross 1989. On *Egil's Saga*, see Tulinius 2002.

7 I cite Sigurður Nordal's edition of *Egils saga* (1933) in this article. It should be noted that the wording of the verse is sometimes reconstructed, especially when Möðruvallabók and the other manuscripts preserve a corrupt text. A review of the text of Egil's verses would be necessary, but is outside the scope of this paper.

8 Laurence de Looze (1989, 127–8) and William Sayers (1995, 34–5) have most recently discussed this scene.

9 *The Third Grammatical Treatise* ch. 15; verse 80: "Eitt er sverð þat er sverða / sverðauðgan mik gerði" (Ólsen 1884, 98). Helgason and Holtsmark (1941, 125–7) drew attention to Latin parallels for the stylistic variant of *dunhent*.

10 McKenzie 1981, 350.

11 Body imagery in skaldic verse is discussed in detail in chapter 7 of my book *Tools of Literacy* (Nordal 2001, 271–308).

BIBLIOGRAPHY

Clunies Ross, Margaret. 1989. "The Art of Poetry and the Figure of the Poet in Egils saga." In *Sagas of the Icelanders: A Book of Essays*. Ed. John Tucker, 126–49. First printed in 1978. New York: Garland.

de Looze, Laurence. 1989. "Poet, Poem and Poetic Process in *Egils Saga Skalla-Grímssonar*." *Arkiv för nordisk filologi* 104: 123–42.

Einarsson, Bjarni, ed. 2001. *Egils saga Skallagrímssonar*. Vol. 1, A–Redaktionen. Editiones Arnamagnæanæ, Series A, vol. 19. Copenhagen: Reitzel.

Faulkes, Anthony. 1992. "The Use of Snorri's Verse-Forms by Earlier Norse Poets." In *Snorrastefna. 25.-27. júlí 1990* (Rit Stofnunar Sigurðar Nordals 1). Ed. Úlfar Bragason, 35–51. Reykjavík: Stofnun Sigurðar Nordals.

Fidjestøl, Bjarne. 1985. "On a New Edition of Scaldic Poetry." In *The Sixth International Saga Conference 28. 7. - 2. 8. 1985. Workshop Papers*, 319–35. I Copenhagen.

Foote, Peter. 1984. "Wrecks and Rhymes." In *Aurvandilstá. Norse Studies*. The Viking Collection. Studies in Northern Civilization 2. Ed. Michael Barnes, Hans Bekker-Nielsen, and Gerd Wolfgang Weber, 222–35. Odense: Odense University Press.

Helgason, Jón. 1956. "Athuganir um nokkur handrit Egils sögu." In *Nordæla. Afmæliskveðja til prófessors, dr. phil. & litt. & jur. Sigurðar Nordals ambassadors Íslands í Kaupmannahöfn sjötugs 14. september 1956*. Eds. Halldór Halldórsson, Jón Jóhannesson, Steingrímur J. Þorsteinsson, and Þorkell Jóhannesson, 110–48. Reykjavík: Helgafell.

– 1969. "Höfuðlausnarhjal." In *Einarsbók. Afmæliskveðja til Einars Ól. Sveinssonar 12. desember 1969*. Eds. Bjarni Guðnason, Halldór Halldórsson and Jónas Kristjánsson, 156–76. Reykjavík: Nokkrir vinir.

Helgason, Jón, and Anne Holtsmark, eds. 1941. *Háttalykill enn forni*. Bibliotheca Arnamagnæna 1. Copenhagen: Ejnar Munksgaard.

Kuhn, Hans. 1983. *Das* Dróttkvætt. Heidelberg: Winter.

McKenzie, Bridget Gordon. 1981. "On the Relation of Norse Skaldic Verse to Irish Syllabic Poetry." In *Specvlvm Norroenvm. Norse Studies in Memory of Gabriel Turville-Petre*. Eds. Ursula Dronke, Guðrún P. Helgadóttir, Gerd Wolfgang Weber, and Hans Bekker-Nielsen. Odense: Odense University Press.

Nordal, Guðrún. 2001. *Tools of Literacy: The Role of Skaldic Verse in Icelandic Textual Culture of the Twelfth and Thirteenth Centuries*. Toronto: University of Toronto Press.

– 2007. "The Art of Poetry and the Sagas of Icelanders." In *Learning and Understanding in the Old Norse World. Essays in Honour of Margaret Clunies Ross*. Eds. Ritstjórar Kate Heslop, Judy Quinn, and Tarrin Wills, 219–37. Brepols: Turnhout.

Nordal, Sigurður, ed. 1933. *Egils saga Skalla-Grímssonar*. Íslenzk fornrit 2. Reykjavík: Hið íslenzka fornritafélag.

Pálsson, Heimir. 2012. "Introduction." In *Snorri Sturluson: The Uppsala Edda*. DG 11 4to. London: Viking Society for Northern Research.

Ólsen, Björn Magnússon, ed. 1884. *Den tredje og fjærde grammatiske afhandling i Snorres Edda tilligemed de grammatiske afhandlingers prolog og to andre tillæg*. Samfundet til udgivelse af gammel nordisk litteratur 12. Copenhagen: Knudtzons.

Sayers, William. 1995. "Poetry and Social Agency in *Egils saga Skalla-Grímssonar*." *Scripta Islandica* 46: 29–62.

Scudder, Bernard, trans. 2005. *Egil's Saga*. London: Penguin.

Sigurðsson, Gísli. 2002. *Túlkun Íslendingasagna í ljósi munnlegrar hefðar: Tilgáta um aðferð*. Reykjavík: Stofnun Árna Magnússonar.

Sturluson, Snorri. 1931. *Edda Snorra Sturlusonar udgivet efter håndskrifterne*. Ed. Finnur Jónsson. Copenhagen: Gyldendalske boghandel, Nordisk forlag.

– 1987. *Edda*. Trans. Anthony Faulkes. London: Dent.

– 1991. *Edda. Háttatal*. Ed. Anthony Faulkes. Oxford: Clarendon Press.

Tulinius, Torfi H. 2002. *The Matter of the North. The Rise of Literary Fiction in Thirteenth-Century Iceland*. The Viking Collection. Studies in Northern Civilization 13. Odense: Odense University Press.

Identity

4 The Concept of the Self in *Egil's Saga*: A Ricoeurean Approach[1]

LAURENCE DE LOOZE

The Sagas of Icelanders are a unique treasure in world literature, although severely understudied in comparison to the attention lavished on other medieval corpora. This imbalance is due more to the small number of scholars who study Icelandic than to any objective evaluation of the saga literature. Indeed, the Sagas of Icelanders are filled with remarkable events and, even more, with complex and memorable characters. Who could ever forget Njal or Hallgerd? Or Grettir? Or, for that matter, Egil Skallagrimsson?

But if these personages are so memorable, it is worth asking some questions about them – about their identities and their selves. The present essay attempts to animate discussion about the concept of the self in the Sagas of Icelanders by focusing on one work in particular and appropriating a couple of approaches by French scholars to the question of identity. The saga that will serve as my object of study is that of Egil Skallagrimsson, and I shall approach it through the theories of the French philosopher and narratologist Paul Ricoeur, as well as, to a lesser extent, the French classicist Jean-Pierre Vernant.

Egil's Saga is a choice work in which to study the self of the skald protagonist for a number of reasons. First, whether or not we accept that the author was Snorri Sturluson, *Egil's Saga* is nevertheless one of the earliest Sagas of Icelanders, and probably the earliest skaldsaga, if we choose to include it among that group.[2] Indeed, regardless of how we construct the generic taxonomies, the eponymous hero of *Egil's Saga* still holds a prime position for our understanding of both the Sagas of Icelanders genre and the skaldsagas subgenre. One can legitimately argue that *Egil's Saga* sets the pattern for subsequent narratives about skalds (a variant of this view would see the saga as an early "working out" of an already-existing genre or subgenre). Moreover, all readers will agree that *Egil's Saga* is the work of a consummate literary craftsman and that the intertextual relationship between it and subsequent Sagas of

Icelanders, the skaldsagas above all, is equally profound whether we see successor texts as imitating the pattern set down in *Egil's Saga* or actively seeking to modify it.

Many aspects of the protagonist Egil Skallagrimsson have been taken up in critical discussions of the saga,[3] so I will only pass over them lightly here. Scholars have noted the Odinic aspects of both Egil's character and that of other skald protagonists. They have also commented on Egil's ugliness, his aggression and even cruelty, and his skill with words from a very early age (upon introduction he is called "talkative" [54: *málugr*, 80]; he composes his first poem at age three during an incident of surprising audacity; and he commits his first killing at age seven). Some traits of Egil are to be found in the other skaldsaga protagonists Gunnlaug, Kormak, Bjorn, and Hallfred, though the love triangle that figures prominently in the other four skaldsagas plays only a minor role in *Egil's Saga.* While some critics see Egil's absence from his brother Thorolf's wedding to Asgerd and his subsequent marriage to the widowed Asgerd as revealing deep-seated amorous feelings,[4] Egil does not display anything like the love-longing we find in other skald protagonists such as Hallfred, Kormak and Gunnlaug; nor is the saga structured around a love triangle of the sort one finds in other skaldsagas or in continental medieval literature. Egil does, however, appear to display many of the traits that will characterize the skald-protagonists more generally: he is an outsider, hostile to society, cantankerous, and violent, and while he attempts to control events through his use of language he also lives in fear of falling prey to another's language.

Still, the protagonist of *Egil's Saga* has proven difficult to assess in any definitive manner. Both good and bad, generous and selfish, Egil has struck readers at times as being downright bizarre. His is an enigmatic, ambiguous self that does not easily fit into any taxonomy.[5] Some of Egil's traits are unusual, even among the Sagas of Icelanders that take skalds as their protagonists. The putative avarice that some scholars have seen in Egil is one such feature. Moreover, Egil is atypical for living a very long life and dying of old age.[6]

Clearly, Egil continues to hold great fascination for readers and to reward critical attention. As part of my own longstanding interest in *Egil's Saga* I therefore propose to investigate in this essay the self of the protagonist not so much through the historical or cultural background of Icelandic society or through myth, but rather through modern approaches to the construction of selfhood. As already stated, I have chosen to make use of Paul Ricoeur's theories regarding the self. This choice derives above all from the fact that Ricoeur has investigated in detail how the construction of the self is related to questions of narrative, which renders his observations especially à propos for a literary work that encapsulates the full life course of the protagonist. Furthermore, Jean-Pierre Vernant is of use to me here because he has investigated the nature of the individual in heroic cultures, especially ancient Greece. I recognize the risk of transposing observations about ancient Greece into a very different cultural context; however, some of Vernant's suggestions regarding heroic cultures may be instructive for our understanding of the Icelandic material, especially if we frame our discussion within a narratological approach – which is where I wish to begin.

The Sagas of Icelanders are celebrated in part for their admirable depiction of the quotidian. While there has been much debate regarding the degree to which they depict a Settlement-era mentality or a Sturlunga-era one, few would quibble with the assertion that the rhetoric in the sagas is one of *mimesis* (I leave aside for the moment the question of whether *mimesis* should refer to a depiction of things as they are or as they ought to be). Into the sagas' much-vaunted "realism" are often set,[7] however, characters who are "larger than life" or who do not quite fit into society. This is especially true of the skalds. Hallfred, Bjorn, Gunnlaug, Kormak – also Gisli and Grettir – are all misfits who contrast sharply with the run-of-the-mill bondsmen who populate the works. Not that this contrast is felt as an attack on verisimilitude. The skald protagonists come across as entirely believable, which, for me, is yet another reason why it behooves us to inquire into their selves and how they are constructed.

Let us consider a classic element of the Sagas of Icelanders, namely the standard introduction of a person: "X hét maðr ..." ("A man was called X ..."). This simple articulation that one finds in saga after saga introduces a person as a statement of his existence through an act of naming – a kind of "zero-degree" introduction. It is very different, however, from either the fairytale "Once upon a time" or the sort of realism one finds in nineteenth-century novels. A nineteenth-century work would say something like, "X lived in a small street in the town of Y, where he had a small shop Z. ..." The Icelandic statement, however, is not initially about *who* the person is in terms of social details, but rather *that* he is. It *creates* the personage through a speech-act that equates utterance with existence. But rather than a biblical *fiat* that creates *ex nihilo*, the rhetoric of this simple statement immediately implies a past, whether known to us or not, as well as a present. It states, in other words, the *existence* of a character as a *pre-existence* as well, as though the character were already "there," quite independently of the narrative, and as though the saga author were just now getting around to informing the reader of the person's existence, bringing him into the story and making the person visible to us. The stance of the narrator is therefore not that he is beginning a story – which is the stance one finds in both fairy tales and in nineteenth-century realism – but rather that he is merely picking out a particular strand (to use Carol Clover's term [1982]) from a larger web of ongoing lives. If Coleridge was right that fiction involves a suspension of disbelief, then in the sagas, as Charles Singleton (1957, 129) has said of Dante's *Divine Comedy*, the fiction is that there is no fiction.

The introductory statement that first presents an individual is part of the broader rhetorical technique of the sagas, a rhetoric that treats the narrative as already completely in place from the beginning and part of a larger reality of which the narrator is simply giving a portion.[8] If we were to adopt the terms of J.L. Austin, we would have to say that although this statement ("A man was called X …") looks like a simple indicative utterance, it is in fact profoundly performative, having an illocutionary and even perlocutionary force.[9] The narrator imposes on the reader the existence of this character, establishing the there-ness of the personage and of his world, and while the character may be undifferentiated when introduced by that initial phrase, the text already establishes him as a *self.*

This is perhaps the moment to bring in Paul Ricoeur. Ricoeur has reflected on the relationship between the self and narrative, first in his trilogy *Temps et récit* (*Time and Narrative*) and then in a more sustained fashion in his book *Soi-même comme un autre* (*Oneself as Another*).[10] Because Ricoeur has investigated the role of narrative in the construction of the self, his model proves useful for examining the nature of the self in literary works as well as in real life. Indeed, many of Ricoeur's examples come from literature. Moreover, if he (and others such as David Carr in *Time, Narrative and History* [1986]) is correct that the self is conceived or created as a function of temporal narrative, then the construction of the self, whether "real" or "literary," is subject to the same narrative laws.

Let me briefly review two key poles of Ricoeur's theory of the self as he posits it in *Oneself as Another*. In the construction of the self Ricoeur distinguishes between what he terms the *ipse* (the deep "what-ness" of the self) and the *idem* (the self as [re]iteration). If Ricoeur chooses to use Latin terms, it is because some modern vernacular languages – particularly French, the language in which Ricoeur writes – present semantic or grammatical complications for these ideas. *Ipse* or, as Ricoeur often puts it, the *ipséité* of a person, refers to the core sense one has of one's own existence. This *selfness* is not affected by the fact that since one's birth one has changed enormously. One is somehow still the "same" person after ten or even forty years, despite the passage of time. But this matter of sameness versus difference over time introduces the other pole, namely that of *idemeté* (Ricoeur often uses the French form *mêmeté*), which is temporal. To suggest that one is the "same" person today as yesterday is to propose identity as reiteration. We assume that there will be a high degree of sameness between who one is today and who one was yesterday and, perhaps even more importantly, between a person today and that person tomorrow. That sameness-as-reiteration is taken as a sameness-of-self. The complete self is thus a negotiation between the deep sense of self (*ipséité*) that continues even in the face of obvious change and the expectation of sameness (*mêmeté*) from day to day. A crucial task of Ricoeur's theory of the self is to account for how *ipséité* obtains when *mêmeté* is weakened or when there seems to be a disjunction between the two aspects. How can the self remain the "same" in the face of massive change?

Here narrative will intervene.

Let me mention one subset of distinctions that Ricoeur also makes, and which have primarily to do with *mêmeté*. Ricoeur makes an important distinction between what he calls "two models of permanence": one's "character" and "keeping one's word." The former, which he defines as "the set of the distinctive marks that permit the re-identification of a human individual as being the same" (119; "l'ensemble des marques distinctives qui permettent de réidentifier un individu humain comme étant le même," 144) implies, he says, an almost complete overlapping of *ipse* and *idem*. One's dispositions, attitudes, personality, etc., tend to be deeply rooted in the self (*ipse*) and are not, presumably, subject to (sudden) change. The promissory "keeping one's word" is quite different, however. Ricoeur argues that "the fidelity to the self [soi] in the maintenance of one's given word marks the extreme gap between the permanence of the self [soi] and that of the same [même]" ("la fidélité à soi dans le maintien de la parole donnée marque l'écart extrême entre la permanence du soi et celle du même," 143; my translation). Ricoeur argues that an intervention of "narrative identity" mediates between the pole of deep character and that of maintaining consistency to the self. One's character contributes to *who* one is by designating *what* one is: a kind person, a difficult person, a brave person, a cowardly person.

The importance of durable character traits and fidelity to one's word in the Sagas of Icelanders is evident. Readers have often remarked that the initial characterization of a personage in the sagas is almost invariably a definitive assessment of his or her character, and the traits enunciated at the beginning will in general persist until the end of the narrative. Moreover, in the saga, fidelity to one's word or reputation becomes an important marker of *mêmeté*. Many are the instances, for example, of a man who refuses to turn back from danger, despite learning of threats that await him; this "keeping of one's word" is what bestows heroism on the man, even though it may cost him his life. Ditto the ability of an Icelander to make light of his predicament in a life-or-death situation; whether or not a person proves to be "true to his self" at that critical moment (and by this we mean "true to the sort of person he has claimed to be") will define what sort of man he is and how he will be remembered.

This refusal to embrace change on the part of major actors in the sagas would seem to frustrate narrative, and yet the Sagas of Icelanders are rich in narrative. Often the narrative events "try" the principal characters, and during their trials they prove their *mêmeté*: for example, in *Njal's Saga* a key question for a large part of the narrative is whether Njal and Gunnar can stay true to their core selves (*ipse*) and also maintain their promises to each other (*idem*) in the face of escalating violence.[11] Heroic cultures can be unforgiving regarding a breakdown of *mêmeté* in a crucial moment of "reiteration." In the sagas the final word regarding one's *ipse* is not really given until one can judge a person's final acts in terms of his *mêmeté.* In *The Saga of Gunnlaug*, Hrafn's betrayal of Gunnlaug in their final battle proves decisive in determining who he is at his core. Likewise, to lie about how a person has met his death, as Gunnar Lambason does regarding the death of Skarphedin in *Njal's Saga*, is to invent a change in *mêmeté* in order to attack a person's *ipséité*; not surprisingly, to do this is viewed as an egregious offence and for this reason Kari is relentless in pursuing Gunnar and re-imposing the true version of events.

Given this brief overview and application of Ricoeur's ideas, largely drawn from the First, Fifth, and Sixth Studies in his book, we can now return to *Egil's Saga*. I could choose almost any passage at random that begins "There was a man called X" ("X hét maðr"). Indeed the first sentence of *Egil's Saga*, like the first sentence of most Sagas of Icelanders, is of precisely this form: "There was a man named Ulf" (3: "Úlfr hét maðr," 3).[12] This initial presentation is followed in many instances by genealogical information, key to establishing the character, since in a heroic culture who a man is is defined in a profound sense by who his forefathers were. Next comes a statement of character, either expressed directly or obliquely. In the case of Ulf, the genealogy is given. In chapter 7, by contrast, the introduction of Bjorgolf does not give a genealogy, and his introduction is followed directly by a characterization of him. We are told that "[He was] a powerful and wealthy landowner who was descended from a mountain giant, as his strength and size bore witness" (10: "hann var lendr maðr, ríkr ok auðigr, en hálfbergrisi at afli ok vexti ok kynferð," 16).

Further on, in chapter 31, we get to the main characters. Thorolf Skallagrimsson is introduced as handsome, a "[very] cheerful character" (54: "gleðimaðr mikill," 80) and "popular" (54: "brátt vinsæll," 80) while Egil is ugly, "talkative at an early age" (54: "brátt málugr" 80), and "difficult to deal with" (54: "illr viðreignar" 80). This introduction establishes the traits that will characterize the two men for the duration of the narrative. In Ricoeurean terms, these introductions mark an almost complete overlapping of *ipse* and *idem* since one of the goals of the Sagas of Icelanders is to show that there is no gap between the heroes' *ipse* and their *idem*.[13] Indeed, one could read many of the Sagas of Icelanders as staging a deep fear of disjunction in terms of these two aspects. Major figures in the narrative may grow older, but there is anxiety about the possibility that a person might not be "reiterated" as continuing to possess the same traits.

Egil's character is established early on. His audaciousness, his violence, and his skill with words are displayed from the first. His first egregious act takes place at the age of three, when he disobeys his father and rides to Yngvar's gathering; this is also the occasion of his first poem. Egil will then first kill a person when he is seven. In the episode of Egil's trip to Yngvar's feast, Egil seems to conduct himself both as a child and as an older person. Skallagrim's refusal to let Egil make the trip is based in part on the fact that, as he says, Egil is a handful even when he is "sober" (55: *ódrukkinn*, 81). This seems a comment more fitting for an adolescent or an adult than for a three-year-old boy. By contrast, Yngvar's recompense of three shells and a duck's egg for Egil's poem seems well suited to a child, not to a sophisticated poet.

If we nuance slightly Ricoeur's reading of character, I think we can make sense of this duality in the treatment of Egil here. One of the prominent features of the sagas is the interest in genealogy, in part because traits are seen as inhering in the bloodline. Ricoeur's "distinguishing marks" of character are seen in the sagas as passed down from generation to generation and therefore not just characteristic of a particular person; the traits that appear repeatedly (*mêmeté*) are also deeply imbedded in one's *ipse*. Egil's physical appearance and traits of personality characterize him as an individual but they also characterize him as the inheritor of a series of Odinic features that have come down from Kveldulf and Skallagrim, his grandfather and father, and these traits contrast strongly with those of his brother and uncle (see Hallvard Lie 1946 and Bo Almqvist 1961). A number of years ago I made some suggestions regarding the cluster of traits that situate Egil on one side of the bloodline and his brother Thorolf on the other (see de Looze 1989). It is no surprise for the reader, therefore, that Egil is already audacious at only three and a poet, etc., because he carries with him the traits of Kveldulf and Skallagrim. His propensity for violence and aggression is already stamped on him – fully grown and adult, if you will – and the reader knows this from the initial description. We also suspect, of course, that Egil will have run-ins with authority, as he first does with his own father and later with King Eirik.

The identity of a personage, however, is more than just his character or predispositions. For Ricoeur the identity of a person is always constructed in tandem with that of the plot. I quote:

> The person, understood as a character in a story, is not an entity distinct from his or her "experiences." Quite the opposite: the person shares the condition of dynamic identity peculiar to the story recounted. The narrative constructs the identity of the character, what can be called his or her narrative identity, in constructing that of the story told. It is the identity of the story that makes the identity of the character. (148)

> [La personne, comprise comme personnage de récit, n'est pas une entité distincte de *ses* "experiences." Bien au contraire: elle partage le régime de l'identité dynamique propre à l'histoire racontée. Le récit construit l'identité du personnage, qu'on peut appeler son identité narrative, en construisant celle de l'histoire racontée. C'est l'identité de l'histoire qui fait l'identité du personnage. (175)]

The narrative is the arena in which Ricoeur considers how one's *ipse* can endure even when there is change in terms of *mêmeté*. Ricoeur here separates out what he calls "concordance," which he defines as "the principle of order that presides over what Aristotle calls 'the arrangement of facts'" (141: "le principe d'ordre qui préside à ce qu'Aristote appelle 'agencement des faits,'" 168) – which is to say, the ordering principle that holds together the events of the life-narrative and makes them credible. In contrast to this concordance, according to Ricoeur, are the "discordances," which are the unexpected events or "reversals of fortune" (141: "renversements de fortune," 168) that alter the configuration of the plot and can change a character. Every narrative and every life, Ricoeur maintains, is a "discordant concordance" – that is to say, the narrative has to find a way to synthesize the improbable discordances into a larger configuration such that changes in terms of *mêmeté* do not seem to vitiate the *ipséité*. The discordances that would seem in fact to disrupt the order have to be made constituents of that order. The events of a life do not simply hold meaning as an intelligible configuration; they become meaningful through their relation to the narrative that negotiates between discordance and concordance, heterogeneity and homogeneity. This is why a person can change radically, and yet the life can still, as Wilhelm Dilthey would put it, "hang together" (the German expression from Dilthey is quoted by Ricoeur: "Zusammenhang des Lebens," 168).

The full complexity of the self, then, is lodged in how the events (Ricoeur calls them *actions*) of the narrative – the discordances that arise – are made part of a meaningful configuration. This configuration is what prevents a change in *ipséité* despite turbulence in terms of *mêmeté*. The full self, then, is the narrative of this "discordant concordance." Some of the most radical changes in terms of *idemeté* or *mêmeté* are, as both Ricoeur and Vernant would argue, conversionary narratives, such as those of Saint Paul in the Bible and Saint Augustine in his *Confessions*, in which the protagonist becomes a "new man," having broken radically with who he had been. Ricoeur would argue that the extraordinary discordance of Saul becoming Paul on the road to Damascus or Augustine in a garden in Milan is made concordant by the narrative that harmonizes these sudden changes – that is, the discordances – into a larger narrative configuration. The complete "selves" of Saints Paul and Augustine are expressed by and through this "discordant concordance" of the narrative.

Before returning to Egil, I would like to turn to my second French scholar, Jean-Pierre Vernant. In his work on ancient Greece, Vernant distinguishes between the selves that are *in* and/or *of* this world, and those that renounce this world (the distinction comes from Louis Dumont's *Homo hierarchicus*). Certainly selves that turn away from this world have little place in the Sagas of Icelanders. Clearly, the Icelandic commonwealth was not the same sort of "egalitarian" society that ancient Greece was, at least in theory – that is, one in which "each individual ... is in principle able to fulfill all social functions" (Vernant 1989, 213–14: "chaque individu ... est en principe apte à remplir toutes les fonctions sociales"). Thus, it may be risky to extrapolate ideas from Vernant's work and apply them to the world of the Icelandic sagas. Still, Vernant's reformulation of Michel Foucault's own treatment of the individual in his book *Le Souci de soi* may prove useful to us here. Vernant isolates three elements of the self in ancient Greek culture (1989, 214–16):

1) The role of the individual in his group or groups and the relative autonomy s/he has,
2) The role of the subject expressing himself in the first person and making utterances of his singular self,
3) Practices that express interiority.

As in the Greek epics, there are very few examples of interiority in the prose of the Sagas of Icelanders: Gunnar's glance in *Njal's Saga* at the beauty of Iceland and his reflections on whether the fact that he is slower to anger than other men might taint his masculinity are rare instances. However, the Sagas, like Greek culture, have a large corpus of poetry in which the subject expresses himself in first-person declamations. Indeed, Icelandic culture juxtaposes the two in the same text, whereas in Greece lyric poetry and epic narrative occupy quite different realms.

Several of Egil's first-person poems are rightfully famous. Certainly much ink has been spilled on the *Sonatorrek*, and that long lament, together with the York-episode in which the *Hǫfuðlausn* is declaimed, have undoubtedly received more attention in *Egil's Saga* than any other portions. I think it is safe to say that the *Hǫfuðlausn* and the *Sonatorrek* can be viewed as the fictional Egil's first-person expression of his singular self;[14] the many critical considerations of the contradictions between Egil's version of his arrival at York and the saga narrator's version, like the arguments regarding the exact meaning of certain passages, reveal that the poem has been viewed by scholars as an expression of Egil's subjectivity. The *Sonatorrek* is an even more stunning example of Egil's self-articulation. The issues surrounding the poems and their meanings are thorny, and they have occupied scholars who have devoted major portions of their careers to the intricacies of Icelandic verse.[15]

I want, instead, to consider here the events that lead *up to* the York-episode and to place them against the thinking of both Ricoeur and Vernant. Though they are less studied, the series of events that make Egil such a complete enemy of King Eirik follow a narrative trajectory that is common in the sagas – one in which offences gradually escalate until they bring on the death of one of the two parties to the conflict. Following on the initial tension between Eirik's clan and Skallagrim's family, there is first the killing of Bard (chapter 44); at issue here is not whether the killing is justified but rather the way it first makes Egil into an enemy of Eirik and Gunnhild. As a result, Eirik declares Egil a persona non grata in Norway, and when four chapters later Egil shows up again in Norway at his friend Thorir's, Eirik makes clear that it is only out of his great respect for Thorir that he is letting his interdiction be crossed. In the next chapter, Egil attacks Gunnhild's brother Eyvind, kills all his men, and takes Eyvind's ship (again, I am not considering justifications here). Finally, and most seriously, in chapter 57 (chapter 58 in the English translation) Egil attacks and kills both Berg-Onund and Eirik's own son Rognvald; this in fact happens when, after having made an attack and left, Egil decides to go back and, as he says, "kill everyone" (118: "drepa menn þá alla," 169). Had Egil not returned, he would not have crossed paths with Rognvald.

The killings in this series become increasingly grave; they escalate from killing a supporter of the king, to attacking the queen's brother and killing his men, and finally to the most egregious crime of all, killing the king's own son. As I have already noted, this narrative pattern is well known in the sagas: the escalation continues until the final showdown, at which point the character will finally die. One is reminded of Njal's warning to Gunnar not to kill twice in the same family or to break a settlement; things of course escalate until Gunnar *does* kill twice in the same family and then he also fails to respect the settlement that sends him abroad. Similar is the case of Grettir, who is killed shortly before he marks twenty years of outlawry.

The curious thing in *Egil's Saga* is that this series goes in a very different direction. It leads to the strange confrontation in York for which the outcome is not at all in line with the usual expectations (Ricoeur would call this a discordance). Egil escapes with his head, which is to say with his life, and does so after committing a killing that cries out for blood vengeance and for which no lord would normally accept compensation. It is neither in keeping with the pattern of saga narratives for Eirik to fail to kill Egil when he has him under his power, nor, for that matter, is it typical for a protagonist in the Sagas of Icelanders to die of old age, as Egil in fact does. The demands of the narrative code generally oblige the protagonist to die heroically in a fight, and the nature of the death is usually critical to the definition of the self. Egil alludes to this ethos when he expresses shame for living to an old age – blind, hard of hearing, and with unsteady legs (chapter 85; chapter 88 in the translation) – and yet he goes down as a larger-than-life figure all the same.

Intercalated into these escalating events is another series of episodes that mitigates them somewhat. The almost ten chapters between Egil's attack on Eyvind and his killing of Berg-Onund and Rognvald are taken up by the episodes of Egil's and Thorolf's participation in Athelstan's wars against King Olaf of Scotland. What may seem a digression is, I suspect, strategically placed in order to prepare for the York episode. Several elements need to be underlined here. First, Egil does great service to Athelstan, particularly in relation to the recovery of Northumberland. When Athelstan subsequently grants Northumberland to Eirik, he is giving the Norwegian a region that Egil effectively won for him. I think it important, as a result, that the next meeting between Egil and Eirik takes place in England, not in Norway; Eirik is the latest arrival in England, both he and Egil are subjects of Athelstan, and Egil enjoys great legitimacy in Athelstan's England, above all in Northumberland. In addition, there is the fact that the Northumberland campaign has cost Egil's brother Thorolf his life. To be sure, there is a certain irony in the fact that Egil is quite discontented until he gets "compensation" from Athelstan for the loss of his brother.

All of this gives to Egil's presence in England a legitimacy that is at least equal to Eirik's. The saga narrator makes every effort, in other words, to prepare for the extraordinary discordance that is coming a few chapters later. For the narrative is going to break radically with the normal configuration one finds in the Sagas of Icelanders, and, as Ricoeur would argue, this discordance will become what he calls a "discordant concordance" and hence part of the (extraordinary) self of Egil. As many critics have intuited, the York episode is crucial to our sense of who Egil is, which is to say that the discordance of this extraordinary sequence, by being harmonized into the narrative, becomes a key element of Egil's identity.

What changes the normal pattern of events is of course Egil's composition of *Hǫfuðlausn*. I have some years ago suggested that this episode says a great deal about how poetry and poetic composition are viewed in the sagas (de Looze 1989). I suggested at the time that the performative aspect of Egil's composition and declamation is powerful, and that the illocutionary dimension has a strong effect, obliging Eirik to compensate the poet. In a sense, Egil "re-writes" the course of the narrative by imposing his own first-person discourse on events and determining their course.

If Ricoeur is right that the self is a configuration in which the discordances are mediated by a narrative that makes them concordant within a larger configuration, the York episode is indispensable for our understanding of Egil's self. The unexpectedness of Egil's saving of his "head" when by rights he should lose it goes against the normal pattern of the sagas. It tells us not only about the role of poetry, but about Egil as well. Only such an extraordinary "self" as Egil could impose language so effectively on events that, against all reasonable expectation, the escalating violence does *not* result in death. Moreover, this discordant act becomes a defining moment in terms of Egil's core *ipse* (which would have been obliterated had Egil been put to death) and his character (*mêmeté*), and the discordant event is assimilated into the series of audacious incidents that mark Egil's life and that are made part of the overall narrative configuration of Egil. Indeed, this episode forms part of a string of events in which Egil does not triumph through the use of arms but by using his mouth; the series begins with his poem at three years old, continues through the York episode, and is gruesomely parodied in his killing of Atli when, his sword having proved worthless, he bites through Atli's throat. The narrative configuration makes these discordances concordant, but it does so in moments when the protagonist takes over in the first person (i.e., using his mouth) and stamps himself onto events. Egil is, in a sense, the proto-writer or proto-poet of his own life. His poetic act at York is a discordant event and yet also an event that becomes concordant in the configuration of the whole life narrative.

Ricoeur, in the second of his "studies of the self," returns to Benveniste's notion of *énonciation* (58–65; see also Benveniste 1974) and considers how a personage, at the textual level of the *énoncé*, can become an active force by making use of the illocutionary nature of utterances. Ricoeur is right to remind us that, as Austin also pointed out (1962), at a certain level all utterances are illocutionary and none is simply locutionary. Using different terms, Mieke Bal has pointed out much the same thing in her book on narratology (1985): when one says, "The book is on the table," there is an unspoken "I declare that …" or "I insist that the book is on the table"; indeed, for Mieke Bal all third-person narrative is covertly first person.[16] More interesting, I think, is the fact that in *Egil's Saga* at the level of the *énoncé* the protagonist, through an illocutionary, first-person act of discourse, not only extends his life when he is condemned to death, but actually creates the very discordance that will become concordant through the configuration of a narrative that incorporates that unexpected event as a constituent part of his self. In Ricoeurean terms, Egil's *ipséité*, that person/self he most profoundly is, is one who can effect changes in terms of *mêmeté* such that discordance characterizes the actions of both Eirik and Egil in this episode. The ability to impose discordance is, if you will, at the very core of Egil's *ipséité*. Egil never becomes predictable; rather, he is forever surprising the reader – generous when we least expect it, astonishingly cruel at other times – and in so doing he also repeatedly challenges the pattern of the protagonist's life story in the Sagas of Icelanders. What could be more fitting for a person who comes from a long line of shape-changers?

In terms of Vernant's three aspects of the self in a heroic society, Egil proves to have greater autonomy than the norm; moreover, he carves out this greater freedom by means of his first-person self-expression. We can trace this same movement in the *Sonatorrek* in which Egil's first-person utterance about why he does not wish to go on living becomes both the reason for his continued life and the expression – the "proto-writing," if you will – of that continued life. The first-person poetic composition again allows Egil to effect an about-face, harmonizing this sudden change in terms of *mêmeté* with Egil's *ipséité*.

If we place *Egil's Saga* within the context of the Sagas of Icelanders more generally, how representative is it? On the one hand it does what all narratives of the self do, according to Ricoeur: the discordances become concordant by means of a narrative configuration. As a result, sudden and/or unexpected changes – moments of betrayal, interiority, about-face, etc. – become keys to a particular *ipse*, and almost more so when they would seem, in the absence of a narrative that configures them, to mark an inexplicable rupture in terms of the self. In the case of the skaldsagas I think a case can be made for the poet-figures putting their mark on events by exploiting the illocutionary power of language. By their use of language they affect – and occasionally alter greatly – the course of their lives. As a result they become, in a profound way, people who both affect and effect their lives through language. What is perhaps unique in *Egil's Saga* is the almost paradoxical nature of the self in which the most concordant actions are the seemingly discordant ones.

In the context of European literature more broadly conceived, I believe that comparison can be made with a whole series of medieval literary works that cast poet-figures as protagonists. In such thirteenth-century French narratives as the *Guillaume de Dole* and the *Chatelain de Couci* the protagonists write their lives, in a sense, from within the narrative, and in *Le Bel Inconnu* and *Le Roman de la Rose* it is the narrator who self-consciously proposes to write discontinuities into the protagonist's self, challenging the reader to render them concordant; this self-conscious construction of the self through literary art also continues through most of the fourteenth century in Spain, France, and England (in Guillaume de Machaut, Jean Froissart, the Arcipreste de Hita, and Geoffrey Chaucer, etc.). As for characters whose core self (*ipse*) comprises a series of alterations in terms of *idem*, I know of only two such personages: Faux Semblant in the *Roman de la Rose* and the narrator of the Spanish *Libro de buen amor*.

In closing, let me return to the question of genealogy. I think, in truth, that I need to nuance somewhat the Ricoeur-Vernant approach I have been taking. In their respective books, both Paul Ricoeur and Jean-Pierre Vernant are thinking of the self as an individual. It would be a mistake, however, to consider the self in the sagas in quite the same individualistic terms. As Bo Almqvist and Hallvard Lie have taught us, the Icelandic sagas are resolute in their depiction of the self as characterized by traits that have come through the bloodline and from which there is virtually no escape. Certainly in the sagas there is no self-fashioning of the sort Stephen Greenblatt has discovered in Renaissance culture (1980). Egil, as a character, is inevitably a re-vision and a re-version of Skallagrim and Kveldulf; he will repeat certain types of experiences that either his forefathers have had or that he himself has had at an earlier point in his life. Many of the episodes in the saga are linked analogically rather than by cause and effect, as in the more modern narratives Ricoeur is thinking of: the scene in Armod's hall recalls the earlier episode with Bard; Egil's appearance at Arinbjorn's in Norway repeats his arrival at both Thorir's and Arinbjorn's dwellings earlier; Skallagrim's murderous impulses towards Egil (chapter 40) are echoed in Egil's avowed intention to kill the filial poet, Einar Skalaglamm; and of course the York episode harkens back to Egil's first transgressive appearance at Yngvar's feast.

Egil's final "appearance," if I can call it that, in the saga is in the form of his skull during an episode that graces the penultimate chapter (86; 87 in the English translation). Egil's almost indestructible cranium is, of course, a humorous return to the *Hǫfuðlausn*, as I have suggested elsewhere (see de Looze 1989). The "head-ransom" is one of the many instances of *mêmeté* in which the dispositions of Egil's character – his daring, his audacity, his agonistic stance – are reiterated. But the enduring, indestructible quality of the skull – the locus of speech – long after Egil is dead suggests that it is also an expression of Egil's core being, which is to say of his *ipséité*. The head/skull that survives is not only *what* Egil is on repeated occasions (*mêmeté*), but also *who* he is (*ipséité*): Egil is, in a sense, the hard skull made narrative. He does not live and die as other saga heroes do. He is also the most audacious of them all, and yet, in spite of his egregious risk-taking, he lives (and lives on) longer than just about anyone else.

NOTES

1 An earlier version of this essay was presented orally at the University of Iceland on 5 April 2011. I am grateful for the comments and suggestions by the scholars in attendance and in particular by Jón Karl Helgason, Ármann Jakobsson, and Torfi Tulinius.

2 Although Egil Skallagrimsson is one of the great skalds, there is debate among critics as to whether *Egil's Saga* should be included in the subgenre of Sagas of Icelanders generally called the "skaldsagas" (Icelandic *skáldasögur*) or "sagas of poets." Bjarni Einarsson includes it in the list he provides in his *Skáldasögur* (1993, 589). Margaret Clunies Ross (2001, 36–8), by contrast, excludes *Egil's Saga* from what she calls the "core group" of skaldsagas, placing it in a secondary taxonomy that she calls the "Outliers."

3 See, in particular, Albertsson 1976, Clunies Ross 1978, Dronke 1978, Lie 1946, Sørensen 1980, and Wright 1973.

4 See Falk's essay in this volume.

5 Torfi Tulinius has pointed to the fascination with "uncertain identities" (2000, 242) and the "uncertain ontological status" (2000, 260) of protagonists in the Sagas of Icelanders, and particularly in the skaldsagas. As regards Egil Skallagrimsson, Tulinius, like other scholars, has called attention to his "paradoxical character" as both a "brutal warrior" and a "poet of profound sentiments" ("caractère paradoxal de guerrier brutal et de poète aux sentiments profonds," 1995, 211). Alison Finlay (1992, 33) also underscores the strange combination of "creative genius" and "ugliness, aggression and troublesomeness." While I am not wholly convinced by a Christianizing of Egil (see Tulinius 1997), I am indebted to Torfi Tulinius' sensitive reading of Egil in several of his publications, especially his 2000 essay.

6 Margaret Clunies Ross (1978, 4–9) has suggested that Egil's longevity, as well as some other features, derives from the paradigm of saints' lives. Some features of his temperament she sees as derived from medieval treatises on melancholy.

7 Aristotle defines mimesis as the imitation of things as they should be, not necessarily exactly as they are. Perhaps rather than speaking of "realism" we would do well to speak à la Roland Barthes of a "reality effect" (Barthes 1968).

8 Similarly the comments that "X is now out of the story" and "Now a man Y enters the story" and the allusions to certain events covered in other sagas are of the same order. The narrative voice implies that the characters and events have an existence independent of the particular narration. The narrative is just that: a narrative. But the rhetoric is of an extra-textual reality that continues independently.

9 I draw the terms "performative," "illocutionary," and "perlocutionary" from J.L. Austin (1962), though I understand them as subsequently nuanced by other linguists, in particular John Searle.

10 *Oneself as Another* (1992) is the title of the English translation of Ricoeur's *Soi-même comme un autre* (1990). I will cite both the original French text and the English translation.

11 In Anglo-Saxon texts this sometimes takes the specifically promissory form that Ricoeur mentions, as when a retainer boasts of the prowess he will have on the battlefield the next day and then must live up to his boast or else be shamed: the danger for the construction of the self of failing to keep one's word could not be greater.

12 The English paraphrase of Icelandic sentences of this type cannot do justice to them. Not only is the paraphrase wordier, but the syntax is very different. The Icelandic begins with the character's name, bringing him before the reader as an act of enunciation. One could of course translate as "X was the name of a man," though this would not solve the problem of the wordy paraphrase. The rhetoric of the Icelandic is that the man exists and the narrator is simply alerting us to his existence and giving us his name.

13 "Character" is a thorny issue for Ricoeur. The sedimentation, he argues, of the traits we consider to be part of one's character give it a sense of permanence over time that Ricoeur views as a process of *ipse* "covering over" or subsuming *idem*, even though it does not erase these two poles. "[M]on caractère, c'est moi, moi-même, *ipse*; mais cet *ipse* s'annonce comme *idem*" (146: "[My] character is me, myself, *ipse*; but this *ipse* presents itself as *idem*," 121). I should note that, in English, "character" can refer to a person's traits as well as simply to a person who figures in a narrative. I have tried to be clear at all times in which sense I use the word in my essay, though in general I have avoided the latter meaning.

14 The question of whether or to what extent the saga author may have added or reworked Egil's compositions cannot, of course, be known.

15 See in particular Frank 1978; See 1977; Poole 2001a, 2001b; on the authenticity and authorship of the verses in the skaldsagas more generally, see Gade 2001. We should bear in mind that modern editions of *Egil's Saga* tend to present more of the poetry, including Egil's most famous poems, than any single medieval manuscript of the work does. For recent discussions, see Michael Chesnutt 2001 and Margaret Clunies-Ross 2005, along with her essay in this volume.

16 If we follow Bal, there is, however, a danger of infinite regress. After all, who says "I declare that the book is on the table?" The narrator, of course. But someone has to insist that the narrator says this, and so forth.

BIBLIOGRAPHY

Albertsson, Kristján. 1976. "Egill Skallagrímsson í Jorvik." *Skírnir* 150: 89–97.

Almqvist, Bo. 1961. "Um ákvæðaskáld." *Skírnir* 135: 72–98.

Austin, J.L. 1962. *How to Do Things with Words*. Oxford: Oxford University Press.

Bal, Mieke. 1985. *Narratology: Introduction to the Theory of Narrative*. Trans. Christine van Boheemen. Toronto: University of Toronto Press.

Benveniste, Emile. 1974. *Problèmes de linguistique générale, II*. Paris: Gallimard.

Barthes, Roland. 1968. "L'Effet de réel." *Communications* 11: 84–9.

Carr, David. 1986. *Time, Narrative, and History*. Bloomington: Indiana University Press.

Chesnutt, Michael. 2001. "Preface." In *Egils saga Skallagrímssonar. I. A-Redaktionem*. Ed. Bjarni Einarsson. Editiones Arnamagnæanæ A 19. Copenhagen: Reitzels.

Clover, Carol. 1982. *The Medieval Saga*. Ithaca: Cornell University Press.

Clunies Ross, Margaret. 1978. "The Art of Poetry and the Figure of the Poet in *Egils Saga*." *Parergon* 22: 3–12.

– 2001. "The Skald sagas as a Genre: Definitions and Typical Features." In Poole 2001b: 25–49.

– 2005. "A Tale of Two Poets: Egill Skallagrimsson and Einar skálaglamm. *Arkiv för nordisk filologi* 120: 69–82.

de Looze, Laurence. 1989. "Poet, Poem and Poetic Process in *Egils Saga Skalla-Grímssonar*." *Arkiv för Nordisk Filologi* 104: 123–42.

Dronke, Ursula. 1978. "The Poet's Persona in the Skalds' Sagas." *Parergon* 22: 23–8.

Einarsson, Bjarni. 1993. "*Skáldasögur*." In *Medieval Scandinavia: An Encyclopedia*. 589–90.

Finlay, Alison. 1992. "*Egils saga* and Other Poets' Sagas." In *Introductory Essays on Egils Saga and Njáls Saga*. Ed. John Hines and Desmond Slay, 33–48. London: Viking Society for Northern Research.

Frank, Roberta. 1978. *Old Norse Court Poetry: The dróttkvætt Stanza*. Islandica, 42. Ithaca: Cornell University Press.

Gade, Kari Ellen. 2001. "The Dating and Attributions of Verses in the Skald Sagas." In Poole 2001b: 50–74.

Greenblatt, Stephen. 1980. *Renaissance Self-Fashioning: From More to Shakespeare*. Chicago: University of Chicago Press.

Lie, Hallvard. 1946. "Jorvikferden. Et vendepunkt in Egil Skallagrimssons liv." *Edda* 33: 145–248. Reprinted in *Om Sagakunst og skaldskap*. Øvre Ervik: Alvheim & Eide, 1982.

Poole, Russell. 2001a. "Introduction." In Poole 2001b: 1–24.

– ed. 2001b. *Skaldsagas: Text, Vocation, and Desire in the Icelandic Sagas of the Poets*. Berlin: Walter de Gruyter.

Ricoeur, Paul. 1990. *Soi-même comme un autre*. Paris: Seuil.

– 1992. *Oneself as Another*. Trans. Kathleen Blarney. Chicago: University of Chicago Press.

See, Klaus von. 1977. "Skaldenstrophe und Sagaprosa: Ein Betrag zum Problem der mündlichen Überlieferung in der altnordischen Literatur." *Medieval Scandinavia* 10: 58–82. Reprinted in *Edda, Saga, Skaldendichtung: Aufsätze zur Skandinavischen Literatur des Mittelalters*. Heidelberg: Carl Winter Verlag, 1981. 461–85.

Singleton, Charles. 1957. "The Irreducible Dove." *Comparative Literature* 9: 124–35.

Sørensen, J.S. 1980. "Komposition og værdiunivers i *Egils Saga*." *Gripla* 4: 260–72.

Tulinius, Torfi. 1995. *La "Matière du nord". Sagas legendaries et fiction dans la literature islandaise en prose du XIIIe siècle*. Paris: Presses de l'Université de Paris-Sorbonne.

– 1997. "Le Statut théologique d'Egill Skalla-Grímsson." In *Hugur. Mélanges d'histoire, de literature et de mythologie offerts à Régis Boyer pour son soixante-cinquième anniversaire*. Ed. C. Lecouteux and O. Gouchet, 279–88. Paris: Presses de l'Université de Paris-Sorbonne.

– 2000. "The Matter of the North: Fiction and Uncertain Identities in Thirteenth-Century Iceland." In *Old Icelandic Literature and Society*. Ed. Margaret Clunies Ross, 242–65. Cambridge: Cambridge University Press.

Vernant, Jean-Pierre. 1987. *Sur l'individu*. Paris: Seuil.

– 1989. *L'individu, la mort, l'amour*. Paris: Gallimard.

Wright, Dorenna Allen. 1973. "The Skald as Saga-Hero." *Parergon* 6: 13–20.

5 Self-Description in Egil's Poetry

MARGARET CLUNIES ROSS

Egil's Saga is what I have elsewhere (Clunies Ross 2001) called "an outlier" of the subgroup of Sagas of Icelanders usually referred to as skaldsagas (*skálda-sögur*, or "sagas of poets"). It is an outlier because it conforms in some respects, but not in others, to a common structural and conceptual pattern in the group of sagas that includes *Kormak's Saga, The Saga of Hallfred the Troublesome Poet, The Saga of Bjorn, Champion of the Hitardal People*, and the *Saga of Gunnlaug Serpent-Tongue*. These sagas are quasi-fictional biographies of Icelandic skalds, who began life as social misfits in Iceland but became successful poets at the courts of foreign kings. The skaldsagas include a considerable amount of poetry, mostly in the form of "loose stanzas" (*lausavísur*) within a prose context, where the poets express their thwarted love for young Icelandic women, whereas the poetry they composed for foreign rulers is for the most part recorded in other saga genres, chiefly in kings' sagas.

The principal compositional pattern of *Egil's Saga* modifies the formula just outlined in three important ways. In the first place, there are only two *lausa-vísur* (23 and 24) ascribed to Egil in his saga that could be termed love poetry, and these relate to his desire for his dead brother's widow, Asgerd. Otherwise, his poetry is free from any heterosexual love interest, although the *lausavísur* about his friendship with the Norwegian Arinbjorn *hersir* Thorisson and the long poem *Arinbjarnarkviða*, "Poem for Arinbjorn," celebrate male friendship, a theme absent from the other poets' sagas, which instead feature male-to-male rivalry. The second major difference between Egil's life-history and his poetry and those of the other protagonists of sagas of poets is that whereas the latter are depicted developing positive personal relations with foreign, mainly Norwegian, kings and becoming their court poets, Egil's relationship with the one king of Norway with whom he has close contact, Eirik Blood-axe Haraldsson, is of a decidedly negative kind. His relationship with the

Anglo-Saxon king Athelstan is equivocal, though it develops some positive qualities after the king has compensated him sufficiently – in his view – for his brother Thorolf's death. As if to underline this difference between *Egil's Saga* and the other poets' sagas, all the poetry ascribed to Egil, whether personal or public, has been recorded in manuscripts containing *Egil's Saga* or in the poetic treatises, Snorri Sturluson's *Edda* and *The Third Grammatical Treatise* of Óláfr Þórðarson, although there is strong evidence that Egil's long poems, *Hǫfuðlausn* ("Head Ransom"), *Arinbjarnarkviða*, and *Sonatorrek* ("Hard Loss of Sons"), may not originally have formed part of the saga prosimetrum (Clunies Ross 2010). By contrast, there is not a trace of Egil's poetry in manuscripts of kings' sagas, implying that he did not rate as a court poet in the eyes of the medieval compilers of historical sagas. The Möðruvallabók version of *Egil's Saga* does its best to stress at least vestigial elements of courtliness in Egil's poetic oeuvre by attributing to him fragments of *drápur*, long skaldic poems that are otherwise unrecorded (cf. Clunies Ross 2005a), but this aspect of his life-history remains insignificant in contrast to his private persona.

A third difference between the poets' sagas and *Egil's Saga* is the subject of this essay. It concerns the remarkably rich element of self-description in Egil's poetry, which complements the other personalized themes to be found both there and in the prose saga. I use the term "personalized" rather than "personal" here to signal the at least partly conventional nature of this poetry. By "self-description" I mean the representation of a character's physical self, together with the attributes that are said to accompany it, rather than references to that character's inner thoughts about the events of the saga in which he is a protagonist. It has been observed many times (e.g., by Ólason 1998, 124–9) that one of the functions of skaldic poetry within both sagas of Icelanders and other genres is as a literary device to reveal the thoughts and feelings of the character in the narrative who is depicted as speaking the verse. While there is obviously a connection between self-description in skaldic poetry and the more general use of skaldic verse to reveal the thoughts and feelings of saga characters, my primary purpose here is to focus on poetry in which the poet describes his own appearance and behaviour and endows them with certain specific values.

In *Egil's Saga* concern with self-image, physical and mental, is found in both the prose and the poetry, whereas in the other sagas of poets it appears mostly in the prose text and is presented as the words of the saga narrator or of another character in the story. The relative absence of self-description in their verses by poets such as Kormak and Hallfred may seem surprising, given their near-obsession with their lovers' beauty and their keenness to denigrate their male rivals in verses that involve unflattering physical descriptions of these men and images comparing them to unpleasant birds and animals. While the prose texts of the skald sagas are notable for their stereotypical descriptions of the poets as usually dark in colouring and troubled in personality, a characteristic shared with *Egil's Saga*'s description of its protagonist (cf. Clunies Ross 1978 [1989]), relatively little of this element is given expression in their poetry. Kormak, for example, spends many lines of moving verse describing his girlfriend's beauty but devotes parts of just two stanzas to his own self-description, and the first of these is a reflex of what he reports she has said about him.

A substantial group of Egil's references to his physical self clusters round the topic of his head ransom (*hǫfuðlausn*), his release from the threat of death at the hands of King Eirik Blood-axe at York as his reward for composing a flattering poem in the king's honour. This topic does not appear in the encomium *Hǫfuðlausn* itself, which represents the poet coming over the sea to visit Eirik of his own free will in order to present him with a praise poem, but it occupies several stanzas (3–9) of the first part of *Arinbjarnarkviða* and is the subject of four stanzas (33–6) among Egil's *lausavísur*.

The name *Hǫfuðlausn*[1] indicates that this poem belongs to a conventional Old Norse skaldic topos, and is as much a description of the convention as a title proper. So-called head-ransom poems were traditionally composed by skalds who had incurred the anger of their patrons in some way and who offered to compose a praise poem in honour of the offended ruler in order to mollify him and save their own lives.[2] From Odd Nordland's thorough study of this topos in Old Norse literature and Nordic folk tradition, it is clear that it incorporates folktale motifs but may well also have been a skaldic "reality."[3] By contrast with the duress under which the prose text of *Egil's Saga* places the poet in his composition of *Hǫfuðlausn*, the encomium itself stresses the voluntary nature of the skald's act. Whereas the saga prose attributes Egil's second visit to England to the effects of Queen Gunnhild's sorcery and represents his personal circumstances as dire, the first two stanzas of the poem have the speaker state that he came "west over the ocean" ("vestr of ver," 1/1: 185) in a ship carrying a cargo of praise and that Eirik offered him hospitality ("buðumk hilmir lǫð," 2/1: 186) and a hearing for his praise poem (2/5–8). In *Hǫfuðlausn* itself the dynamics of compulsion and danger are completely obliterated and the poem focuses – in rather vague and general terms – on Eirik's prowess in battle and the sights and sounds of warfare. Only the final three stanzas (19–21) return the emphasis to the poet himself, and they refer to his poetic achievement, not to his personal predicament at Eirik's court.

The prose of *Egil's Saga*[4] and the poem *Hǫfuðlausn* are thus at variance in their presentations of the circumstances under which Egil composed a poem in praise of a ruler he hated. It may, of course, have been part of the head-ransom convention for the poet not to allude to his forced praise of his lord, as that may have been thought to lessen the depth and apparent sincerity of the praise itself. Óttarr svarti's *Hǫfuðlausn*, the only extant independent example with which to compare Egil's head ransom, alludes fleetingly to its circumstances of composition in the first two stanzas, when Óttarr first urges the king to listen to "the recollection of the dark black one" ("minni myrkblás," 1/1–2) and then affirms his need for the approval of both the king and his retinue.[5] Otherwise, he does not refer to his personal circumstances in this poem, at least as extant.

The necessity not to reveal that his act of praise was other than voluntary and the restraint not to allow the praise itself to go beyond what Kries and Krömmelbein (2002, 127) have called "the semantic necessities characterizing the text as a praise poem" were probably the two main factors that led to the absence of self-description in Egil's *Hǫfuðlausn* and the poem's lack of narrative detail about Eirik's exploits (cf. Noreen 1926, 195; Poole 1993, 101). Egil's own view of his visit to Eirik's court at York, on the other hand, is the main subject of the first part of *Arinbjarnarkviða*.

Whether *Arinbjarnarkviða* was originally part of the saga prosimetrum or a separate composition cannot be determined definitively. Certainly the saga mentions a "poem" (*kvæði*) that Egil composed about his friend Arinbjorn and the Möðruvallabók version adds "and this is the beginning of it" (177: "ok er þetta upphaf at," 257), but the space the scribe left that was big enough for a single stanza was never filled. In the C redaction the text adds "and sent it [the poem] to him in Norway" (177: "ok sendi honum til Noregs," 257, n. 2), while the B redaction has very similar wording.[6] The only medieval record of this poem is on the verso of the final leaf (99) of *Egil's Saga* in Möðruvallabók, where it is now almost illegible. It is in a fourteenth-century hand different from, but probably contemporary with, those of the chief scribe of the manuscript and his assistants (Einarsson 2001, xxxix; English summary by Michael Chesnutt, lxx). Codicologically speaking, *Arinbjarnarkviða* is not part of the A redaction of the saga proper, but an addition to the codex.[7]

In spite of the vagaries of its preservation, *Arinbjarnarkviða* is thematically and stylistically a counterpart and an antithesis to *Hǫfuðlausn*. It is a less formal poem than *Hǫfuðlausn*, being in the metre *kviðuháttr* and lacking a refrain (*stef*). It has two main subjects, which are anticipated in the poem's opening stanzas (1–2: 258), where the poet declares that he likes to praise generous men and those who do not lie and that he will sing the praises of his friends, although he has sought out many princes. The praise of friends is thus implicitly contrasted with the praise of princes, and the first part of the poem (stanzas 3–9: 258–61) is a recollection of Egil's visit to a prince who was not a friend, Eirik Blood-axe, and the circumstances in which he composed *Hǫfuðlausn*.

Here we find the frankness that was missing from *Hǫfuðlausn* and, with it, the poet's description of his own person and the peril in which he found himself. The link between the first and second parts of the poem is the figure of Arinbjorn, a true friend, who was with Egil in York and advised him, according to the saga prose (176–80), on how to go about composing his head ransom. The poem's second part (stanzas 16–23: 263–7), which celebrates Arinbjorn's universal generosity, is preceded by an interlude of five stanzas (10–15: 261–3) that intertwine praise of Arinbjorn with reflection on Egil's own powers as a poet.

Although, as mentioned earlier, the subject of the head ransom was a conventional topos in Old Norse poetry, the way in which that topos is expressed in Egil's poetry has unique characteristics, to judge by the available evidence. This comprises stanzas 3–9 of *Arinbjarnarkviða* (258–67) and *lausavísur* 33–6 attributed to Egil in the saga (180, 193–4, and 200). These stanzas reflect on Egil's appearance before Eirik at York and his redemption of his head as a reward for composing and reciting *Hǫfuðlausn*. The first thing to notice is the great emphasis laid on the head and its parts – hair, eyes and eyebrows, ears, nose, mouth, tongue, and teeth. This is to be expected, given the sense of the Old Norse compound *hǫfuðlausn*, "head ransom *or* head redemption," which stresses not the redemption of a threatened person's whole body or his life, but of his head as symbol of his person. In the case of a poet such as Egil the emphasis upon the head, and upon the mouth in particular, is linked to the importance of those parts as conduits for poetry, conventionally represented in skaldic verse, particularly through kennings, as an intoxicating liquid, a mead or ale, the gift of the god Odin, whose mythic regurgitation of this precious liquid functioned as the prototypical act of poetic composition to which all skalds aspired (cf. Clunies Ross 2005b, 91–6).

Egil's verses, both those in *Arinbjarnarkviða* and the *lausavísur*, combine kennings for the head and its parts with direct references to these body parts. Often the nouns are qualified by adjectives such as "dark," "ugly," or "wolf-grey" that find parallels in the saga's initial description of Egil: "And as he grew up it could readily be seen from him that he would be very ugly, and, like his father, dark of hair" (cf. 54: "En er hann óx upp, þá mátti brátt sjá á honum, at hann myndi verða mjǫk ljótr ok líkr feðr sínum, svartr á hár," 80). There are also numerous references to Egil's dark, ugly head and the physical signs of his dark, brooding disposition throughout his poetry, including three kennings for his dark eyebrows in *lausavísa* 23 (148), two for his head, drooping from sorrow at the loss of his sons, in *Sonatorrek* 19 (253), and two uses of the adjective *svartbrúnn* ("having dark eyebrows") to refer to himself in *lausavísur* 35 (194) and 49 (231–2). *Lausavísur* 40 and 58 also reveal that Egil has inherited another of his father Skallagrim's physical characteristics, his baldness, in their use, respectively, of the words "before the hairless bald one" ("fyr rotnum skalla," 204–5) and "I am in danger of falling onto my bald head" ("váfallr em ek skalla," 294), the latter a self-description in old age to which I shall return presently.

For the most part the kennings Egil uses to describe his ransomed head conform to typical Old Norse kenning structures. In *Arinbjarnarkviða* 7 (260) he refers first to his head as his "poet-payment" (*skáldfé*), which, he admits, "did not seem handsome of form" ("né hamfagrt þótti") to the men at Eirik's court. In the second half of the same stanza he expands on this subject by using the head-kenning "wolf-grey lump of the hood" ("ulfgrátt hattar staup"), which may be compared with the head-kenning "the crag of helmets" ("hjalma klett") used in *lausavísa* 34 (193–4) to describe the same event. The second of these kennings is quite conventional, though its relevance to Egil's person is emphasized by the qualifying subordinate clause "though it is ugly" ("þótt ljótr séi"). The first is likewise particularized by the adjective *ulfgrátt*, which may serve to remind the hearer of the connections of Egil's paternal grandfather Kveldulf ("Evening-Wolf") with shape-shifting, while the base-word *staup*, which means a lump of metal, is a variation on the usual base-word types in head-kennings, which denote prominent natural features of the landscape like cliffs, slopes, and mountains (cf. Meissner 1921, 128). Determinants of head-kennings, like Egil's here, are usually words for parts of the head or of objects, such as helmets and hoods, that one wears on or over the head. In *lausavísa* 35 (194) there is a more elaborate head-kenning of a self-congratulatory kind, as Egil reviews his success in wresting his head from Eirik's grasp. He asserts that now, as before, he is in command of "the lineage-ennobled inheritance seat of the hat of Ali <legendary king>" [helmet → head] ("áttgǫfguðum arfstóli hattar Ála"). Having described Eirik at the beginning of the same stanza as "truth-sparing" (*sannsparr*) and, in the following stanza (36) as showing "ugly anger" ("en ljóta reiði," 200), along with some other unflattering remarks, Egil exacts the verbal revenge on Eirik that it was not possible to express in *Hǫfuðlausn*.

Stanzas 7, 8, and 9 (260–1) of *Arinbjarnarkviða* exhibit a somewhat comical, self-deprecatory catalogue of the various features of the head that Egil managed to release from Eirik's control. After he had got his head back, he says in stanza 8, two things followed, namely his two eyes, the "dark sinkings [*or* 'jewels'] of the drooping eyebrows" [eyes] ("sámleit sǫkk [or søkk] síðra brúna"), and his mouth, "that mouth that bore my head-ransom before the prince" ("sá muðr es mína bar hǫfuðlausn fyr hilmis kné"). Stanza 9 follows the same cataloguing vein, listing other features that Egil redeemed: a "tooth-multitude" (*tannfjǫlð*), "tongue" (*tunga*), and ears, "listening-tents ennobled with hearing" ("hlertjǫld hlustum gǫfguð"). The comic effect of this catalogue of treasures climaxes in the assertion that "that gift" ("sú gjǫf") was better than gold.

It is possible that these three stanzas of self-description are a variation on another literary topos which is found in some descriptions of beautiful women. The topos, which may well be a literary universal,[8] involves enumerating the monetary value of specific body-parts of the woman and of her whole person. In *Kormak's saga*, two of Kormak's *lausavísur* (7 and 8: Sveinsson 1939, 212–13) discuss Steingerd's physical virtues in these terms. According to the saga prose, a slave woman provokes Kormak into estimating his girlfriend's worth, and he claims in verse 7 that he would give three hundred silver pieces for one eye, while valuing her hair at five hundred. In verse 8 he turns to even greater hyperbole, saying that the price he would put on Steingerd's whole person would equal the combined value of Iceland, Denmark, Germany, England, and Ireland.

Self-description in Egil's poetry persists into the verse of his old age and the themes with which it is associated in his earlier life also continue, including his preoccupation with his head and the organs of perception that allowed him to compose poetry.[9] The last three *lausavísur* (58–60) cited in *Egil's Saga* (294–6), one of which (58) is also in *The Third Grammatical Treatise*, are devoted to Egil's old age. These *lausavísur* paint a pathetic picture of an enfeebled old man ("karl afgamall"). Along with his bald head, they include mention of his wavering gait, limp penis, deafness, blindness, and cold feet. In a series of figures, kennings for the head and eyes are prominent. *Lausavísa* 58 also alludes to his sexual impotence, with a kenning for the flaccid penis unparalleled in the skaldic corpus, which was the reason why the verse was included in *The Third Grammatical Treatise*.[10] In two verses (*lausavísur* 58 and 59) in which he laments the failure of the organs of his physical body, he contrasts his present weak and lonely state, in which he finds himself bossed around by household servants on the farm in Iceland, with the glamour and rich rewards of his life as a poet in the service of kings. Yet the verses themselves, though full of self-pity, are also playful and witty in their use of kennings and the punning poetic device of *ofljóst*, which occurs probably twice in the final verse.[11]

The stanzas attributed to Egil in his old age are unusual in the skaldic corpus, especially in their references to his failing bodily organs and the kennings used to describe them. Although the final chapters of a number of sagas describe the old age of their protagonists, very few use skaldic poetry to do so and there are no precedents for such a continuing emphasis upon the head, the eyes, and eyebrows as we find in Egil's final verses, which detail the decline and ultimate failure of the organs of perception that served him so well in his career as a poet.

The strongly somatic character of Egil's self-description in the poetry that relates to his head-ransom experience has another, important dimension and that is its intertwining with the topos of poetic composition. Indeed, as mentioned earlier, the whole concept of the head ransom in Nordic tradition is predicated on the importance of the poet's head, especially his mouth and tongue, as the vehicle for the transport of poetry from his breast, where it was thought to reside, to the listening audience who receive it. This idea is expressed in the opening stanza of *Sonatorrek*, where the poet complains that great sorrow has made it hard for him to draw poetry "from the hiding-place of thought" [breast] ("ór fylgsni hugar," 246). It is not accidental, therefore, that the stanza (6) of *Arinbjarnarkviða* immediately preceding the description of the actual moment at which Egil redeems his head celebrates his delivery of *Hǫfuðlausn* to Eirik's court in imagery that recalls the originary mythic acquisition of poetry by Odin in the form of an intoxicating mead stolen from the giant Suttungr and his daughter Gunnlǫð. He states that he dared to bring "the bolster-price of the match of the he-salmon" [snake = Odin → poetry] ("bólstrverð maka hœings," 259–60) to Eirik.[12]

For Old Norse skalds, as a number of studies have shown (cf. Kreutzer 1977, 257–60; Clover 1978), poetic composition was a visceral act, involving the outpouring of Odin's mead, often likened to vomit in Egil's poetry, as the poet imitated the god's act of swallowing the intoxicating liquid and regurgitating it for the gods and good poets to use, as Snorri Sturluson narrated in *Skáldskaparmál* (Sturluson 1998, I, 5). In the same stanza 6 of *Arinbjarnarkviða*, Egil employs the common poetry-kenning type "drink of Odin," but he gives it a topical twist by means of an extended metaphor, bringing its relevance home to Eirik's court: "so that Yggr's (Odin's) toast [poetry] came foaming to every man's mouths of the ears [earholes]" ("svát Yggs full ýranda kom at hvers manns hlusta munnum," 259–60).

Egil was by no means the only Old Norse skald to employ the conventional imagery of poetic composition and invoke the mead myth in his poetry. What is distinctive in his compositions is the frequency and elaboration of his references to his acts of poetic composition, conveyed especially through kennings, and their interrelatedness with acts of physical self-description. There are three dimensions to these interrelated passages and they turn on three basic connections: between poetry and the animal, between poetry and drunkenness, and between poetry and craftsmanship. The first two of these three dimensions are amply presented in the prosimetrum of *Egil's Saga*, while the third is mainly conveyed in the poetry alone, particularly in two of Egil's long poems, *Sonatorrek* and *Arinbjarnarkviða*.

The association between Egil and the animal is at the heart of several of the most violent episodes in *Egil's Saga* and in each of these the saga represents Egil as being moved to compose poetry about his violent actions. It can be seen that clusters of *lausavísur* belong to each of these episodes, including the encounter with Bard, the steward of Eirik and Gunnhild on the island of Atley (*lausavísur* 8–11: 108–13); the elaborate and murderous revenge that Egil, pretending to be a bear, takes on Berg-Onund and the related but delayed revenge he takes on Berg-Onund's brother Atli the Short (*lausavísur* 25, 26, 30, and 42: 156, 159, 169, and 210); the fight with the berserk Ljot the Pale (*lausavísur* 30–4: 202–6); and the encounter with the Vermaland farmer Armod (*lausavísur* 37–9: 222–8).

To a modern sensibility the brutal violence of these acts is shocking,[13] but neither the prose text nor the poetry conveys any sense of regret on Egil's part for his actions. In fact many of the verses are self-justificatory; Egil is self-righteous about his violence against Bard, who denied him proper hospitality and tried to poison him; against Berg-Onund, who tried to steal his wife's inheritance; against Ljot, who threatened to abduct a relative of Arinbjorn's; and against Armod for his lack of hospitality. Several of the verses associated with these episodes consist of Egil's first-person account of his physical acts of aggression. In *lausavísa* 42 (210), for example, he describes how, after he discovered that Atli the Short had tried to use magic to blunt his sword in a duel, he threw his sword aside and grabbed hold of Atli with both hands, forced him to the ground, and bit through his windpipe, killing him. The verse proclaims:

> I caused the molar-brother [incisor tooth] to destroy the windpipe [*ek bar* = *bark* + *sauð* = *á* → *barka*] out of necessity.
>
> [jaxlbróður létk eyða
> ek bar sauð af nauðum.][14]

There is a pervasive semiotic field associating members of Egil's family with predatory wild animals and with supernatural powers in Old Norse tradition. Both the prose saga and its poetry are created with this background semiotic in mind, beginning with the opening chapter's description of Kveldulf's shape-changing propensities, the troll-like Skallagrim, and the damaging rages that both he and his son Egil fly into (cf. Jakobsson 2008, 3–9). The saga audience is also reminded in the very first paragraph of the prose text that Kveldulf's ancestry stretches back to the legendary "men of Hrafnista" (*Hrafnistumenn*), who included Ketil Haeng "Salmon," Grim Ketilson Hairy-cheeks, and, according to some sources, Arrow-Odd, about all of whom narratives and poetry existed. These became the basis of "sagas of ancient times" (*fornaldarsögur*) if not already at the time *Egil's Saga* was composed, then certainly not very long afterwards. The association with the world of wild animals arguably expresses the aggressive, almost superhuman strength of Egil's family, just as it does of Hrolf Kraki "Pole-ladder" in the legendary *Saga of Hrolf Kraki*, of Beowulf in the Old English poem *Beowulf*, and of Starkad in parts of the *Víkarsbálkr* ("Vikar's Section") in the *Saga of Gautrek*, especially the final stanzas in which Starkad describes how courtiers at Uppsala laughed at his appearance, his "ugly snout, long muzzle, wolf-grey hair" ("ljótan skolt, langa trjónu, úlfgrátt hár").[15]

Aggression and poetic creativity are linked in Egil's psyche, and this connection is most clearly expressed in his poetry. Several of his most violent acts are carried out when he and his opponents are drunk. Given the general Old Norse cultural connection between poetic creation, conceived of in physical form as an intoxicating liquid, and the commonest circumstances in which alcoholic liquor would have been consumed in early Scandinavia, namely at feasts where poetry was commonly recited, the close link between poetic composition, feasting, drunkenness, and aggression was all but pre-ordained. The drinking contest between Arrow-Odd and his two rivals, Sjolf and Sigurd, in the *mannjafnaðr* in the *Saga of Arrow-Odd* (Boer 1888, 159–67) demonstrates the same cultural connection: as the rivals become drunker, their ability to compose poetry peters out, while Odd continues to drink and compose insulting verses about them, thereby winning the contest and demonstrating his superior merits as both a man and a poet.

Egil's poetry also shows an awareness of this nexus, that he who can drink most is also the best man and – particularly – the best poet. The *locus classicus* for this concept is *lausavísa* 10 (110), one of the verses Egil recites during his drinking contest with a man named Olvir on the island of Atley. Its first half features a witty repetition of like-sounding words linking the name Olvir (*Ǫlvir*) with the noun *ǫl* ("ale"), implying the man's growing incapacity, but the opening verbal phrase "I am getting drunk" ("ǫlvir mik") asserts gleefully that the speaker, Egil, is just getting into his stride as he lets the ale ("the moisture of the halberd of the aurochs" [horn → ale]: "atgeira ýrar ýring") shower over his lips. The final couplet makes the connection between drunkenness and poetic creativity absolutely clear, when Egil claims that "it is raining [*or* 'I am raining'] with the rain of the thanes of the High One" [poetry] ("rigna getr at regni … Háars þegna").[16]

By contrast, the comparison between the creation of poetry and the skills of a craftsman or labourer, which occurs in a number of places in Egil's poetic oeuvre, is not much noted in the prose saga, except perhaps in the anticipatory vignette of his father Skallagrim as a skilful blacksmith (78–9) whose craft provokes a stanza attributed to him, and Egil's own prowess as a rune-master. This practical aspect of the art of the poet finds expression in two episodes of the saga (109 and 228–30) and in two *lausavísur* (9 and 48) in which Egil asserts his ability to deal with practical problems by carving runes (in the first case providing an antidote to poisoned ale and in the second counteracting poorly executed runic magic that has been making a young girl sick).[17] While the runic inscriptions Egil carved need not have been in verse, and the saga does not indicate whether they were or not, many Old Norse runic inscriptions were metrical, and there was in any case a close traditional connection between the skills of the poet and those of the rune-master, as the Loddfáfnir section of the eddic poem *Hávamál* ("Words of the High One," stanzas 111–37) makes clear.

Within the verse, we find complex, metaphorical descriptions of poetic activity that, in evoking the work of a craftsman or labourer, differ markedly from the many skaldic kennings that refer to poetry in terms of the mead of poetry myth as "Odin's drink" and the like (cf. Meissner 1921, 427–30). They are confined to two of the long poems, *Arinbjarnarkviða* and *Sonatorrek*.[18] In *Sonatorrek* 5 (248) the poet begins to enumerate his family members who have died and to celebrate their loss in poetry, and he describes his act of poetic creation and recitation (the two are combined) as follows:

> I carry out of the word-temple [mouth] the timber of praise [poem], made leafy with speech.
>
> [þat berk út
> ór orðhofi
> mærðar timbr
> máli laufgat.]

Although the first of the two kennings here, "word-temple" (*orðhof*), conforms to a normal type for the mouth [place (e.g., house, seat, gate) + poetry/praise/speech], the use of the base-word *hof* ("sanctuary, [heathen] temple") is unusual, as is the apparent underlying extended imagery conveyed by the notion of the poet carrying timber (= a poem) out of a sacred place, which causes it to burst into leaf. In *Arinbjarnarkviða* 15 (263) the poet once again chooses an extended metaphor in which to express his act of composition, and this time again the imagery belongs to the domain of wood-working[19] – the act of smoothing and shaping a length of untreated wood with a plane. He states that "material for praise" ("efni mærðar") of his friend Arinbjorn "is easy for me to smooth with the voice-plane" [tongue] ("erum auðskœf ómunlokri") because he already has suitable lengths lying ready on his tongue, out of which the poem can be crafted.

In the stanza of *Arinbjarnarkviða* conventionally numbered 25 and usually placed last in the poem (267) it is again a kenning for the tongue that is treated in an extended metaphor. This time the poet describes himself as awake early (*árvakr*) and putting words together "with the morning works of the language-servant" [tongue] ("með málþjóns morginverkum"). He appears to imagine himself as a farm manager collaborating with a labourer or a servant to get tasks done around the farm, and this impression is confirmed by the last four lines of the stanza:

> I built a praise-pile [praise-poem], which will stand for a long time not likely to be broken on the home field of poetry [poetic corpus?].
>
> [hlóðk lofkǫst,
> þanns lengi stendr
> óbrotgjarn
> í bragar túni.]

The metaphorical identity of the image informing the "praise-pile," certainly intended as a kenning for the poem *Arinbjarnarkviða*, has been debated; Sigurður Nordal (1933, 267–8, note) thought it was a sacred cairn of stones, but Egil may have been imagining any ordered pile of stones or wood lying in the farm's home field. It is also uncertain whether the phrase "on the home field of poetry" ("í bragar túni") should be understood as a kenning and, if so, what its referent might be. Some possibilities are either the mind, the memory, or, as suggested here, the whole corpus of skaldic verse.

In addition, there is another theme, usually connected with that of the poet as craftsman, that is unprecedented in skaldic verse from the pre-Christian age outside Egil's work, and that is his reference to his art as ennobling and connected to the divine. The best-known of these passages is the penultimate stanza of *Sonatorrek* (24), in which the poet claims that Odin gave him "a skill devoid of blemish" ("íþrótt vammi firrða," 256). Similar sentiments are expressed in *Arinbjarnarkviða* 2 (258).

The foregoing analysis of the self-description in the poetry attributed to Egil has examined a cohesive and consistent body of stanzas which carry several intertwined themes that are also central to the saga's presentation of the character of Egil. Yet they are independently cohesive: over and above the saga prose the verses exhibit a tight focus on several characteristics of the protagonist as a poet: his physical ugliness, dark eyes, and beetling brows which correlate with his outstanding gift of poetry. The centre of the audience's attention in these verses falls undoubtedly upon the poet's head and all its organs of perception and vocal expression – eyes, ears, mouth, tongue, and teeth. Further associations in the verses lead to characterizations of Egil in terms of drunkenness and animal aggression. Then finally we find an imagistic nexus between the ideas of labour and craftsmanship and the poet's speech and tongue. In the context of the saga narrative the focus on Egil's head relates to the circumstances in which Egil was obliged to compose a *Hǫfuðlausn* ("Head Ransom") to save his life when he was at the mercy of King Eirik Blood-axe at York. However, in the poetry itself this focus becomes symbolic of a wider grouping of concepts which express in concentrated form the fundamental Norse association between poetic creativity and paranormal mental states, of which Egil's somatic condition is the external manifestation.

NOTES

1 Secure medieval evidence for the poem's title, *Hǫfuðlausn*, "Head ransom," comes principally from the introductory rubric to the text of the poem in the Wolfenbüttel manuscript of c. 1330–70 (WolfAug 9 10 4° fol 49v, l. 27) "her hefr hòfvðlausn." Stanza 8/7 of *Arinbjarnarkviða* (261) is often drawn on as a presumably contemporary witness to the head ransom poem's name, but the presence of the word *hǫfuðlausn* there is in fact an emendation, first proposed by Rasmus Rask (1818, 260), and, while probably correct, cannot be regarded as fully reliable.

2 The narrator of *Egil's Saga* is fully aware of this tradition, and makes the character Arinbjorn refer to the precedent of his own kinsman, Bragi Boddason, who, he claims, composed such a "praise poem" (*lofkvæði*) of twenty stanzas about Bjorn, king of the Swedes (182). *Skáldatal* ascribes this head ransom poem to Bragi's father-in-law, Erpr lútandi "the bending," and says he composed verse about the king's dog Saurr (Sigurðsson et al. 1848–87, III, 252, 260). On this and another head ransom poem attributed to Gísl Illugason, but not preserved, see Nordland 1956, 60–7. Two other known poems called *Hǫfuðlausn* (both later than Egil's) are ascribed to respectively Óttarr svarti and Þórarinn loftunga.

3 In addition to Nordland, cf. Stith Thompson 1955, J1185, Execution escaped by storytelling; Boberg 1966, 194, M234.5, Life bought for poem; also Harris 1996, 114–21 and note 16.

4 The A version of the saga, represented by Möðruvallabók (AM 132 fol), does not record the poem at all, while it is present in the B and C versions. For an account of the three major versions of the saga, see Einarsson 2001, xix–lxxv.

5 The interpretation offered here follows the recently published edition of Óttarr's *Hǫfuðlausn* by Matthew Townend for Volume I of *Skaldic Poetry of the Scandinavian Middle Ages*, ed. Diana Whaley (2013), Part 2, 741–2. The translation of *myrkblás* as "dark black one" (referring to Óttarr's nickname) is an emendation based on a suggestion of E.A. Kock 1923–44, §721. The fact that Óttarr was changing patrons from Óláfr Eiríksson of Sweden to Óláfr Haraldsson of Norway was probably as important as his supposed offence in producing an especially conciliatory opening to his encomium.

6 I cite Scudder's translation of *Egil's Saga* (1997).

7 The two stanzas 24 and 25, which have conventionally been placed at the end of the poem, are cited only in *The Third Grammatical Treatise*. Editors have assumed from their subject matter that they were part of *Arinbjarnarkviða*.

8 Cf. Roberta Frank's discussion (1978, 168) of this and similar themes in Old Norse poetry.

9 See Alison Finlay's essay in this volume for detailed discussion of this section of the saga.

10 There the kenning, *borr bergifótar* (or *bergis fótar*) "borer of the tasting-limb (?)" or "borer of the drink of the leg" is given as an example of the rhetorical figure *karientismos*, explained as *ef úfǫgr nǫfn talask grannligar* "if ugly names are mentioned more delicately" (Ólsen 1884, 114).

11 For an explanation, see Einarsson 2003, 180, note to verse 60. The second of these puns, on *ekkjur*, a noun that means both "widows" and "heels," is yet another reference to Egil's body, his cold feet which he tries to warm by the fire.

12 This kenning alludes to the myth in which Odin, in the form of a snake, enters the bed-chamber of Gunnlǫð and gains one draught of the poetic mead from her for each of three sexual encounters; cf. the account in *Skáldskaparmál* (Sturluson 1998, I, 4–5).

13 As further discussed by Jón Karl Helgason in his essay in this volume.

14 The citation here is not from *Egils saga* 1933 but from Helgason (1957), who proposed a satisfying explanation of this extremely clever but obscure confession by Egil of his animal-like act. *Ek bar*, "I carried," must be read as *bark*, with the suffixed personal pronoun, and combined with *á*, the accusative singular form of the word *ær*, "ewe," as a substitute for *sauðr*, "sheep," to give the noun *barka*, "windpipe." As Egil wished to gain his wife's inheritance from Atli's family by challenging the man to a duel, he could not afford to admit openly that he had killed him in such a barbaric way.

15 Ranisch 1900, 33; on the comparison with Starkad, see Grimstad 1976 and Meulengracht Sørensen 1977.

16 The wording *getk rigna*, "I am raining," is from AM 162 A fol. The other manuscripts have *getr at rigna*, "it is raining."

17 See also Knirk 1994, 411–13.

18 Those scholars who have been sceptical of the authenticity of these two poems, especially *Sonatorrek* (cf. Helgason 1969; See 1998), as products of a Viking-Age sensibility, might dismiss these expressions as influenced by Christian concepts of poetry as God-given, yet they have no parallel in Christian skaldic verse any more than in the poetry of an earlier period. On the other hand, the use of extended metaphors, such as we find in both poems, is not uncommon in *kviðuháttr* verse, and Þjóðólfr of Hvinir's *Ynglingatal* (c. 900) makes very effective and frequent use of this literary device.

19 Sayers has drawn attention to the importance of wood-working imagery in skaldic poetics, but refers only tangentially to Egil's poetry. His one detailed discussion (Sayers 2002, 8) of the first stanza of *Hǫfuðlausn* is misleading, as it is not based on an accurate understanding of the verse's meaning.

BIBLIOGRAPHY

Boberg, Inger M. 1966. *Motif-Index of Early Icelandic Literature*. Bibliotheca Arnamagnaeana 27. Copenhagen: Munksgaard.

Boer, R.C., ed., 1888. *Ǫrvar-Odds saga*. Leiden: Brill.

Clover, Carol. 1978. "Skaldic Sensibility." *Arkiv för nordisk filologi* 93: 68–81.

Clunies Ross, Margaret. 1978. "The art of poetry and the figure of the poet in *Egil's saga*." *Parergon* 22: 3–12, reprinted 1989 in *Saga of the Icelanders,* ed. J. Tucker, 115–30. New York: Garland.

– 2001. "The Skald Sagas as a Genre: Definitions and Typical Features." In *Skaldsagas: Text, Vocation, and Desire in the Icelandic Sagas of Poets*. Ed. Russell Poole, 25–49. Berlin: De Gruyter.

– 2005a. "A Tale of Two Poets: Egil Skallagrímsson and Einarr skálaglamm." *Arkiv för nordisk filologi* 120: 69–82.

– 2005b. *A History of Old Norse Poetry and Poetics*. Cambridge: D. S. Brewer.

– 2010. "Verse and Prose in *Egils saga Skallagrímssonar*." In *Creating the Medieval Saga: Versions, Variability and Editorial Interpretations of Old Norse Saga Literature*. Ed. Judy Quinn and Emily Lethbridge, 191–211. The Viking Collection 18. Odense: University Press of Southern Denmark.

Einarsson, Bjarni, ed. 2001. *Egils saga Skallagrímssonar*. Vol. I. *A-Redaktionen*. Editiones Arnamagnæanæ Series A, vol. 19. Copenhagen: Reitzel.

– ed. 2003. *Egils saga*. London: Viking Society for Northern Research.

Frank, Roberta. 1978. *Old Norse Court Poetry: The dróttkvætt Stanza*. Islandica XLII. Ithaca, NY: Cornell University Press.

Grimstad, Kaaren. 1976. "The Giant as a Heroic Model: The Case of Egil and Starkaðr." *Scandinavian Studies* 48: 284–98.

Harris, Joseph. 1996. "Romancing the Rune. Aspects of Literacy in Early Scandinavian Orality." *Atti Accademia Peloritana dei Pericolanti. Classe di Lettere Filosofia e Belle Arti.* 70: 111–40.

Helgason, Jón. 1957. "Ek bar sauð." *Acta Philologica Scandinavica* 23: 94–6.

– 1969. "Höfuðlausnarhjal." In *Einarsbók. Afmæliskveðja til Einars Ól.Sveinssonar. 12. desember 1969*. Ed. Bjarni Guðnason, Halldór Halldórsson,and Jónas Kristjánsson, 156–76. Reykjavík: Útgefendur Nokkrir Vinir.

Jakobsson, Ármann. 2008. "*Egil's Saga* and Empathy." *Scandinavian Studies* 80: 1–18.

Jónsson, Finnur, ed. 1912–15. *Den norsk-islandske skjaldedigtning*. Vols. AI, AII (tekst efter håndskrifterne) and BI, BII (rettet tekst). Copenhagen: Gyldendal. Rpt. 1967 (A) and 1973 (B). Copenhagen: Rosenkilde og Bagger.

Knirk, James E. 1994. "Runes from Trondheim and a Stanza by Egill Skalla-Grímsson." In *Studien zum Altgermansichen: Festschrift für Heinrich Beck*. Ed. Heiko Uecker, 411–20. Berlin: De Gruyter..

Kock, E.A. 1923–44. *Notationes Norrœnæ: Anteckningar till Edda och skaldedikt-ning*. Lunds Universitets årsskrift . New Series, sec. 1. Lund: Gleerup.

Kreutzer, Gert. 1977. *Die Dichtungslehre der Skalden*. 2nd edn. Meisenheim am Glan: Hain.

Kries, Susanne, and Thomas Krömmelbein. 2002. " 'From the Hull of Laughter': Egill Skalla-Grímsson's 'Hǫfuðlausn' and Its Epodium in Context." *Scandinavian Studies* 74: 111–36.

Meissner, Rudolf. 1921. *Die Kenningar der Skalden. Ein Beitrag zur skaldischen Poetik*. Bonn: Schroeder. Reprinted Hildesheim: Olms, 1984.

Meulengracht Sørensen, Preben. 1977. "Starkaðr, Loki og Egill Skalla-Grímsson." In *Sjötíu ritgerðir helgaðar Jakobi Benediktssyni 20 júli 1977*. Ed. Einar G. Pétursson and Jónas Kristjánsson, II, 759–68. 2 vols. Reykjavík: Stofnun Árna Magnússonar á Íslandi.

Nordal, Guðrún, and Tarrin Wills, eds. forthcoming. *Skaldic Poetry of the Scandinavian Middle Ages*. 9 vols. Volume V: *Poetry in Sagas of Icelanders*. Turnhout: Brepols.

Nordal, Sigurður, ed. 1933. *Egils saga Skalla-Grímssonar*. Íslenzk fornrit 2. Reykjavík: Hið íslenzka fornritafélag.

Nordland, Odd. 1956. *Hǫfuðlausn i Egils Saga. Ein tradisjonskritisk studie*. Oslo: Det norske samlaget.

Noreen, Erik. 1926. *Den norsk-isländska Poesien*. Stockholm: Norstedt.

Ólason, Vésteinn, 1998. *Dialogues with the Viking Age. Narration and Representation in the Sagas of the Icelanders*, trans. Andrew Wawn. Reykjavík: Heimskringla.

Ólsen, Björn Magnússon, ed. 1884. *Den tredje og fjærde grammatiske afhandling i Snorres Edda tilligemed de grammatiske afhandlingers prolog og to andre tillæg.* Samfund til udgivelse af gammel nordisk litteratur 12. Copenhagen: Knudtzon.

Poole, Russell 1993. "Variants and Variability in the Text of Egil's *Hǫfuðlausn*." In *The Politics of Editing Medieval Texts. Papers given at the Twenty-Seventh Annual Conference on Editorial Problems University of Toronto 1–2 November 1991.* Ed. Roberta Frank, 65–105. New York: AMS Press, Inc.

Ranisch, Wilhelm, ed. 1900. *Die Gautrekssaga in zwei Fassungen.* Palaestra XI. Berlin: Mayer & Müller.

Rask, Rasmus. 1818. *Anvisning till isländskan eller nordiska Fornspråket.* Stockholm: A. Wiborg.

Sayers, William. 2002. "Scarfing the Yard with Words (*Fóstbrœðra saga*): Shipbuilding Imagery in Old Norse Poetics." *Scandinavian Studies* 74: 1–18.

Scudder, Bernard, tr. 1997. *Egil's Saga.* London: Penguin.

See, Klaus von. 1998. "Das Phantom einer altgermanischen Elegiendichtung. Kritische Bemerkungen zu Daniel Sävborg, 'Sorg och elegi i Eddans hjältediktning'." *Skandinavistik* 28: 87–100.

Sigurðsson, Jón., et al., eds. 1848–87. *Edda Snorra Sturlusonar: Edda Snorronis Sturlaei.* 3 vols. Copenhagen: Legatum Arnamagnæanum. Reprinted Osnabrück: Zeller, 1966.

Sturluson, Snorri. 1998. *Snorri Sturluson, Edda. Skáldskaparmál*, ed. Anthony Faulkes. 2 vols. London: Viking Society for Northern Research.

Sveinsson, Einar Ól., ed. 1939. *Vatnsdœla saga.* Íslenzk fornrit 8. Reykjavík: Hið íslenzka fornritafélag.

Thompson, Stith. 1955. *Motif-Index of Folk Literature.* 6 vols. 2nd rev. edn. Copenhagen: Rosenkilde og Bagger.

Whaley, Diana, ed. 2013. *Skaldic Poetry of the Scandinavian Middle Ages.* 9 vols. I. *Poetry from the Kings' Sagas 1: From Mythical Times to c. 1035.* Turnhout: Brepols.

Emotions and Affiliations

6 Thorolf's Choice: Family and Goodness in *Egil's Saga*, Ch. 40[1]

ÁRMANN JAKOBSSON

Emotions and Saga Narratives

This may well be the unhappiest home in Iceland. With two dominating characters, both men, one in his late fifties, the other on the brink of adolescence, both extremely large and extravagant in behaviour, the other members of the household must be overwhelmed by this psychological dictatorship. The two men are not speaking to each other. Their silence is neither good nor meaningless and harmless. It is, in fact, pregnant with ill feeling and fuelled by the cruel and senseless crimes that each has perpetuated against the other. The mother of the house is absent, we do not know why. No one else in the household has the social status or the strength of character to mediate between the two; they are extras who hardly even matter. Then a happy, vibrant, handsome, and buoyant young man enters this miserable house. He has been travelling the world, has befriended princes, and enjoyed a brilliant social life among aristocrats and the most capable men of the age. His old family home in rural Iceland would perhaps seem claustrophobic, even if it were filled with mirth and laughter. It most assuredly is not.

The Sagas of Icelanders, composed in the thirteenth, fourteenth, and perhaps to some extent in the fifteenth century, are psychological dramas. This trait has been long acknowledged, and yet there are surprisingly few recent scholarly analyses of the characters' emotions and interpersonal relationships in the sagas (with the notable exceptions of Miller 1992, Hoyersten 1998, and Poole 2004). This situation may in part be explained by the fact that saga scholars are typically trained in philology, language, and history, but not, for example, in psychology. However, not analysing the personal relationships in the Sagas of Icelanders is doing them a disservice since character depiction is a vital component of the art of the sagas and one of the reasons they are still read and enjoyed today. Whenever the sagas are taught at university level, the first questions with which the student reader wrestles pertain to the characters in the sagas. The emotional relationship explored in the sagas is thus an area of serious scholarship that should not be abandoned. Hence one of my aims in this experimental essay is to try to say something serious about character depiction in a well-known saga.

Egil's Saga is one of the longest of the sagas, encompassing not only the long life of Egil Skallagrimsson – chieftain, warrior, and poet – but also a lengthy narrative about the previous generation of his family, his father, Skallagrim, and his uncle.[2] I will mostly concern myself with chapter 40, which takes place during Egil's childhood at Borg.[3] I believe that psychological readings, along with close readings of the sagas, which take a relatively small narrative segment and pay close attention to detail, are much too rarely attempted.[4] Chapter 40, along with chapter 78 in which Egil, late in his life, mourns for his two sons, justifies this focus, as a close reading of the two is essential to any study of the family relationships in the saga and the emotional life of Egil Skallagrimsson.

The Family at Borg

Chapter 40 of *Egil's Saga* consists of two linked narratives, both accounts of murders committed by Egil. The first, when he is seven years old, involves his killing of a slightly older boy, Grim Heggsson, after having been treated roughly in a game. This death causes a bloody quarrel among the relatives of the dead boy and some of Skallagrim's friends and allies in the district, but the Borg household mysteriously takes no part. In the second narrative, Egil is twelve years old and kills his father's cherished foreman and paymaster in revenge for the death of his only two friends in the world, whom his father has slain. This reprisal results in father and son breaking off relations while still remaining in the same house: "þeir feðgar rœddusk þá ekki við, hvárki gott né illt, ok fór svá fram þann vetr" (102: "father and son did not speak to each other, neither kind nor unkind words, and so it remained through the winter," 69). Nothing is said about how this tension affected the household; that has to be imagined. Borg was a large farmstead, but any Icelandic farm during the Middle Ages would be a constricted space, especially during the bleak winters. The atmosphere would have been claustrophobic, even if it were not dominated by two large men with overwhelming personalities vigorously ignoring each other. After all, three people are dead, and these deaths remain present in the heavy silence.

Skallagrim is introduced at the beginning of the saga as a "svartr maðr ok ljótr" (5: "swarthy and ugly [man]," 4], and he is "líkr feðr sínum, bæði yfirlits ok at skaplyndi" (5: "resembl[ing] his father in both appearance and character," 4; see also 50: 33). His father, Ulf, had already been introduced as a big, strong man. Although his wife is "kvenna vænst" (4: "a beautiful woman," 3), he manifestly does not match her in looks. And although Ulf is a devoted farmer, who rises early and takes a keen interest in every small and menial task his men perform, he is also *styggr* (4: "bad-tempered," 3) in the evening and thus is nicknamed Kveldulf. Ulf is not just any given name, but means "wolf." Moreover, it is suggested in *Egil's Saga* that Kveldulf and his family are actually shape-shifters, although the saga never makes this point quite clear (see Sørensen 1977, 766; Pálsson 1994, 60–3; and Kristjánsdóttir 1997, 75–81). It is as if the saga author challenges those who would like to do so to identify them as shape-shifters, whereas others can see the recurrent references to wolves as metaphors.

Grim (as Skallagrim is called in his youth) is a carpenter and is often seen fishing with the farmhands (Nordal 1933, 5). When invited to join the service of King Harald of Norway, he refuses, whereas his brother Thorolf eagerly accepts (13–14: 8–9). Grim stays at home but goes to see the king after Thorolf's death even though he claims he is not *orðsnjallr* (61: "eloquen[t]," 41) enough to speak to the king. As it turns out, Skallagrim's only visit to a royal court is not a success. He takes with him eleven men, most of whom have strange nicknames, and they are said to be more like trolls than ordinary humans (63: 43). As unsuitable as his companions are at court, Skallagrim himself does not feel at home there either, and his feelings never change. When facing the king, he again refuses to enter his service and goes as far as to express a treasonous desire to kill him. After this ugly confrontation, Kveldulf and Skallagrim do the sensible thing and immediately leave Norway for Iceland. Kveldulf dies on the voyage, so Skallagrim comes to Iceland alone and immediately starts farming and working as a blacksmith. He is at one and the same time a quite ordinary, if unusually dedicated, farmer and a trollish figure who can dive to the bottom of the fjord to find a suitable stone for his smithy (75 and 78–9: 49 and 53).

Like his father, Skallagrim marries a woman who seems not quite as strange as he is. We do not know much about Bera and have to infer much from the silence. No mention is made of a bestial streak in her,[5] and she is not said to be swarthy and ugly. Her father is a former royal retainer who seems to be a jovial and friendly man. The only time he is really portrayed in the saga, he is welcoming his troublesome three-year-old grandson to a party by giving him small presents and encouraging him to recite poetry (81–3: 54–6). Bera herself only makes one explicit appearance after Egil's first killing: "Bera kvað Egil vera víkingsefni ok kvað þat mundu fyrir liggja, þegar hann hefði aldr til, at honum væri fengin herskip" (100: "Bera said that he had the makings of a true Viking when he was old enough to be put in command of warships," 68).

Chapter 31 states that Skallagrim and Bera had several children, but they all died in infancy until Thorolf, Egil's older brother, was born. Then the couple had two more daughters, Sæunn and Thorunn, and last a son, Egil, born when Skallagrim was close to fifty. This last son is obviously not as eagerly awaited as the first, nor does he show as much promise as his siblings, at least not as unambiguously (80: 54). Skallagrim's reaction to his youngest child also seems lukewarm at best. It is later noted that Skallagrim's foreman and paymaster – Egil's second victim – is *kærstr* (102: "[the] favourite," 69); no such statement is ever made about Egil. Skallagrim is a workhorse: he loves work and also loves his foreman and paymaster, who assists him in the productive business of managing the farm. He also loves his eldest son Thorolf – as does Bera – as the saga explicitly states: "unni honum ok vel faðir ok móðir" (80: "his father and mother were very fond of him," 54). But as I will discuss below, Egil is not quite as lovable as Thorolf.

The first clash between Skallagrim and Egil happens when Egil is three years old and is not allowed to go with the rest of the family to the party at his grandfather's house, even though he was invited. This refusal is sharpened by Skallagrim's prickly statement that Egil would not be able to behave himself in public especially with drinking going on: he is bad enough when sober (81: 55).[6] Even after Egil has not only chosen to disobey him but also performed the spectacular feat of riding alone over the moors from Borg to Alftanes and then composing two complicated stanzas of skaldic verse, Skallagrim still does not say anything (81–2: 55–6). His reaction to his son's first killing – when Egil kills the older and larger boy Grim Heggsson in anger – is equally indifferent: "lét Skalla-Grímr sér fátt um finnask" (100: "Skallagrim seemed indifferent to what had happened," 68). What Egil has done is morally dubious, and Skallagrim might have a reason to be angry, especially since some of his friends run into trouble as a result of Egil's actions. Seen in that light, Bera's praise of Egil's promise as a Viking might be regarded as slightly irresponsible. But Skallagrim simply does not seem to care either way. He is neither angry nor pleased, just emotionally distant from his son.

At this time, Skallagrim is said to be "heldr hniginn at aldri" (99: "fairly advanced in age," 67), and five years later, he is older still. In spite of his old age, he is still very strong and takes part in some unspecified *leikum* (101: "games," 68) that seem to rely heavily on physical prowess, though he has a hard time matching the combined strength of his son Egil – now twelve and according to the saga bigger and stronger than most adults – and Thord Granason, Egil's best friend, who is in his twenties. But when night falls, Skallagrim, suddenly "gerðisk ... sterkr" (101: "filled with ... strength," 68), kills Thord Granason in a frenzy and then turns on Egil. The boy is saved by his foster-mother, Thorgerd Brak, who distracts Skallagrim by accusing him of behaving like a shape-shifter,[7] with the result that he lets go of Egil and chases and eventually brutally kills her instead (101–2: 68–9).

Skallagrim is no longer merely cold and indifferent towards his son. In this episode, he threatens his life. And by the time his anger subsides, he has deprived Egil of both his foster-mother and his best friend, the only two people who have supported him. After that tragic loss and Egil's killing of the foreman, however, Skallagrim returns to his earlier passive-aggressive tactics: for a whole year, this old and powerful chieftain of sixty stops talking to his teenage son. The cruelty of his previous animalistic and possibly supernatural rage is replaced by a different, more down-to-earth, and much colder cruelty, which he has demonstrated before: the cruelty of indifference.

In this narrative, Skallagrim is the aggressor. But where is the mother? In light of her previous praise of Egil, it might be tempting to conceive of this as a family in which a cold and indifferent father is countered by a loving and doting mother. But, alas, that is not so in this case. During the whole episode of Skallagrim's rage resulting in the killing of the three bystanders, Bera plays no part in the action. She is not said to have died, although she has clearly done so by the time Egil returns to his father after twelve years in Norway (151), but Egil certainly does not owe his life to her. If she is still present, she does not say anything about her husband's attack on Egil or their later behaviour. Nor does she mediate in the dispute. It is not she but the foster-mother, Thorgerd Brak, who protects Egil and sacrifices her life for his.

This family does not consist of a hostile father and a benevolent mother but rather of a cold and menacing father and an absent mother. Even though Bera has shown Egil more affection than Skallagrim in the past, she is not there for him at this moment. Even her previous praise of Egil was morally dubious, since she was pleased with her son's Viking ways in spite of the fact that his actions had not only caused controversy but also resulted in the death of seven more men in the region (100: 68).[8] Bera is not a loving and supportive mother comparable to Grettir Asmundarson's mother, Asdis. Perhaps she is the type of remote parent who pats a child on the head, praises him, and is mistakenly regarded by the child as loving and kind, but who is not there for him in a crisis and does not do him much good in the long run.[9]

In effect Egil has no one to rely on but Thord Granason and Thorgerd Brak, both of whom Skallagrim kills on the same night. Thord is a strange friend in that he is much older than Egil. When Egil is seven, Thord is "á ungum aldri" (99: "a … young man," 67) and when the boy is twelve, he is "á tvítugs aldri" (101: "in his twentieth year," 68). Unlike Skallagrim, this young man "var elskr at Agli" (99: "was very fond of Egil," 67). This expression of affection suggests that the saga does not shy away from making statements of love when there is cause to do so, which means that Skallagrim's love for Egil is likely not mentioned because it is not demonstrated.

This friendship between the young man and the small boy is not in itself so strange and may be attributed to Thord's kindness of heart, but the fact that Egil seems to have no other friends most assuredly is. And if Thord is an unusual best friend for a little boy, so is Thorgerd Brak, Skallagrim's slave, who is "mikil fyrir sér, sterk sem karlar ok fjǫlkunnig mjǫk" (101: "an imposing woman, as strong as a man and well versed in the magic arts," 69). She is not a glamorous mother figure, this magical manly woman who is not even free, just a slave, almost a non-person. It is thus a curious pair that stands up for Egil, a young man who has befriended a little boy and a trollish slave woman, and nobody else. And when Skallagrim has killed both, Egil has no one.

It is shown from the outset that Egil is not lovable. First his parents have Thorolf, who is "inn vænsti sýnum … íþróttamaðr … gleðimaðr mikill … vinsæll af alþýðu" (80: "handsome … accomplished … cheerful … popular with everyone," 54), and, as the saga has it, is loved by both his parents. Then, late in life, they have this other son who is "mjǫk ljótr ok líkr feðr sínum, svartr á hár" (80: "very ugly and resembl[ing] his father, with black hair," 54). When he is three, this ugly child is as big as six- or seven-year-olds. He is also "málugr ok orðvíss" and "heldr … illr viðreignar, er hann var í leikum med ǫðrum ungmennum"' (80: "talkative … and had a gift for words, but tended to be difficult to deal with in his games with other children," 54).

There is an insight here into the emotional life of Skallagrim. It is mentioned that Thorolf looks like his late uncle Thorolf, the one whose death resulted in Skallagrim threatening the king. Egil, on the other hand, looks like his father, but Skallagrim, apparently not a narcissist, does not seem to care much for seeing his own ugly visage perpetuated in this little boy. And there is, of course, one important difference. Not only is this unnecessary second son big and ugly, he is also bothersome and he talks all the time. Skallagrim does not talk much himself. Like many taciturn people, he may perhaps not care much for people who talk constantly. And there is a good case to be made that he likes them even less when they look like himself.

Egil, however, cannot be reduced to a stereotype. An ugly duckling he may be, but he is also a child prodigy (see Stein-Wilkeshuis 1970, 88–9; cf. Hansen 2003; and Jakobsson 2003). His merits are recognized by his grandfather, who, as previously mentioned, presents him with three sea-snail shells and a duck's egg for composing a skaldic stanza at the age of three.[10] And, as we have also seen, when Egil kills the boy Grim after having been bullied and threatened by him, his mother is pleased and calls him a Viking. But in both cases, Skallagrim sees no accomplishments, only trouble. This son of his is not only ugly as sin, he cannot even behave himself. And that is the only thing Skallagrim has to say to Egil in both chapters 31 and 40, before ceasing all communication with him for a whole winter.

The last character in this family drama is the least conspicuous one, Thorolf the good-looking older brother, the handsome and happy son whom Skallagrim loves. The old man's affection for his elder son is mentioned from the outset, as we have seen, and further established when Thorolf intercedes with him on behalf of Bjorn Brynjolfsson, who had quarrelled with Skallagrim's friend and ally Thorir in Norway and then had the impudence to stay at Borg for the winter (88–9: 60–1). It is clear that Skallagrim is grievously affronted by this situation and equally clear that Thorolf is able to persuade him not only not to harm Bjorn but also to act as negotiator between Bjorn and Thorir. Thorolf is such a favourite with his father that he will do almost anything for him.

Thorolf Skallagrimsson is a somewhat neglected figure in *Egil's Saga*, perhaps eclipsed by his uncle, Thorolf Kveldulfsson, who dominates the first quarter of the saga. Scholars have often treated the second Thorolf as a repetition of an already well-established type (see Nordal 1942, 169; Grimstad 1976, 286; Sørensen 1977, 766; Clover 1982, 4–6; Ólason 1991, 54; Hafstað 1985, 138–9, and others). But while the second Thorolf may resemble the first Thorolf physically, there is an important difference. The first Thorolf was arrogant and ambitious, and behaved in such a way that King Harald was bound to become suspicious when Thorolf's malcontents began to slander him after having been treated less than generously by him (14–54, esp. 27; 9–38, esp. 17; see also Sørensen 1993, 140–2; for a different view, see Andersson 1967, 107; and Ólason 1991, 50). The second Thorolf is, as I will demonstrate, a morally superior character, and this character is, in fact, well exemplified in chapter 40 of *Egil's Saga*.

Thorolf and Empathy

Skallagrim is taciturn, but his son Egil is talkative. The frosty silence between the two for a whole winter must have been a much more severe punishment for Egil than for his father. In addition, while Skallagrim may have lost his foreman he still retains the majority of what is most important for him: his work, his household, and all his loyal workmen. One can imagine him as an important chieftain, regularly going to assemblies and enjoying the good life that only those in the upper echelons of Icelandic society did. Egil, on the other hand, is neither a worker nor a chieftain. He is stuck at home, a garrulous, brilliant, completely underestimated teenager full of life but with no role and no friends. He is unpopular throughout the district, the only communication mentioned between him and the other local boys being when they "œpðu at honum" (100: "jeered at him," 67) after he was hurt by Grim Heggsson. In short, although the saga does not say so directly, Egil is close to being, at least in his own head, the most miserable teenager in the whole world when his brother Thorolf – for Egil probably an almost mythical figure – returns from Norway after a decade abroad.

Thorolf had gone to Norway as a youngster to live with Skallagrim's friends and allies in Aurland. As luck would have it, Skallagrim's friend and ally Thorir has fostered Eirik Blood-axe, the son of the now old King Harald of Norway. One day, Thorolf meets young Prince Eirik standing and admiring young Thorolf's beautiful ship. Thorolf presents this ship to the prince, who promises Thorolf in return to be his friend for life. Then Thorolf heads for court, is accepted, albeit reluctantly, by the old king, and soon joins Eirik on his voyages to Permia as one of his most respected men. Thorolf has a new life now. It is a life in the company of kings and courtiers. It is a sophisticated life, full of parties, merriment, exciting adventures, and foreign raids. As an accomplished youngster, he enjoys admiration and respect. He returns home in triumph. One cannot imagine he has often thought of Skallagrim and his family at home, but he knows that he enjoys their love and respect as the favourite son. In fact, we are given no grounds to believe that Thorolf has ever been disliked. It has been specified that he was loved from the outset by his parents and that he is a good-looking man with pleasant manners. A person like Thorolf hardly knows what it means to be alone, unpopular, or despised. There is, in fact, no greater gap than exists between his big and bright world and the life of his younger teenage brother, whom he has never really known.

When Thorolf has been at his old home for a year and wants to return to Norway, Egil goes to him and asks to be allowed to accompany him. Thorolf's reaction is normal and understandable. Even the most charming of younger brothers would be a nuisance to a popular and handsome young Viking and merchant who wants to see the world and be received by kings and princes. And what is there to say about the ugly, unpopular, uncontrolled, and misunderstood troll-descendant with whom he is now faced, whom his father detests and who has already killed two largely innocent people? This outlandish stranger cannot have been prepossessing when he turned to his older brother in desperation and asked to accompany him, likely not too skilfully, as it is hard to imagine young Egil exhibiting any impressive social graces.

Faced with this monstrosity, Thorolf Skallagrimsson is indeed put to the test. And, at first, he says no. He says: "ef faðir þinn þykkisk eigi mega um þik tœla hér i hýbýlum sínum, þá ber ek eigi traust til þess at hafa þik útanlendis með mér, því at þér mun þat ekki hlýða, at hafa þar slíkt skaplyndi sem hér" (102: "if your own father doesn't feel he can manage you in his house, I can't feel confident about taking you abroad with me, because you won't get away with acting there the way you do here," 69). The short and abrasive version of this would be: "You mean trouble, and I don't want you around."

But Egil does not give up. He cuts the mooring ropes of his brother's ship so that it drifts out into the fjord, and when confronted with his act he claims that he will do Thorolf further harm if he does not take him with him to Norway. Egil is desperate, and that is understandable enough. But if Egil's motives are understandable, what about Thorolf's? Why does he give in to his brother? It would be easy to jump to the conclusion that Egil has forced his hand: he has to take Egil with him, and there is no way out. But that solution is not logical and must be dismissed. After all, Egil has no allies at Borg, and in spite of his cleverness and unruliness Thorolf would definitely have been able to get out of taking him with him. He could have conceived some ruse with plenty of allies to help him. Or he could simply have forced Egil to stay at home, by fetters if needed. Thorolf does not absolutely have to take Egil with him. He has a choice and, although Egil is indeed trying to force his hand, Thorolf does not merely yield to superior force but decides, upon reflection, to take this uncontrolled and monstrous younger brother with him.

At this juncture, we get an important insight into the character of Thorolf Skallagrimsson that decisively distinguishes him from Thorolf Kveldulfsson and makes it possible for us to grasp his character. It must be admitted that Thorolf is not only in danger of being eclipsed by the previous Thorolf as his supposed double, he even seems a slightly duller version. The previous Thorolf created trouble with his ambition, and there is an interesting disagreement between him and his father, who does not want him to go to the court of King Harald, whereas the second Thorolf, like his father Skallagrim, knows his place, mostly stays out of trouble, and, unlike most of the other major characters in *Egil's Saga*, gets along very well with his father. Indeed, as a character, he has the great narrative flaw of having no obvious flaw, and I can imagine that this is the reason he has been so often overlooked. Egil is naturally a much more colourful character in the story, whereas there is a distinct lack of drama in Thorolf's life.

I would contend that Thorolf's decision to take Egil with him to Norway is actually quite remarkable and sheds significant light on Thorolf, on the assumption that my argument – that his hand was not forced – is accepted. It must also be kept in mind that it would be difficult for Thorolf to empathize with Egil's situation in Iceland. Indeed, Thorolf does seem to take some time to grasp it fully, and perhaps it is Egil's desperate act of vandalism followed by his (somewhat empty, as I have argued) threats that really opens his eyes. But what is it that Thorolf is doing in taking Egil abroad with him?

He Ain't Heavy

Whereas parents are supposed, and usually legally required, to take responsibility for their children, siblings do not necessarily share this duty. If two brothers are in good health, they have the choice of not really speaking to each other and of not taking responsibility for each other's actions. This scenario frequently plays itself out in modern urban societies but can also be seen in thirteenth-century Iceland, for instance in the case of Snorri Sturluson and his brothers, who were effectively estranged.[11] Bonds between siblings often tend not to be as binding as those between a parent and a child

The lack of firm rules about how siblings are supposed to behave towards each other makes the relations between them an interesting subject that is frequently explored in stories, and brotherhood has long been established as an important theme in *Egil's Saga* (see Einarsson 1975, 114–23). The author and audience of *Egil's Saga* would have been familiar with the biblical narrative of Cain and Abel, as has been argued by Torfi H. Tulinius (2004, 77), as the contemporary Icelandic interpretation of the Danish dynastic troubles of the 1240s and the 1250s readily shows (see Hoffmann 1975, 188–92). According to the Bible, Cain and Abel are the first brothers in history and their narrative, like all Bible narratives, is exemplary. At the end of the narrative, Cain poses an interesting question to God: "er ek nǒckut skipadr geymslumadr brodur mins" (Unger 1862, 42: "Am I my brother's keeper?"). Even though Cain's question may be construed as an attempt to cover his crimes, it is still valid and has remained unanswered; God very cleverly gave Cain no reply, and every single brother and sister is now stuck with this question, which has no simple answer. Siblings do not need to take responsibility for each other but are free to allow their siblings to be responsible for themselves. In addition, some siblings behave in such a way that it is far from easy to be their brother or sister, and that can be certainly said of young Egil when he confronts Thorolf.

When Thorolf takes Egil on he does take responsibility for him, and that is quite remarkable in light of what has previously happened. When Egil killed Grim, this deed resulted in bloodlettings in the districts, but Egil's parents took no part in them and effectively refused to accept responsibility for their son. It landed instead on Oleif Hjalti, Skallagrim's friend. By taking Egil, Thorolf is thus doing what his parents have failed to do. Thorolf's decision to take Egil is even more remarkable because he has nothing to gain from it (and indeed Egil soon starts to cause him a great deal of bother) and, as we have seen, has no prescribed duty to do so. As already noted, it must have cost Thorolf some effort to relate to Egil's situation and his capacity for empathy is tested to the utmost. I would indeed argue that the word empathy is a key concept in any interpretation of Thorolf Skallagrimsson. Thorolf definitely has the ability to feel the pain of others; this capacity is the only explanation for his actions.[12] He can feel Egil's pain, even though it is vastly different from anything he has experienced. Thus he seems to possess imaginative powers that his older namesake never demonstrated and which make the younger Thorolf a more attractive character.

He thus becomes the first person to make a sacrifice for Egil and not pay with his life, or at least not immediately. For Thorolf is indeed making a sacrifice: he is exchanging a happy and relatively trouble-free existence for a totally different and much more bothersome life with Egil. And Egil is desperate, he needs saving, his life is so miserable that it can scarcely be regarded as a life. Thus Thorolf's actions echo the recent actions of Thorgerd Brak and those of Thorgerd Egilsdottir later in the saga (see Torfi Tulinius 2004, 83). All three save Egil's life, but whereas the acts of the two women have been noticed and lauded, what Thorolf is doing has remained less conspicuous, although, upon reflection, it is no less important or impressive.[13]

Thorolf's choice is not dramatized or commented upon in the narrative. Its significance has to be inferred from the situation. But I would still contend that my interpretation of the events is neither free nor fanciful but the only possible way to explain this narrative. The only question is the extent to which the author and the audience were aware of Thorolf's dilemma, choice, and sacrifice and its importance to Egil. I would argue that the ramifications of Thorolf's choice would have been clear, and that his action would have been the main reason why the audience of the saga was meant to see Thorolf as an uncommonly noble and kind man. Since a thirteenth-century audience would be familiar with the Bible, as Torfi H. Tulinius has argued (see 1994; 1997; 2004), they would also have been aware of the fact that Thorolf was actually answering Cain's question in deciding to become his brother's keeper.

Empathy and goodness are key concepts in the interpretation of these events. Thorolf would not have been able to assist Egil if he did not have a capacity for empathy, which is in this case was prompted not by any past experience but only by his imagination. Imagination is not usually seen as a virtue in itself and certainly was not regarded so in the Middle Ages. But it might be fruitful to contrast Thorolf's reaction to Egil with the "banality of evil" that Hannah

Arendt later observed in the Eichmann trials in Jerusalem. For Arendt, Eichmann's evil was a lack of empathy and imagination. He was unable to think an original thought and had a very hard time envisaging events from a different point of view than his own (Arendt 1963, 47 ff.). In contrast, Thorolf Skallagrimsson is able to adopt a position vastly removed from his own and imagine himself in the shoes of an ugly, unloved, temperamental, and murderous child, although he has never himself been any of these. He is also able to transform this feeling into the good deed of saving his brother. To act so kindly is an ability not given to all, and we, like the thirteenth-century audience, cannot but be impressed by what Thorolf does here.

The Altruist and the Egoist

Having taken Egil along, Thorolf keeps standing up for him throughout his life. After Egil has killed the king's representative in Atley, Thorolf takes him east on Viking raids, during which time they are constantly together and Egil continues to run into trouble. Thorolf does not ever reproach him, although he does once comment that Egil seems to be deliberately making it impossible for them to stay in Norway (Nordal 1942, 127). There is nothing of the earlier Thorolf's excessive ambition in Thorolf Skallagrimsson; he does not even seem to resent the fact that, owing to Egil's unruly disposition, he himself is no longer popular in Norway and has gained powerful enemies (123: 85–6). He has, in fact, dedicated his whole life to becoming his brother's keeper, to the extent that Egil is now the more dominant of the two brothers.

Thorolf's goodness highlights the fact that Egil himself remains an egoist. He becomes jealous of his brother's marriage and, in spite of his violent and expressive grief after Thorolf's fall in England,[14] promptly marries his widow, whom he had probably always desired (105, 143–50: 71, 100–4).[15] Later, when grieving for his own sons, he seems unable to fathom that this loss might affect his wife as well; the only loss Egil feels is his own (242–5: 167–71).[16] Thus the empathy Thorolf shows when he takes Egil with him to Norway and stands by his troublesome brother is sadly not repaid by Egil. Egil is arguably not a simple character; even his behaviour in his great grief differs from that demonstrated by other elderly Viking fathers (see Jakobsson 2005a, 315–21). There is no lack of emotion or of poetic imagination in Egil, but he does not seem to feel much empathy. To the contrary, it can be argued that throughout his life Egil Skallagrim chooses to remain oblivious to the pain of others.

How, then, can we characterize the role of Thorolf Skallagrimsson in *Egil's Saga*? I have argued here that far from emulating the former Thorolf, he makes different choices and plays a fundamentally different role. The only trait that the two Thorolfs have in common is serving as opposites to their surviving brothers. The first Thorolf was ambitious, highlighting Skallagrim's lack of ambition. The second Thorolf is, on the other hand, kind, generous, and caring, whereas Egil lacks all of these qualities. If any character in *Egil's Saga* personifies goodness, it is Thorolf Skallagrim. Egil, even though he looks like his father, ends up imitating his uncle Thorolf in amassing wealth and challenging kings. The younger Thorolf, however, is a good and true brother to Egil, just as Skallagrim was a loyal and devoted son to his father. Egil survives because of Thorolf and owes his greatness to him – although this greatness, like perhaps all greatness, is morally dubious and obtained, ultimately, at the expense of others.

NOTES

1 This is a new version of a study originally published in *Scandinavian Studies* 80.1 (Spring 2008): 1–18.

2 *Egil's Saga* is usually believed to have been composed in Iceland in the first half of the thirteenth century, and, in fact, the oldest manuscript of the saga is only slightly younger. Most twentieth-century scholars believed that Snorri Sturluson authored the saga. For the arguments for this conclusion, see Nordal 1933, liii–xcv. The age and authorship of *Egil's Saga* are not important for my study so I will not pursue this question here.

3 I follow the Íslenzk fornrit edition, but the number of chapters in the saga actually varies, see *Egils saga* (A-version; Einarsson 2001) 58; *Egils saga* (C-version; Chestnutt 2006) 48–52.

4 Although there are some significant exceptions: see Cook 1984–5.

5 This despite the fact that her name means "she-bear."

6 In modern Iceland, this mean-spirited comment has developed into the view that Egil Skallagrimsson was drinking alcohol at the age of three. That is never stated in the saga and the only "evidence" is Skallagrim's statement to Egil before the party: "þykkir ekki góðr viðskiptis, at þú sér ódrukkinn" (81: "[you seem] enough trouble when you're sober," 55). I have argued before (Jakobsson 2005b) that taking this statement as evidence for Egil's inebriation is a classic case of over-interpretation.

7 Literally, *[h]amask* (101: "shape-shift," 68).

8 While the word "Viking" is frequently bandied about when medieval Iceland is discussed, it is important to keep in mind that this was not a Viking society in any real sense of the word and not exceptionally violent, but rather a mostly peaceful society of farmers (with some feuds and killings that, of course, were felt to have more historical significance than everyday life and thus tended to make it into the

sagas). The only Vikings in Iceland were retired ones, sons of chieftains who had gone on raids in distant countries, like Egil himself. This point is well demonstrated by the fact that after killing Grim Heggsson and his father's foreman, Egil kills several people abroad during his adulthood but none in Iceland, until he kills two of his de facto son-in-law's slaves in his extreme old age (297: 195–6). Thus, after Grim, Egil does not do any killing in Iceland that might result in a lawsuit or feud, proving himself able to adapt rather better to the restrictions of his own society than Skallagrim would perhaps have anticipated.

9 Bera is sometimes mistakenly seen as a doting and loving mother who refuses to see any wrong in her son's actions (Guðmundsson [2012, 86] diagnoses her as "dependent") but this interpretation ignores her lack of involvement in Egil's struggle with Skallagrim in ch. 40.

10 This composition of skaldic poetry at such a tender age is often considered wildly unbelievable, but the saga relates this in a matter-of-fact fashion. There is no apparent reason to expect that the author did not want his audience to take this prodigious feat at face value.

11 An especially interesting point for those who want to believe in Snorri as the author of *Egil's Saga* (see Tulinius 2004, 177–80).

12 For a good recent essay on empathy, see Sontag 2004. Empathy is a relatively recent concept, perhaps influenced by romantic nineteenth-century ideas about the imagination. It might be defined as the ability to imagine oneself as another person, to think and feel oneself into the inner life of another. Unlike sympathy, empathy is characterized by the ability to comprehend the state of another without necessarily experiencing that state. And whereas sympathy is a moral concept, empathy is not. It is more a cognitive process, a way of understanding rather than of relating. Thus, sympathy is altruistic but empathy does not necessarily lead to altruism (see Kristjánsson 2004, 288–9).

13 In addition it can be argued that Egil's friend Arinbjorn also saves his life later in the narrative, when he successfully pleads his case with King Eirik in York.

14 Admittedly Egil does show a very rare generosity when he buries two gold rings with Thorolf (142), which indicates that he did appreciate what Thorolf had done for him. Later, when Skallagrim dies, it is noted in the saga that Egil buries him without any gold (175: 119).

15 Cf. Torfi H. Tulinius's interpretation of *Egil's Saga* as a narrative of incest, fratricide, guilt, and salvation (2004, 54–82). It must be noted that Egil's desire for Asgerd before the death of Thorolf is far from unambiguous. Much rests on the fact that Egil became "sick" and couldn't attend Thorolf and Asgerd's wedding (105). While his love for Asgerd could explain this sickness, it could, of course, also be caused by his anxiety that he is now going to lose his brother, the only person in the world who has shown himself to be firmly on Egil's side.

16 After the death of Thorolf Skallagrimsson, there are no more Thorolfs in the Borg family. Egil has three sons but does not use the name.

BIBLIOGRAPHY

Andersson, Theodore M. 1967. *The Icelandic Family Saga: An Analytic Reading.* Cambridge: Harvard University Press.

Arendt, Hannah. 1963. *Eichmann in Jerusalem: A Report on the Banality of Evil.* New York: Viking.

Chesnutt, Michael, ed. 2006. *Egils saga Skalla-Grimssonar III: C-redaktionen. Editiones Arnamagnaeanae A, 21.* Copenhagen: Reitzel.

Clover, Carol J. 1982. *The Medieval Saga.* Ithaca: Cornell University Press.

Cook, Robert. 1984–5. "The Reader in *Grettis saga.*" *Saga-Book* 21: 133–54.

Einarsson, Bjarni. 1975. *Litterære forudsætninger for Egils saga.* Reykjavik: Stofnun Árna Magnússonar.

– ed. 2001. *Egils saga Skalla-Grimssonar I: A-redaktionen. Editiones Arnamagnaeanae A, 19.* Copenhagen: Reitzel.

Grimstad, Kaaren. 1976. "The Giant as a Heroic Model: The Case of Egill and Starkadr." *Scandinavian Studies* 48: 84–98.

Guðmundsson, Óttar. 2012. *Hetjur og hugarvíl. Geðsjúkdómar og persónuleikaraskanir í Íslendingasögum.* Reykjavík: JPV.

Hafstað, Baldur. 1985. *Die Egils saga und ihr Verhaltnis zu anderen Werken des nordischen Mittelalters.* Reykjavik: Rannsoknarstofnun Kennaraháskola Íslands.

Hansen, Anna. 2003. "The Precocious Child: A Difficult Thirteenth-Century Icelandic Saga Ideal." In *Scandinavia and Christian Europe in the Middle Ages. Papers of the 12th International Saga Conference, Bonn/Germany, 28th July–2nd August 2003.* Ed. Rudolf Simek and Judith Meurer, 220–8. Bonn: Universität Bonn.

Hoffmann, Erich. 1975. *Die heiligen Könige bei den Angelsachsen und den skandinavischen Völkern: Königsheiliger und Königshaus.* Neumunster: Karl Wachholtz Verlag.

Hoyersten, Jon Geir. 1998. *Personlighet og avvik: En studie i islendingesagaens menneskebilde, med særlig vekt pa Njala.* Bergen: Regionsenter for barne- og ungdomspsykiatri og Psykiatrisk institutt, Universitet i Bergen.

Jakobsson, Ármann. 2003. "Troublesome Children in the Sagas of the Icelanders." *Saga-Book* 27: 5–24.

– 2005a. "The Specter of Old Age: Nasty Old Men in the Sagas of Icelanders." *Journal of English and Germanic Philology* 104: 297–325.

– 2005b. "Á ég að gæta bróður míns? Innlifunin og Þórólfur Skalla-Grímsson." *Skíma* 28.2: 35–41.

Kristjánsdóttir, Bergljót S. 1997. "Primum caput: Um höfuð Egils Skalla-Grímssonar, John frá Salisbury o.fl." *Skáldskaparmál* 4: 74–96.

Kristjánsson, Kristján. 2004. "Empathy, Sympathy, Justice, and the Child." *Journal of Moral Education* 33: 291–305.

Miller, William Ian. 1992. "Emotions and the Sagas." *From Sagas to Society: Comparative Approaches to Early Iceland.* Ed. Gisli Palsson, 89–109. Enfield Lock: Hisarlik.

Nordal, Sigurður, ed. 1933. "Formáli." In *Egils saga Skalla-Grimssonar*. Íslenzk fornrit 2. Reykjavik: Hið íslenzka fornritafélag.

– 1942. *Íslenzk menning* I. Reykjavik: Mál og menning.

Ólason, Vésteinn. 1991. "Jórvíkurför í Egils sögu: Búandkarl gegn konungi." *Andvari new ser*. 33: 46–59.

Pálsson, Hermann. 1994. "Fornfræði Egils sögu." *Skirnir* 16: 37–72.

Poole, Russell. 2004. "Myth, Psychology, and Society in *Grettis saga*." *alvissmál* 11: 3–16.

Sontag, Susan. 2004. *Regarding the Pain of Others*. New York: Picador.

Sørensen, Preben Meulengracht. 1977. "Starkaðr, Loki og Egill Skalla-Grímsson." *Sjötíu ritgerðir helgaðar Jakobi Benediktssyni 20. júlí 1977.* 759–68. Reykjavik: Stofnun Árna Magnússonar.

– 1993. *Fortælling og ære: Studier i islændingesagaerne*. Aarhus: Aarhus University Press.

Stein-Wilkeshuis, Martina W. 1970. *Het kind in de oudijslandse samenleving.* Groningen: Wolters-Noordhoff.

Tulinius, Torfi H. 1994. "Mun konungi eg þykja ekki orðsnjallr: Um margræðni, textatengsl og dulda merkingu í Egils sögu." *Skirnir* 168: 109–33.

– 1997. "Egla og Biblían." *Milli himins og jarðar: Maður, guð og menning í hnotskurn hugvísinda: Erindi flutt á hugvísindaþingi guðfræðideildar og heimspekideildar 18. og 19, okt. 1996.* Ed. Anna Agnarsdóttir, Pétur Pétursson, and Torfi H. Tulinius. 125–36. Reykjavík: Háskólaútgáfan.

– 2004. *Skáldið í skriftinni: Snorri Sturluson og Egils saga.* Reykjavík: Hið íslenska bókmenntafélag.

Unger, Carl Rikard, ed. 1862. *Stjorn: Gammelnorsk bibelhistorie fra verdens skabelse til det babyloniske fangenskab.* Christiania: Feilberg & Landmark.

7 Elegy and Old Age in *Egil's Saga*

ALISON FINLAY

Introduction

Egil Skallagrimsson claims the reader's attention as one of the most active and assertive of saga heroes. Yet the devoting of nearly a quarter of his saga to his decline into helpless and friendless old age could be seen as anti-climactic, not least because this section is made up largely of a collection of loosely assembled anecdotes. In this paper I consider the narrative of Egil's old age, attempting to point to various formative influences in its composition. I argue that the accumulation of these anecdotes is likely to have been stimulated by the elegiac poem *Sonatorrek.* This poem and its companion piece *Arinbjarnarkviða*, together with some of the *lausavísur* ("loose verses"), which can reasonably be assumed to have originated at an earlier stage than the extant saga prose, delineate the general contours of the protagonist's decline into helplessness and disappointment, universalize his plight in terms of older mythology and legend, and infuse qualities of the lyrical and the elegiac into the saga as a whole. Also significant in shaping the final third of the saga are themes developed in earlier sections of the saga, notably the stylized treatment of Egil's kin in terms of the dichotomy "fair and handsome and good-natured" versus "dark and ugly and ill-natured." A third influence comes from the culture more generally and it is with this aspect that we shall begin.

Depictions of Old Age in the Sagas of Icelanders

It is in the nature of the Viking world-view that the life of the Icelandic saga hero is typically nasty, brutish, and short. A characteristic view of old age is voiced by the old Egil Wool-shirt in the *Saga of Hakon the Good*, rejoicing at the end of a long period of peace:

> I was afraid for a while, during this long peace, that I would die of old age indoors on my bed-straw, but I would rather die in battle and follow my lord.[1]
>
> [Þat óttuðumk ek um hríð, er friðr þessi inn mikli var, at ek mynda verða ellidauðr inni á pallstrám mínum, en ek vilda heldr falla í orrostu ok fylgja hǫfðingja mínum. (Aðalbjarnarson 1941–51, I, 178)]

Saga authors subscribe to this ideology by presenting as heroes men whose lives are cut short by their enemies, their heroism definitively displayed in a final unsuccessful defence. According to the estimates of the editors of the Íslenzk fornrit series, some necessarily more speculative than others, the life expectancy of a heroic Icelander was not high. Grettir and Bjorn Champion of the Hitardal People meet their violent ends at the age of thirty-five, Kjartan Olafsson at thirty-three, while Gisli Sursson achieves a middle-aged forty-five (approximately); Gunnlaug Serpent-tongue must have died aged only 25.[2] In this respect Egil is a conspicuous exception, surviving as he does into advanced old age.

Ármann Jakobsson has analysed depictions of old age, particularly those of old men, in the Sagas of Icelanders against the background of wider medieval conceptions of old age. Many of the most striking examples – Thorolf Blister-pate of *The Saga of the People of Eyri*, Thorarinn in *The Tale of Thorstein Staff-Struck* – are not protagonists but subsidiary characters, whose function in the saga consists largely in the articulation of their relationship with their sons. Here too Egil is exceptional – as is Njal Thorgeirsson, the hero of *Njal's Saga*. Njal is doubly exceptional in falling into the category of "nice old man" (to use Jakobsson's somewhat reductive terminology), whereas Egil shares many features with the contrasting "nasty" old men whose predicament, according to this analysis, is essentially that they have outlived not only the physical prowess that offered an outlet to the aggression proper to a successful Viking hero but in some cases also a warlike ideology that has become anachronistic in more peaceable times. A former Viking is almost an "ex-human being" (Jakobsson 2005, 309). Georges Minois, in his analysis of medieval perceptions of old age, finds a discrepancy in the sagas between elders who enjoy prestige and a reputation for wisdom – among whom he includes Olaf Feilan (*The Saga of the People of Laxardal*), Hoskuld Dala-Kollsson and Snorri the Godi (*The Saga of the People of Laxardal, The Saga of the People of Eyri*), and Thorfinn Karlsefni and Flosi Thordarson (*Njal's Saga*) – and "deposed old chieftains" who are "maltreated without any consideration" (Minois 1989, 190–1). He surmises that the difference between the types epitomizes a "transition from a warlike way of life to a more peaceable agrarian economy which no longer admired this bravado. … [T]he realistic style of sagas of the thirteenth century made fun of such belligerent old men" (Minois 1989, 192). In sagas that incorporate poetry that can be argued to date authentically from the tenth-century *milieu* of the early saga heroes – such as some of the poetry attributed to Egil Skallagrimsson – the clash of cultures identified by Minois could perhaps be more pointedly expressed in terms of the transition from a pagan to a Christian culture.

Such a cultural shift may underlie the variation in the treatment of old age in the sagas, although it should be pointed out that sagas present a range of character types among the elderly, as is the case with other age groups. The sagas also employ different modes, some satirical, as in the characterization of old Thorarinn in *The Tale of Thorstein Staff-Struck*, and others more idealistic, as in the characterization of the hero of *Njal's Saga.* An important conduit for these variations in mode, which is not taken into account by these analyses, is the poetry, usually older than the saga text in which it has been incorporated, and the varying strategies adopted by the prose authors in integrating these verses into their text can intensify the discrepancies. In those texts where an old warrior reflects on the contrast between his prowess at the height of his powers and the physical decline brought on by age, a lyrical impulse can be detected that seems to be strongly traditional and indeed perhaps to have roots in a common Germanic heritage, if it is not rather to be seen as universal in human culture.

Saga authors differed in the ways they chose to bring this contrast between youthful prowess and senile decline into play. Take for example the anecdote of the venerable warrior Bersi the Dueler, who in old age fosters Halldor, the son of Olaf Peacock. *The Saga of the People of Laxardal* has a cameo of the sick old man, too infirm to rescue the child when he falls out of his cradle, speaking a verse in which he likens his own lack of strength to that of the babe in arms:

> We lie both unable to move, Halldor and I; we have no strength. Old age does it to me, youth to you; you will be cured of it, I never will.

> [Liggjum báðir
> í lamasessi
> Halldórr ok ek,
> hǫfum engi þrek:

veldr elli mér,
en œska þér,
þess batnar þér,
en þeygi mér.] (Sveinsson 1934, 76)
…

Bersi plays no other role in this saga; the verse simply stands as a rueful observation on a warlike man's descent into the second childishness of old age. But the same verse also occurs in *Kormak's Saga*, where Bersi plays a much larger part and recites a number of verses which tend to tally obsessively the number of people he has killed. At first sight the verse is less suitably placed here, for Halldor is twelve years old, rather than a babe in arms; Bersi adopts him specifically as a defence against the numerous enemies his aggressive lifestyle has ensured for him. The verse, in much the same form as that in which it appears in *The Saga of the People of Laxardal*, is spoken as one of a group that form a preamble to Bersi's last killing, in which the boy assists his foster-father, using the famous sword Hviting with which Bersi had killed many of his enemies. The boy's comment makes clear what the saga author wants it to demonstrate: "You aren't aging much in courage, foster-father" ("Lítt eldisk þú enn í huginum, fóstri minn," Sveinsson 1939, 262). The verse has a valedictory function, marking the point where the man who has lived by the sword is forced to give up his weapon to the succeeding generation. The adoption of a son to take on this role only highlights the old warrior's lack of the natural son who should step into his shoes – a classic predicament that will be discussed in more detail presently. It is this more elegiac view of old age, stemming likewise from incorporated poetry, that has its counterpart in *Egil's Saga*, and indeed dominates there, despite the fact that the protagonist definitely belongs at the nastier end of the spectrum of aged males.

Difficult Vengeance

As noted above, the narrative of Egil's old age takes its chief inspiration from Egil's great elegy *Sonatorrek*. In it Egil laments the death of his sons, reproaching the deceitful god Odin, and in doing so finds consolation in his own gift of poetic articulation, attributed to the same god. Like Egil's two other long poems, *Hǫfuðlausn* and *Arinbjarnarkviða*, the poet's tribute to his friend, *Sonatorrek* is included in full in modern editions of the saga, but it is not clear that they were originally intended to form part of its text. The best surviving version of the saga, the fourteenth-century Möðruvallabók (M), follows the practice common in other poets' sagas of citing only the first stanza, introduced by the formula "and this is the beginning of the poem" ("ok er þetta upphaf kvæðis," 245). The poem's full text is found only in later copies.[3] Nevertheless *Sonatorrek* echoes many of the saga's principal concerns. Turville-Petre's comment that "It gives a clear insight into the mind of Egill in his advancing years, showing him as an affectionate, sensitive, lonely man, and not the ruffianly bully which he sometimes appears to be in the Saga" (Turville-Petre 1976, 24) is superficially true, but ignores the complexity with which Egil's inner life has been represented, perhaps even prefigured, at earlier stages of the saga.

The generality of the elegy itself has been somewhat overshadowed by the dramatic occasion given for it in the saga's prose, in which Egil, intending to starve himself to death in his grief, is tricked by his daughter Thorgerd into drinking milk instead of water, and so lives on to hold the funeral feast for his drowned son. Torfi Tulinius, for instance, has applied a Christian reading to this scene, seeing Thorgerd as a type of the Virgin Mary, saving Egil – ambiguously situated between paganism and Christianity by the rite of *prima signatio* which he had undergone some years earlier – from the sin of suicide (Tulinius 1997). While this hypothesis seems to me to go beyond the evidence of the text, it is a useful reminder that the saga was produced by a thirteenth-century Christian author, whose discomfort with the overt paganism evidenced, for instance, in *Sonatorrek,* can perhaps be detected in elements such as the emphasis Tulinius notes in the saga on the disposal of the hero's body (Tulinius 1997, 280–2).[4]

Sonatorrek, like many elegies, uses the occasion of a particular loss as a springboard for a much wider evocation of grief. The lament for the drowned Bodvar, which the prose context foregrounds as the occasion for the poem, is generalized into a more universal sense of loss, encompassing the passing of the poet's whole family and his abandonment or betrayal by friends and, indeed, by his tutelary god. Readers have been struck by the uniquely personal quality of *Sonatorrek,* by the access that it seems to give to the poet's own mental state and to the process of healing – underwritten by the power of poetic expression – that its composition seems to enact. This psychological insight has been considered strangely modern: Sigurður Nordal remarked that it is not until the later nineteenth century that we encounter an Icelandic poem as personal as this one (1924, 146). Contradictorily, the poem has also been accepted as a genuine manifestation of very deep-rooted traditions including pagan belief. Joseph Harris has explored ways in which the poem may function as ritual, suggesting that certain types of *grátr* ("lament") might require, of a devotee of Odin, "re-enactment of the mythological experience" attributed to Odin himself (2010). It is important to bear in mind here Russell Poole's point that "Vikings … were not 'pagan' in any absolute sense, since they moved freely within Christian as well as non-Christian milieux, especially once prime-signed" (Poole 2010, 193). His own hypothesis, that there were thematic and rhetorical parallels between Egil's longer poems and Carolingian poetry, which Egil might have been exposed to at the court of the English king Athelstan, suggests a more complex milieu than either Harris's postulation of a tradition of ritual lament re-enacting the myth narrated in *Gylfaginning* or Tulinius's theory of Egil as a proto-Christian wholly fashioned by the thirteenth century.

Speaking to the strongly traditional elements in the poem, Harris's interpretation places primary emphasis on those aspects of the poet's mourning for the death of his son that parallel Odin's loss of his son Baldr. The most fundamental parallel is the father's inability to avenge his son, since the "slayer" of Egil's son Bodvar was the inanimate sea: "The sea has robbed me of much" ("Mik hefr marr / miklu ræntan," 250, v. 10).[5] Stanza 8 of the poem is difficult to understand, but in it Egil seems to tell of his inability to use traditional weapons against the "brewer" (*ǫlsmiðr*), apparently the sea-god Ægir (who brewed beer for the gods) and his wife Ran:

> You know that if I could avenge that injury with the sword, the brewer's days would be over; if I could fight, I would go against the brother of the storm [i.e., Ægir, god of the sea] and the wife of Ægir. (Turville-Petre 1976, 32–3)

> [Veizt, ef þá sǫk
> sverði of rækak,
> vas ǫlsmiðr
> allra tíma;
> hroða vágs brœðr,
> ef vega mættak,
> fórk andvígr
> ok Ægis mani.] (249)

The impossibility of taking vengeance against the sea may be alluded to in the poem's title. *Sonatorrek* is often translated "Grievous loss of sons," although Nordal and others have argued that it could mean "Difficult vengeance for sons" (1933, 257 n.).[6] According to *Gylfaginning*, Odin's son Baldr was killed accidentally by his brother Hod (Sturluson 1982, 45–6). Although Odin's grief is singled out beyond that of the other Æsir, the father's inability to kill his own son in vengeance is not directly referred to in *Gylfaginning*, where the stated obstacle to vengeance is that the killing has taken place at a sacred assembly site.

Nevertheless, the story seems to have functioned in tradition as a prototype of the particular anguish of the father denied access to the emotional release offered by revenge – a motif that is strongly operative in *Egil's Saga*. What is evidently an older analogue, pointing to the highly traditional nature of such material, occurs in the Old English epic poem *Beowulf*, in the form of the story of old king Hrethel and his sons. This story in turn seems to derive from a legendary recasting of the myth of Odin and Baldr, reflecting the gods' names: *Hæð*cyn (where the first element in the compound corresponds to Hǫðr, i.e., Hod) accidentally shoots his brother Here*beald* (where the second element in the compound corresponds to Baldr):[7]

> That was a fight that could not be compensated, a sinful crime, wearisome to the heart; none the less for that, the prince had to give up his life unavenged.
>
> [þæt wæs feohleas gefeoht, fyrenum gesyngad,
> hreðre hygemeðe; sceolde hwæðre swa þeah
> æðeling unwrecen ealdres linnan.] (*Beowulf*, ll. 2441–3)

In yet a further analogue, Hrethel's distress is compared by the *Beowulf* poet with that of another, nameless, father whose son is killed by the gallows, which (like the sea) is an inanimate agent, so that revenge is thwarted (de Looze 1991; Lindow 1997, 141–4):

> In the same way it is sorrowful for an old man to experience his young son riding on the gallows; then he composes a lament, a sorrowful song, when his son hangs to the benefit of the raven, and he, old and wise, cannot do anything to help him.
>
> [Swa bið geomorlic gomelum ceorle
> to gebidanne, þæt his byre ride
> giong on galgan; þonne he gyd wrece,
> sarigne sang, þonne his sunu hangað
> hrefne to hroðre, ond he him helpe ne mæg,
> eald ond infrod ænige gefremman.] (*Beowulf* ll. 2444–9)

Explicitly rejected is the apparently commonplace solution of awaiting the birth of an alternative heir:

> He is constantly reminded every morning of his son's departure; he cares for no other, nor to await heirs within the courts when the first has experienced evil deeds that enforced his death.

[Symble bið gemyndgad morna gehwylce
eaforan ellorsið; oðres ne gymeð
to gebidanne burgum in innan
yrfeweardas, þonne se an hafað
þurh deaðes nyd dæda gefondad.] (*Beowulf* ll. 2450–4)

The use of this convention may be another submerged allusion to the myth of the death of Baldr in which according to some versions – although not Snorri's account in *Gylfaginning* – Odin sired the god Vali specifically in order to take vengeance on Hod for Baldr's death.[8] Egil also alludes to this notion, though without explicitly rejecting its potential for consolation; the thought may be completed for him, in the context of the whole poem, by the loss of at least one other son besides Bodvar, and the long-ago loss of his own brother, recalled almost immediately before this stanza:

This is also said that no one may get recompense for his son unless he himself begets yet another descendant who will be for others (?) a man born in place of his brother. (Turville-Petre 1976, 36–7)

[Þat's ok mælt
at engi geti
sonar iðgjǫld
nema sjalfr ali
enn þann nið,
es ǫðrum sé
borinn maðr
í bróður stað.] (252–3, v. 17)

Like Egil, the old man in *Beowulf* takes refuge in elegy (*sorhleoð*) as the poem modulates into the generality typical of the elegiac mode of Old English poetry.

Harris may be right to argue that the parallel between Egil's loss of Bodvar and Odin's mourning for Baldr weighed with the saga author in his identification of the poem so specifically with the death of this drowned son. But the suggestion is somewhat weakened by the fact that this emphasis is stronger in the prose than in the poem itself, where a more general sense of loss is expressed. It is intriguing to remember that the author of the saga prose is usually believed to have been none other than the author of *Gylfaginning*, and that it may have been he rather than Egil himself who noted and strengthened the parallel between Egil and Odin. Snorri Sturluson was first mooted as the author of *Egil's Saga* in 1818 by Grundtvig, in the introduction to his translation of

Heimskringla. Since then the attribution has been supported by many including Sigurður Nordal, editor of the 1933 Íslenzk fornrit edition, on the grounds of similarity in style, vocabulary, and theme to the two works generally accepted to be by Snorri, namely *Snorra Edda* and *Heimskringla.* The attribution is often accepted without question, and the argument moved on to the issue of the relative chronology of *Egil's Saga* and *Heimskringla*, which Jónas Kristjánsson argued in 1977 to have been written earlier than *Egil's Saga* rather than later.[9]

The title *Sonatorrek* refers to "sons" in the plural. The other son of the title is, according to the saga prose, Egil's second son Gunnar, who had died a short time before the drowning of Bodvar. In stanza 20 Egil recounts that

> the vicious fire of sickness seized my son from the world. (Turville-Petre 1976, 38)
>
> [son minn
> sóttar brími
> heiptuglegr
> úr heimi nam] (245)

It may be noted that fever is a target as elusive as the sea for revenge by the sword. To add yet further to this pattern, Jón Hnefill Aðalsteinsson has argued that the death of a third son in battle is alluded to in the following stanza:

> This I remember yet, when the friend of the Gautar [Odin] raised up the ash-tree of my race which grew from me and the family branch of my wife into the world of the gods. (Turville-Petre 1976, 39)
>
> [Þat man ek enn
> er upp um hóf
> í goðheim
> Gauta spjalli
> ættar ask;
> þann er óx af mér
> ok kynvið
> kvánar minnar.] (245)

This is usually taken to refer to Bodvar but, as Aðalsteinsson (1991, 16; 1998–2001, 169–70) points out, the raising by Odin to the world of the gods is an honour usually reserved for those who die in battle. The initial line of the stanza, "This I remember yet" ("Þat man ek enn"), seems to refer to an event from the past. If Aðalsteinsson is right, the enumeration of the deaths of three sons from different causes, each impossible to avenge, may further extend a generalizing tendency comparable to that seen in *Beowulf*, where the distress of Hrethel is expressed through the depiction of the grief of an anonymous, emblematic figure and by the empty courts from which a whole community has passed away.

Before the poem refers at all to the drowning, Egil broadens his lament further with an introductory reference to the death of his parents:

> But yet I will first tell of the death of my mother and the fall of my father. (Turville-Petre 1976, 31)
>
> [Þó munk mitt
> ok móður hrør
> fǫður fall
> fyrst um telja] (248, v. 5)

Telja means "to tell," but also "to enumerate"; the poem assembles a list of the losses in a long life that contribute to the poet's grief. After the stanzas narrating the drowning, Turville-Petre says, Egil now turns his thoughts to his brother, Þórólfr, "killed many years earlier" (1976, 35), but this too is expressed as a generality; the poet thinks of "lack of brothers" (*brœðraleysi*) rather than "loss of a brother" (Turville-Petre translates "lack of a brother"). Egil laments the cutting off of his whole line both in general, as in stanza 4:[10] "For my line is at an end, storm-beaten like forest maples" (Turville-Petre 1976, 31: "Þvít ætt mín / á enda stendr, / hræbarnir / sem hlynir marka," 247), but also specifically in relation to his son's drowning: "the sea has cut the bonds of my race, a strong strand of me myself" (Turville-Petre 1976, 32: "sleit marr bǫnd / minnar ættar,/ snaran þátt / af sjǫlfum mér," 248, v. 7).

Sonatorrek locates the poet's distress within his outrage at the breaching of his family (*frændgarðr*), the "cutting of his bonds of race" ("ættar bǫnd"), the ending of his line. Egil's sense of family is one of the most dynamic themes of the saga and of its representation of his personality. It has a political dimension, rhetorically opposed to the dangerous aspiration of serving a king, which proves fatal to his uncle and brother. This contrast is underlined by the division of Egil's family into two strains: the dark, ugly, aggressive, and individualistic side, with mysterious hints of the supernatural, to which Egil belongs, and the fair, sociable, and reasonable side represented by Egil's brother and uncle, both named Thorolf. In *Sonatorrek* family values are more emotionally represented as a bulwark battered and breached by the onslaughts of indiscriminate nature and destiny embodied in the implacable and impersonal pagan deities.

According to the saga narrative, Egil is not an old man when *Sonatorrek* is composed (in the chronology cited by Nordal he is only about fifty years old:

Nordal 1933, liii), but the poet's sense of the falling away of all his kin is coupled with a suggestion of treachery and lack of support in the world, explicitly associated with old age. His assertion of his inability to fight against the sea, which would of course be the same for any man, young or old, modulates into an expression of the helplessness of old age:[11]

> But I thought I did not have power of vengeance against my son's killer, for the old man's lack of support appears before the eye of every man. (cf. Turville-Petre 1976, 33)
>
> [En ek ekki
> eiga þóttumk
> sakar afl
> við sona bana,
> þvít alþjóð
> fyr augum verðr
> gamals þegns
> gengileysi.] (249, v. 9)

The closing stanza, in which the poet, stripped of friends and kin, awaits the goddess Hel with resignation, seems so like the words of closure with which the saga should end that it is disconcerting to realize that, according to the conventional dating, Egil has another thirty years to live. It is ironical that the stimulus for the collection of rather loosely structured anecdotes about the poet's old age with which the saga continues may have been precisely the image of old age which Egil constructed for himself in *Sonatorrek.*

"Now diminish the warriors who diminished gold" ("Þverra nú, þeirs þverrðu … mjaðveitar dag")

Awkward as it is for the overall structure of the saga that Egil's third long poem, *Arinbjarnarkviða*, is placed almost immediately after *Sonatorrek*, the two poems function in some ways as companion pieces. The preoccupation of *Sonatorrek* is with kin; *Arinbjarnarkviða* moves the subject on to friendship. While the opening of *Sonatorrek* shows the poet crippled into inarticulacy by the weight of his grief, the eager praise of *Arinbjarnarkviða* trips off his tongue, his eloquence in itself a measure of his friend's excellence:

> I am quick of speech in praise of the prince, but stumble in speech over misers, fluent about a king's deeds but silent about people's lies.

[Emk hraðkvæðr
hilmi at mæra,
en glapmáll
of gløggvinga,
opinspjallr
of jǫfurs dáðum,
en þagmælskr of þjóðlygi.] (258, v. 1)

Arinbjarnarkviða, at least according to the context it is given by the saga's prose, is not a memorial poem but salutes the poet's friend at a moment of ascendancy: Arinbjorn's exile in service of Eirik Blood-axe is at an end and he has returned to favour in Norway in the train of the new king, Eirik's son Harald Grey-cloak. Yet some scholars, such as Carolyne Larrington, have sensed a note of commemoration about it:

> At times, *Arinbjarnarkviða* sounds very much like the kind of memorial lay that we find in *Glymdrápa*, a praise-poem celebrating the achievements of the dead lord. It is only the saga context, and a small number of present tense verb forms (among a majority of preterite forms) in the text which suggest that Arinbjǫrn is still alive at the time of composition. (Larrington 1992, 50)

Inevitably, since Egil's career at the courts of kings is at an end – "people say that Egil did not leave Iceland … and the main reason was that Egil could not go to Norway because of the quarrels that kings considered they had with him" ("Svá segja menn, at Egill fœri ekki á brott af Íslandi … ok bar þat mest til þess, at Egill mátti ekki vera í Noregi af þeim sǫkum … at konungar þóttusk eiga við hann," 257) – the friendship belongs to the past tense. This is emphasized by the diversion of the poem from generalized praise into a vivid narrative of Egil's encounter with King Eirik in York. As Carolyne Larrington says, this is

> taken … as a single occasion which stands for all; … it is the one moment where Arinbjǫrn, the diplomat and politician, is forced to choose publicly between the lord he has followed faithfully into exile in England and his old friend. (1992, 55)

From the point of view of the saga's construction, this reminiscent mode marks the point where Egil begins to be represented as an old man revisiting the dramas of his past. Arinbjorn's triumph is not allowed to last; almost immediately we hear of his death at the side of Harald Grey-cloak at Limfjord,[12] commemorated by Egil in a strongly elegiac stanza lamenting the loss of friends:

Now diminish the warriors who diminished gold [by giving it away]; where shall I seek generous men, who beyond the island-studded earth's belt [the sea] made crucible-snow [silver] rain over my hawk's high mountains [hands] in exchange for words?

[Þverra nú, þeirs þverrðu,
þingbirtingar Ingva,
hvar skalk manna mildra,
mjaðveitar dag, leita,
þeira's hauks fyr handan
háfjǫll digulsnjávi
jarðar gjǫrð við orðum
eyneglda mér hegldu.] (269–70)

In this stanza the carefully articulated theme of *Arinbjarnarkviða*, in which the *hersir*'s generosity matches the poet's praise, is repeated, but generalized into a lament for all generous patrons; the lyrical repetition of *þverra* and the rhetorical "where shall I find …?" echo are conventional elegiac tropes.

"A senile old man" ("karl afgamall")

It has often been pointed out that the construction of the last part of the saga is episodic, loosely stringing together a variety of anecdotes about Egil's old age. The observation has tended to be related to the discussion of Snorri's possible authorship, since, as argued by de Vries (1967, II, 350), this discursiveness, degenerating at the end into a series of barely connected items, seems at odds with the more purposeful structuring of *Heimskringla*.

A partial explanation of this episodic quality is that this last part of the saga is very specifically rooted in the local landscapes around Egil's homes at Borg and later Mosfell. The saga ends with the enumeration of his numerous descendants, and the anecdotes of the poet's old age presumably derive from local traditions developed and preserved within this extended family; these apparently rely largely on prose accounts, with few verses cited, often tending to show the struggle between Egil's aggressive spirit and his increasing infirmity. The local focus is reinforced by the lengthy account of a boundary dispute between neighbours, mainly involving Egil's surviving son Thorstein. Continuing in the valedictory vein of his final verse tributes to Arinbjorn, there are reminders of the hero's relinquishment of honour and fame beyond Iceland in the stories of the *drápur* he composes in thanks for valuable shields sent to him from abroad. One of these arises out of his friendship with the poet Einar Skalaglamm, with whom Egil enjoys discussing poetry (271–3), one of the few references in Old Norse texts suggesting a culture in which the art of skaldic composition was passed on from one poet to another. In this context it can be read as an element in Egil's relinquishment, a handing on of the public role of poet to a younger successor.

Egil is survived by his son Thorstein, Thorstein's ten children and two further sons born out of wedlock, not to speak of Egil's two daughters and his niece (also step-daughter) and her husband, with whom he is living when he dies. This gives the lie to the theme paramount in *Sonatorrek* of the withering of the family line. In some ways, though, the account of Egil's frosty relationship with Thorstein – "Egil had little love for him; Thorstein was also not affectionate towards him" ("Egill unni honum lítit; Þorsteinn var ok ekki við hann ástúðigr," 274) – is used to elegiac effect, to suggest the replacement of men of heroic stature (in particular Egil himself) by lesser men, and to recall the division of Egil's family into the two character types that we have noted as an earlier theme in the saga. Thorstein is not a negligible figure, as is clear from the summary remark at the end of the boundary dispute: "Thorstein was a straightforward and just man, not touchy, but he held his own if other people were aggressive to him; it was difficult for most who got into a fight with him" ("Þorsteinn var maðr órefjusamr ok réttlátr ok óáleitinn við menn, en helt hlut sínum, ef aðrir menn leituðu á hann, enda veitti þat heldr þungt flestum, at etja kappi við hann," 293). But repeatedly he is shown at a disadvantage beside Egil, as is graphically represented in the episode where he borrows a splendid cloak given to Egil by Arinbjorn (another token of the hero's past glory) and ruins it by wearing it at the Assembly, where it trails in the mud because it is too long for him. This is the occasion for Egil to recite an angry verse, accusing his son of betraying him and using up his inheritance while his father is still alive. In the same vein, in a subsequent verse about his nephew Thorgeir Blund, Egil complains, "my sister's son failed me" ("mér brásk minnar systur mǫgr," 293), contributing to a picture of an embittered old man disappointed by his descendants.

The first of these verses, assuming it was in existence at the time the saga was written, seems likely to be the main source for the poor relationship between Egil and Thorstein. But this is developed into a recapitulation of the contrast made earlier in the saga between the dark, ugly, and turbulent Skallagrim and Egil, on the one hand, and Egil's uncle and brother, both called Thorolf and both fair in appearance and equable in temperament, on the other. The saga casts Thorstein in the latter mould, while insisting on his failure to measure up to his father: he is the most handsome of all men, with fair hair and a bright complexion; "he was big and strong, and yet not to the same extent as his father" ("allra manna fríðastr sýnum, hvítr á hár ok bjartr álitum; hann var mikill ok sterkr, ok þó ekki eptir því sem faðir hans," 274). The negative connotations of fair colouring are exploited by the taunt of one of Thorstein's adversaries: "Are you running away now, Thorstein the White?" ("Rennr þú nú, Þorsteinn hvíti?," 291).

Egil contributes to the boundary dispute only at the end, where he manoeuvres his way into having sole arbitration in the dispute and settles it forcefully in favour of his son. His arrival at the Assembly for this settlement "with eighty men all fully armed as if ready for battle" ("með átta tigu manna, alla vel vápnaða, svá sem til bardaga væri búnir," 284) is clearly designed as a final flourish of warlike display from the old hero. His detailed speech, harking back in formal vein to his father's settlement of the district, inaugurates the saga's insistence, in his descent towards death, on his and his family's identity with the local scene: "I begin the case with the fact that my father Grim came here to this land and settled all the lands around Mýrar and the district beyond, and set up his residence at Borg" ("hef ek þar upp þat mál, er Grímr, faðir minn, kom hingat til lands ok nam hér ǫll lǫnd um Mýrar ok víða herað ok tók sér bústað at Borg," 287).

The last three verses of the saga, one a single half-verse (*helmingr*) and another in the loose *fornyrðislag* metre, record the infirmities of extreme old age, incontinence, impotence, blindness, and susceptibility to cold. In the last of them the poet, in a complex pun, substitutes the word *ekkja* ("widow," or in poetry, "woman" in general) for *hæll*, which also means "widow" but more commonly "heel," the relevant sense here, to convey the humiliation of his confinement to domestic and female companionship in a heated indoors:

I have two very cold heels / women, and those women need flame.

[eigum ekkjur
allkaldar tvær,
en þær konur
þurfu blossa.] (296)

These are the universal plaints of old age, and contribute nothing to the individualization of Egil, but rather belong to the pattern of generalization that we have noted previously. But the sequence of verses acts as a prelude to Egil's last quirky gesture before his death, the mysterious disposal of the two chests of silver given to him long ago by King Athelstan in compensation for his brother's killing. This constitutes another recapitulation of an element from Egil's past, for it closely mimics the last act of his father Skallagrim. After disputing possession of Athelstan's gift with Egil (the king had told Egil first to give the silver to his father and then to share it with the rest of his family as well), Skallagrim had taken his own hoarded money and sunk it in a marsh (174). Egil is thwarted in his first mischievous intention, to scatter the money from the Law-Rock at the Assembly in order to watch people scramble for it, an impulse that could be interpreted as another identification of Egil with Odin, in reference to the story of the god's casting a whetstone up into the air, leading Baugi's slaves to kill each other with their scythes as they try to catch it (Sturluson 1998, I, 4). Egil is believed instead to have hidden the money somewhere around Mosfell, where he had been living with his step-daughter. The saga's references to places where the exotic English coins can still be found are a last reminder of the identification of the hero with the particularities of the local landscape (in this case that of Mosfell), a reminiscence of his days of martial glory in foreign battles, and a device that ensures his continuing influence among the saga author's contemporaries as they continue to turn up evidence of his hoard and speculate on its location.

Conclusion

In *Sonatorrek* Egil gives magnificent poetic expression to a sense of abandonment and loss arising out of a specific personal tragedy but generalized to include his sense of no longer being supported by family loyalties, nor even by the god on whom he had depended. Its evocation of elegiac themes widely current throughout the Germanic world is evident from the parallels with *Beowulf.* Its resolution seems to leave the poet reconciled to imminent death:

> Yet gladly and without fear I shall await the goddess Hel. (cf. Turville-Petre 1976, 41)

> [skalk þó glaðr
> með góðan vilja
> ok óhryggr
> heljar bíða.] (256, v. 25)

With thirty years left to live, however, the poet's anticipation of death turns out to have been more in the nature of a mid-life crisis. In these circumstances the prosaic and episodic last sequence of the saga can hardly fail to be an anticlimax. Nevertheless the anecdotes of Egil's last years develop the poem's elegiac theme in a different register, through the poet's problematic relationship with his son and nephew and his sense of the diminishment not only of his own powers but also of the stature of his family. His tribute to his friend Arinbjorn and the tokens of his heroic ventures abroad – the presentation shields, the cloak, and the hoarded treasure of Athelstan – stand as tangible reminders of his achievements as a Viking hero. And the increased prominence of the local landscape gives a contrasting perspective to the elegiac generalities of *Sonatorrek*, grounding the identity of the aging poet and his legacy, both poetic and material, firmly in western Iceland.

NOTES

1 Unless otherwise specified, all translations are my own.

2 Jónsson 1936, lxvii–lxviii; Nordal and Jónsson 1938, lxxxvii, lix; Sveinsson 1934, lix; Þórólfsson and Jónsson 1943, xlii–xliii.

3 Of the saga's three long poems, *Hǫfuðlausn* is omitted entirely by M, but is cited in its entirety in the fourteenth-century Wolfenbüttelbók (W) ("hér hefr Hǫfuðlausn") and the seventeenth-century Ketilsbók (K) ("ok er þetta upphaf kvæðis þess," 185n.). One stanza of *Sonatorrek* is cited in M; the remainder is found only in K (this part of the saga is missing from W) (Nordal 1933, 245n.). Even the copies of K in which the poem appears introduce it with the formula "ok er þetta upphaf kvæðis." Bernard Scudder's translation (1997, 171) substitutes the sentence "Then Egil composed this poem" as a more appropriate introduction to the following translation of the whole text of the poem, but this is not supported by any manuscript. M introduces *Arinbjarnarkviða* with "then Egil composed a poem about Arinbjorn, and this is its beginning" ("Þá orti Egill kvæði um Arinbjǫrn, ok er þetta upphaf at," 257 and n2), and space is left for a stanza that has not been inserted; the poem survives only in a copy in another hand placed after the end of the saga, and in no other manuscript.

4 Tulinius does not address the content of the poem or its authorship in this article, but elsewhere he argues that it could not be the authentic work of Egil himself (Tulinius 2000, 195–6) and aligns himself with those (Einarsson 1992, Hafstað 1995) who consider all or most of the verse in the saga to be the work of the author (Tulinius 2004). Others, notably Joseph Harris (2010, 152–3, n12), take not only the poem but the saga as a "source for pagan life and ritual." Russell Poole (2010, 174–81) gives a nuanced account of the "probably diverse provenances of the verses and their gradual incorporation into the saga material, giving cautious support to the status of the three long poems attributed to Egil as authentic tenth-century compositions." This position is essentially that followed in this paper.

5 Throughout my discussion of *Sonatorrek* I cite the translation of Turville-Petre (1976, 24–41), although the stanzas themselves are cited from the edition of Sigurður Nordal (1933). The translations are sometimes arrived at through some emendation of the text, which is not noted here. The translations of vv. 9 and 25 are my own.

6 As Harris notes, the word *torrek* occurs elsewhere in poetry only in a verse by Sigvatr Þórðarson (*c.*1030) where it "must refer to loss and not to revenge"

(Harris 2010, 157, n. 28). It is also found in prose with the same sense (Fritzner 1886–96, III, s.v.)

7 For further parallels, and a discussion of the relationship between the Old Norse and Old English stories, see Lindow 1997, 141–4 and Orchard 2003, 116–19. For a detailed analysis of the passage in *Beowulf*, see Georgianna 1987; also Dronke 1969.

8 The clearest reference is in *Baldrs draumar* 11; see Turville-Petre 1964, 110–11. Snorri cites kennings in *Skáldskaparmál* referring to Vali as "hefni-Áss Baldrs" ("Baldr's avenging god") and "dólg Haðar ok bana hans" ("enemy of Hod and his slayer," Sturluson 1998, I, 19).

9 Torfi Tulinius reviewed the debate and argued for Snorri's authorship of *Egils saga* (Tulinius 2002, 234–6). The argument has resurfaced recently after the inclusion of the saga in the "collected works" of Snorri published in Iceland in 2002 as *Ritsafn Snorra Sturlusonar*, ed. Helgi Bernóduson, Jónas Kristjánsson, and Örnólfur Thorsson, 3 vols (Reykjavík, 2002). The naming of Snorri as author was challenged by Guðrún Nordal in a review in *Lesbók Morgunblaðsins* and defended in a reply by Thorsson and Vésteinn Ólason (who was responsible for the introduction to the edition), in which they assert the overwhelming probability of Snorri's authorship of the saga. Ironically the defence rests partly on the uncertainty of attribution also of those works, *Heimskringla* and the *Prose Edda*, which are generally agreed to be by Snorri; and they point out that Guðrún Nordal does acknowledge the origin of the saga in Snorri's own district and circle, while agreeing that even if Snorri is acknowledged as author, the saga as we now know it must have changed considerably from the form in which he left it. In his earlier, somewhat more sceptical article Ólason traces the history of the discussion and analyses the historical, literary, and linguistic grounds for attribution to Snorri, without himself taking a position for or against (Ólason 1968).

10 The text here follows Sigurður Nordal's emendation of ll. 3–4, which read "sem hræbarnar / hlinnar marka." For other suggestions, see Nordal 1933, 247–8n.

11 *eiga* is emended from MSS *eigna*; *sonar bana* is emended from *súðbana.*

12 This effect is increased by the telescoping of events in the saga's chronology, since virtually nothing is told of the reign of Harald Grey-cloak, which according to *Heimskringla* lasted for fifteen years (Aðalbjarnarson 1941, I, 239).

BIBLIOGRAPHY

Aðalbjarnarson, Bjarni, ed. 1941–51. *Heimskringla* I–III. Íslenzk fornrit 26–28. Reykjavík: Hið íslenzka bókmenntafélag.

Aðalsteinsson, Jón Hnefill. 1991. "Synspunkter på *Sonatorrek*." In *Nordisk hedendom En symposium.* Ed. Gro Steinsland et al. 9–17. Odense: Odense University Press.

– 1998–2001. "Religious Ideas in *Sonatorrek*." *Saga-Book* 25: 159–78.

Beowulf. 1950. Ed. Fr. Klaeber. 3rd ed. Boston: Heath.

de Looze, Laurence. 1991. "Frame Narratives and Fictionalization: Beowulf as Narrator." *Interpretations of Beowulf: A Critical Anthology*. Ed. R.D. Fulk, 242–50. Bloomington, IN: Indiana University Press.

de Vries, Jan. 1967. *Altnordische Literaturgeschichte*. 2 vols. Berlin: deGruyter.

Dronke, Ursula. 1969. "Beowulf and Ragnarǫk," *Saga-Book* 17.4: 302–25.

– 1984. "Óminnis hegri."In *Festskrift til Ludvig Holm-Olsen på hans 70-årsdag den 9. juni 1984*. Ed. Bjarne Fidjestøl et al., 53–60. Øvre Ervik: Alvheim & Eide.

Einarsson, Bjarni. 1992 "Skáldið í Reykjaholti." In *Eyvindarbók. Festskrift til Eyvind Fjeld Halvorson, 4 mai 1992*. Ed. Finn Hødnebø et al., 34–40. Oslo: Institutt for nordistikk og litteraturvitenskap.

Fritzner, Johan. 1886–96. *Ordbog over det gamle norske Sprog*. 3 vols. Oslo.

Georgianna, Linda. 1987. "King Hrethel's Sorrow and the Limits of Heroic Action in *Beowulf*." *Speculum* 62,4: 829–50.

Hafstað, Baldur. 1995. *Die Egils saga und ihr Verhältnis zu anderen Werken des nordischen Mittelalters*. Reykjavík: Rannsóknarstofnun

Harris, Joseph. 1999. "Goðsögn sem hjálp til að lifa af' í *Sonatorreki*."In *Heiðin minni: Greinar um fornar bókmenntir*. Ed. Haraldur Bessason and Baldur Hafstað, 47–70. Reykjavík: Heimskringla.

– 2010. "'Myth to Live By' in *Sonatorrek*." In *Laments for the Lost in Medieval Literature*. Ed. Jane Tolmie and M. J. Toswell, 149–71. Turnhout: Brepols.

Jakobsson, Ármann. 2005. "The Specter of Old Age: Nasty Old Men in the Sagas of Icelanders." *Journal of English and Germanic Philology* 104, 3: 297–325.

Jónsson, Guðni, ed. 1936. *Grettis saga Ásmundarsonar*. Íslenzk fornrit 7. Reykjavík: Hið íslenzka bókmenntafélag.

Kristjánsson, Jónas. 1977. "Egilssaga og konungasögur." In *Sjötíu ritgerðir helgaðar Jakobi Benediktssyni 20. júli 1977*. Ed. Einar G. Pétursson and Jónas Kristjánsson. Vol. 2, 449–72. Reykjavík: Stofnun Árna Magnússonar.

Larrington, Carolyne. 1992. "Egill's Longer Poems: *Arinbjarnarkviða* and *Sonatorrek*." In *Introductory Essays on Egils saga and Njáls saga*. Edited by John Hines and Desmond Slay, 49–63. London: Viking Society for Northern Research.

Lindow, John. 1997. *Murder and Vengeance among the Gods: Baldr in Scandinavian Mythology*. Helsinki: Suomalainen tiedeakatemia, Academia Scientiarum Fennica.

Minois, Georges. 1989. *History of Old Age from Antiquity to the Renaissance*. Trans. Sarah Hanbury Tension. Cambridge: Polity Press.

Nordal, Guðrún. 2002."Egill, Snorri og höfundurinn." *Lesbók Morgunblaðsins* (21 December 2002): 8–9

Nordal, Sigurður. 1924. "Átrúnaður Egils Skallagrímssonar." *Skírnir* 97: 145–65.

– ed. 1933. *Egils saga Skalla-Grímssonar.* Íslenzk fornrit 2. Reykjavík: Hið íslenzka bókmenntafélag.

Nordal, Sigurður, and Guðni Jónsson, eds. 1938. *Borgfirðinga sǫgur.* Íslenzk fornrit 3. Reykjavík: Hið íslenzka bókmenntafélag.

Ólason, Vésteinn. 1968. "Er Snorri höfundur *Egils sögu*?" *Skírnir* 142: 48–67.

Orchard, Andy. 2003. *A Critical Companion to Beowulf.* Cambridge: Brewer.

Poole, Russell. 2010. "'Non enim possum plorare nec lamenta fundere': *Sonatorrek* in a Tenth-Century Context." In *Laments for the Lost in Medieval Literature.* Ed. Jane Tolmie and M.J. Toswell, 173–99. Turnhout: Brepols.

Scudder, Bernard, trans. 1997. "Egils saga." In *The Complete Sagas of Icelanders including 49 Tales.* Vol. 1, 33–177. Reykjavík: Leifur Eiríksson.

Sturluson, Snorri. 1982. *Edda. Prologue and Gylfaginning.* Ed. Anthony Faulkes. London: Viking Society for Northern Research (repr. 1988, 2000).

– 1998. *Skáldskaparmál.* Ed. Anthony Faulkes. 2 vols. London: Viking Society for Northern Research.

Sveinsson, Einar Ól., ed. 1934. *Laxdœla saga.* Íslenzk fornrit 5. Reykjavík. Hið íslenzka bókmenntafélag.

– ed. 1939. *Vatnsdœla saga.* Íslenzk fornrit 8. Reykjavík: Hið íslenzka bókmenntafélag.

Þórólfsson, Björn K. and Guðni Jónsson, eds. 1943.*Vestfirðinga sǫgur.* Íslenzk fornrit 6. Reykjavík: Hið íslenzka bókmenntafélag.

Thorsson, Örnólfur and Vésteinn Ólason. 2003. "Snorri og Egils saga. Um höfunda fornsagna." *Lesbók Morgunblaðsins* (1 February 2003): 6–7.

Tulinius, Torfi. 1997. " Le statut théologique d'Egill Skalla-Grímsson." In *Hugur: Mélanges d'histoire, de littérature et de mythologie offerts à Régis Boyer pour son 65e anniversaire.* Ed. Claude Lecouteux and Olivier Gouchet, 279–88. Paris: Presses de l'Université Paris-Sorbonne.

– 2000. "The Prosimetrum Form 2: Verses as an Influence in Saga Composition and Interpretation." In *Skald Sagas: Text, Vocation, and Desire in the Icelandic Sagas of Poets.* Ed. Russell Poole, 191–217. Reallexikon der Germanischen Altertumskunde – Ergänzungsbände. Berlin: de Gruyter.

– 2002. *The Matter of the North. The Rise of Literary Fiction in Thirteenth-Century Iceland.* Odense: Odense University Press.

– 2004. *Skáldið í skriftinni. Snorri Sturluson and Egils saga.* Reykjavík: Hið íslenska bókmenntafélag for Reykjavíkur Akademían.

Turville-Petre, E.O.G. 1964. *Myth and Religion in the North.* New York.

– 1976. *Scaldic Poetry.* Oxford.

8 **Konutorrek*: A Husband's Lament

OREN FALK

For what could be more unbearable than the death of the son before his father's eyes?

["Quid namque esse intolerabilius potest, quam mors filii ante oculos patris?"][1]

The poem in the title of this chapter does not exist. Like so much poetry of the Norse Middle Ages, it could have been forgotten, lost, mutilated in transmission, or scrubbed clean from parchment by censorious hands. In this case, however, we have little cause to think it ever existed. This non-being is a significant historical fact. About sixteen thousand lines of skaldic verse survive (Frank 1985, 159); add the prose sagas and the corpus is many times richer still. Nothing human is foreign to the medieval Norse authors. It is, therefore, all the more revealing to begin peeling away at the crumbling margins around some lacunae in this monumental corpus. What the skalds and saga writers do not discuss may tell us as much about Norse civilization as what they do.

Medieval texts, Norse and otherwise, seldom lend much of an ear to widowers.[2] But *Egil's Saga* in fact provides us with several fleeting widower cameos, which may begin to teach us about what medieval Norsemen thought proper and plausible – not always the same thing – for a widower to do. The saga thus opens up for us the range of responses culturally available to a man like Egil upon the death of a wife.[3]

That Egil was capable of rhapsodizing on the theme of loss is handily confirmed by *Sonatorrek*, "Hard Loss of Sons," an indisputable masterpiece so well known that most medieval manuscripts simply allude to it without quoting more than the opening lines: the saga audience would have been expected to fill the poem in from memory.[4] *Sonatorrek* is an exquisitely narcissistic, yet also movingly plaintive, dirge: "in contrast to other commemorative poems we have the remains of, it deals first and foremost not with the deceased but with the surviving father's grief" (Helgason 1953, 137). The poem dwells at length on the speaker-poet's lugubrious state of mind (vv. 1–3, 25), the severity of the harm he has incurred through attrition of kinsmen (vv. 4–7, 9–10, 13–21), and his own irrepressible spirit (vv. 8, 22–5). Egil does also sing the praises of the dead – primarily his recently drowned son Bodvar, but also another deceased son, as well as his parents and his older brother, Thorolf – though mostly in terms that redound favourably on himself. Once we accept that Egil is constitutionally incapable of eulogizing others except in self-congratulatory terms, however, we may come to see *Sonatorrek* as actually quite a tender elegy to the family members he had lost: "My stock stands on the brink, pounded as plane-trees on the forest's rim; no man is glad who carries the bones of his dead kinsman out for burial" (172, v. 4: "ætt mín á enda stendr, hræbarnir sem hlynir marka; esa karskr maðr sás kǫggla berr frænda hrørs af fletjum niðr," 247).[5]

The more closely we reflect on *Sonatorrek*'s idiom, however, the more an unmistakable gender imbalance asserts itself: Egil's conception of his now defunct kindred focuses almost exclusively on kins*men* – his father, brother, two sons, and an indefinite gathering of "relatives" (*frændr*) characterized in stereotypically martial, masculine terms (e.g., v. 6). According to the enveloping prose, the poem had been commissioned by Egil's daughter, Thorgerd, who deflected her father's death-wish by pretending to share it, then tricking him into composing verse in Bodvar's memory. Yet in the poem itself Thorgerd receives no nod as a member of the injured ingroup. Nor does Asgerd (who presciently sent for Thorgerd post-haste as soon as she realized Egil had lost his will to live), aside from two circumlocutory allusions, which specify Bodvar as Egil's "wife's son" (175, v. 18: "kvánar sonr," 253) and as "the tree of my wife's kin" (176, v. 21: "kynvið kvánar minnar," 255). Alone of Egil's various female kin, Egil's mother gets to count expressly as part of the family, when her cadaver makes a fleeting appearance in the catalogue of the dead (172, v. 5: "móður hrør," 248).

The drowning of his first-born son thus occasions from Egil a moving elegy, in which he achieves in verse "an ancient male goal: a family without women" (or very nearly so; Harris 2007, 169). No such poetry is forthcoming, however, when his wife, Asgerd, likewise predeceases him. There is no question that Egil cares deeply for Asgerd.[6] He is her second husband; the first had been his brother, Thorolf, and it was only some time after Thorolf fell that Egil, speaking in cleverly obscure verse, declared his love for the widow to his friend (and her kinsman) Arinbjorn. Whenever "the head-dress [= *-gerd*] of the rock-giant's earth [= *As*-] … enters the poet's mind," he must bury "in [his] cloak the outcrop between [his] brows," says Egil, adding – lest Arinbjorn miss the encoded pun – "I seldom hide the name of my female relative in the drink of the giant's kin [i.e., in poetry]" (103–4: "verðk í feld, þás foldar / faldr kømr í hug skaldi / berg-Óneris, brúna / brátt miðstalli hváta. / Sef-Skuldar felk sjaldan … / í niðjerfi Narfa nafn aurmýils," 148–9). Arinbjorn correctly deciphers the encryption, endorses Egil's suit, and betrothes Asgerd to him.

"Egill's two verses about his relationship with Ásgerðr," notes Alison Finlay (1992, 34–5), "suggest more emotion than is implied by the prose narrative, in which his marriage to her seems to be partly a commercial transaction, partly a stage in the process of healing the grief at his brother's death." Lucre, as we will see again later, is never far from Egil's mind; and his connection with Asgerd (as well as with Thordis, Thorolf's orphaned daughter by her, whom Egil adopts as his own) undoubtedly contains an element of sublimated grieving for his brother, her husband – but also of Egil's envy of the dead man, and of enduring devotion to the lady whose bed they ultimately share.[7] Egil's convoluted, halting confession of affection supplies a retroactive explanation for his erratic behaviour, many years earlier, when Thorolf set out to wed Asgerd, or, earlier still, when Thorolf had purposed to take her from Iceland to Norway and leave Egil behind: "'In that case,' said Egil, 'perhaps neither of us will get to go'" (69: "'Vera má,' sagði Egill, 'at þá fari hvárgi okkarr'," 102).[8] Surely but subtly, the saga hints at Egil's long-standing infatuation with his more accomplished sibling's spouse. A similarly wispy hint will be dropped again decades later, when, immediately after Asgerd's death, Egil is said to "love Thordis, his step-daughter, most *of all the people who were then alive*" (187: "hann unni mest Þórdísi, stjúpdóttur sinni, *þeira manna, er þá váru á lífi*," 275, emphasis mine). The implication, of course, is that Thordis embodies for Egil a living memento of the two people he had loved the most of all those now no longer alive: his brother and his wife.[9]

This depth of emotion notwithstanding, Egil reacts to Asgerd's death with laconic stoicism, made all the more inscrutable by being reported in indirect speech: we are told only that he hands over his estate to his surviving son, Thorstein, taking up residence with Thordis (187: 275). This celebrated skald and devoted husband, capable of funnelling the most profound emotion into a breathtaking verbal torrent, chooses not to mourn his lifelong love in verse. Why, then, did Egil compose no **Konutorrek*, "Irreparable Loss of a Wife"? Why were other widowers, populating the pages of this and other sagas, similarly muted in their grief?[10]

In the world of the sagas, such impassivity was evidently the norm prescribed for widowed men. Women, in contrast, were expected to experience their loved ones' deaths as high trauma: Egil's granddaughter Helga expires of grief; her counterpart in another saga, Oddny, sinks into stupor; and even the poker-faced Gudrun Osvifsdottir depends, for her cheerful demeanour to lull her husband's killers into complacency, on the expectation that she respond to Bolli's killing with wails and tears.[11]

Men, however, were supposed to take the loss of a spouse on the chin, rebounding quickly into remarriage or accepting conjugal solitude for the rest of their lives. Like Egil, several other saga widowers opt for dependence on grown children in lieu of seeking out a new marital partner; such a recourse may have commended itself especially to those who, on account of advanced age or disability or both, were already ripe for retirement.[12] For the more vigorous, remarriage was the preferred option; that turnover was typically rapid is suggested by the fact that saga narratives tend to introduce a replacement bride immediately upon the death of a well-loved wife.[13] Widowers are expected to move on, and excess grieving is expressly stigmatized. Thus, in *Ágrip af Nóregskonunga sǫgum* ch. 4 (ÍF 29: 6), when Norway's king Harald Fair-hair dotes for three years over the incorrupt body of his witch of a wife, Snjofrid, his subjects stage an intervention. Only devilry, the saga author implies, can make sense of such unreasonable behaviour as the failure of a self-possessed man to recover from his bride's death with alacrity, equanimity, and desire for a new helpmeet.

Between Egil's decorous, taciturn response to Asgerd's demise and King Harald's madness, which marks the outer margins of impropriety, lies a range of reactions that medieval Norsemen deemed plausible for a widower, even if they were socially disruptive or undesirable. *Egil's Saga* contains two curiously similar narratives of malfunctioning widowerhood which illuminate this spectrum.

The first, spanning the middle third of the saga, concerns Asgerd's own parentage (Figure 1). The fortunes of Asgerd's lineage underwrite what is both sequentially and thematically the chief matter of the saga: Egil's family's settlement in Iceland and his own life and times. The young Bjorn Brynjolfsson falls passionately in love with Thora at a party hosted by her brother (and legal guardian) Thorir, but the latter refuses his suit of marriage.[14] Undeterred, the amorous young man returns when Thorir is away from home and abducts his beloved. This precipitate action pits him against his own father (not to mention his unwilling brother-in-law), forcing the young couple into hazardous exile on the high seas and in Iceland. But eventually he and Thora return to Norway, to be reconciled with both Brynjolf and Thorir; Asgerd, the daughter that had been born to them in Iceland, is left behind for Bera and Skallagrim, Egil's parents, to foster.

The saga treats this episode in elaborate detail (56–61: 83–90). By contrast, the next plot development unfolds with such rapidity that only a reader specifically on the lookout is likely to spot it:

Figure 1. Asgerd's lineage

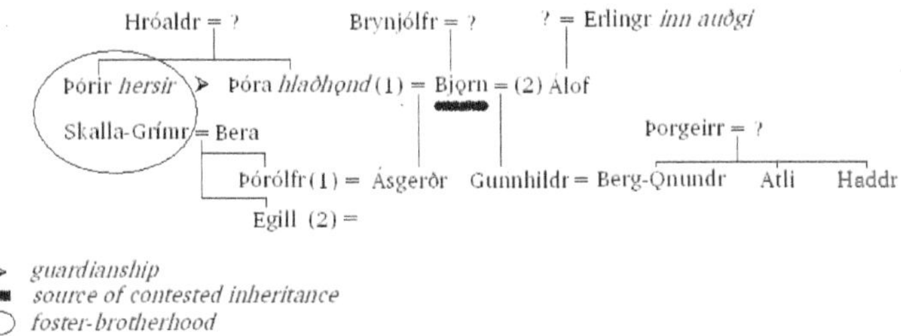

> The next thing that happened was that Bjorn's wife, Thora, fell ill and died. Some time afterwards Bjorn took another wife, Olof, daughter of Erling the Wealthy from Ostero. Bjorn and Olof had a daughter called Gunnhild. (64)

> [Þat varð þá næst til tíðenda, at Þóra, kona Bjarnar, tók sótt ok andaðisk, en nǫkkuru síðar fekk Bjǫrn sér annarrar konu; hon hét Álof, dóttir Erlings ins auðga ór Ostr; þau áttu dóttur, er Gunnhildr hét. (94)]

This telegraphic obituary-*cum*-wedding-and-birth-announcement is followed at once by the introduction of three new characters, the brothers Hadd, Berg-Onund, and Atli. In fact none will play any role in the saga until well into its second half, when Berg-Onund marries Gunnhild (103: 148), and by that point hardly any but the most astute reader will have the faintest recollection of having encountered the newly-weds before. Perhaps medieval audiences were better attuned to genealogical asides and would have had no difficulty placing Gunnhild and Berg-Onund at second sighting. But even such an audience, we may presume, would not have paid much attention to the pivotal role Bjorn's bereavement and swift remarriage play in putting the spouses of his two daughters on an epic collision course of protracted litigation and, ultimately, effusive bloodshed.

Bjorn's conjugal affairs may thus be isolated as a discrete element in the saga's central drama. Bjorn's first coupling produces the child who will grow into Egil's lifelong love interest. His second marriage seems much more straightforward, contracted according to the accepted speedy protocols of widowerhood. During Bjorn's lifetime, all we hear about his relationship with Olof is the bare fact of its inception; after his death, Berg-Onund – admittedly a prejudiced witness – paints this second marriage in normative hues ("Bjorn took [Olof] by law," 108: "Bjǫrn hafði [Álofu] lǫgfengit," 155), in sharp contrast to the first, which he describes with the vocabulary of ravishment, slavery, vagabondage, and outlawry: "[Thora had been] taken as booty and made a concubine without her kinsmen's approval, and shipped from one country to another … by some vikings and outlaws who had been exiled by the king," 108: "[Þóra var] hernumin, en síðan tekin frillutaki, ok ekki at frændaráði, ok flutt land af landi … með víkingum ok útlǫgum konungs," 155).

Yet the tranquil second marriage undergirds one of the saga's key conflicts. It is the friction between Bjorn's two matrimonies that sparks so much trouble. Were it not for the inflammatory fact of Bjorn's widowerhood, his union with Olof would indeed have been as uneventful as Berg-Onund seeks to portray it. But, because of this intervening fact alone – because the marriage to Olof is Bjorn's *second* – Bjorn's liminal bereavement, a status which, as we have seen, he retains for less than a sentence, is the flashpoint for multigenerational conflict.

Bjorn Brynjolfsson's cardinal widowerhood is prefigured, as in a distorting mirror, by an episode in the saga's Norwegian prelude involving a near-namesake father-and-son duo, the magnates Bjorgolf and his son Brynjolf (Figure 2; cf. Bredsdorff 2001, 20; Andersson 1969, 12–18). We find here most of the components that will constitute the later dispute over Asgerd's parentage and inheritance, albeit scrambled into a different configuration; perhaps the only constants across the two episodes are widowerhood (and ensuing claims of illegitimacy) and the messy, homicidal outcome.

In this case, it is not the son's roving eye but the father's that wreaks havoc. At first, all seems to go smoothly, despite the death of the family's (unnamed, hence, from a narrative standpoint at least, unimportant) matron. We do not know how deeply Bjorgolf was stricken by his wife's passing, but he adapts to his new status with remarkable grace. Already old, Bjorgolf sets up his grown son as householder in his place, providing him with a wife. Evidently Bjorgolf envisions the proper care of the family interest as requiring not just an able-bodied man but a *hjón*, a marital unit.[15] Bjorgolf thus ensures that Brynjolf is supplied with the requisite infrastructure to perform optimally in his new role and attempts to avoid any risk of jeopardizing Brynjolf's claim on the patrimony.[16] Having managed matters with care and foresight, he steps aside without a fuss.

But matters do not remain uncomplicated for long:

> One autumn Bjorgolf and his son invited a lot of people to a feast, and they were the most noble of all those present. … One of the guests was a man named Hogni who had a farm at Leka. He was wealthy, outstandingly handsome and wise, but came from an ordinary family and had achieved his position through his own

Figure 2. Lineage of Bjorgolf and his son Brynjolf

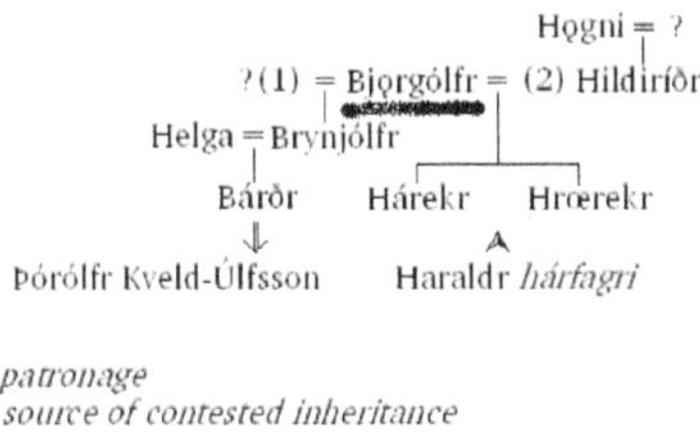

efforts alone. He had an attractive daughter named Hildirid, who was allotted a seat next to Bjorgolf. They talked together at length that evening and he thought the girl was beautiful. (10–11)

[Þat var eitt haust, at þar var gildi fjǫlmennt, ok váru þeir Bjǫrgólfr feðgar í gildinu gǫfgastir menn. ... En þar at gildinu var sá maðr, er Hǫgni hét; hann átti bú í Leku; hann var maðr stórauðigr, allra manna fríðastr sýnum, vitr maðr ok ættsmár, ok hafði hafizk af sjálfum sér. Hann átti dóttur allfríða, er nefnd er Hildiríðr; hon hlaut at sitja hjá Bjǫrgólfi; tǫluðu þau mart um kveldit; leizk honum mærin fǫgr. (16)]

Attraction will soon beget action: just as Bjorn, though initially rebuffed, comes back for his Thora, so also Bjorgolf returns for Hildirid. Where Bjorn's youthful passion has to rely on stealth, however, Bjorgolf's courtship is blunt; there can be no refusing "the most noble of all those present":

The same autumn old Bjorgolf set off from home. ... When they reached Leka, twenty of them went up to the farm. ... Bjorgolf called Hogni over and said: "The reason I have come here is to take your daughter home with me, and I will celebrate a loose wedding with her here now." Hogni saw he had no other choice than to let Bjorgolf have his way. Bjorgolf paid an ounce of gold for Hildirid and he shared a bed with her afterwards. (11)

[Þat sama haust gerði Bjǫrgólfr gamli heimanfǫr sína ...; hann kom fram í Leku, ok gengu þeir heim til húss tuttugu. ... Bjǫrgólfr kallar til sín Hǫgna bónda ok segir honum, at "ørendi er þat hingat, at ek vil, at dóttir þín fari heim með mér, ok mun ek nú gera till hennar lausabrullaup." En Hǫgni sá engan annan sinn kost en láta allt svá vera, sem Bjǫrgólfr vildi. Bjǫrgólfr keypti hana með eyri gulls, ok gengu þau í eina rekkju bæði. (16–17)]

Even now, Bjorgolf does not throw caution entirely to the wind: he makes a point of paying a meagre brideprice in contravention of custom, and the saga text appears to put in his mouth a nonce term (*lausabrullaup*) for the nonce wedding he imposes on his bride.[17] The relationship between the two sons he fathers by Hildirid and their half-brother (himself the father of a son, Bard, equal to them in age) cannot but be rocky from the outset.

"[A]t the heart of [Hildirid's sons' disruptive] existence," Thomas Bredsdorff observes, "lies a manifestation of the *erotic drive* at an abnormal moment, in an abnormal mode," clearly illustrating the kind of complications that might arise if an elderly widower came out of retirement and initiated a new relationship, especially if he sired new children (2001, 22, emphasis in original). Bjorgolf's prudent safeguards for shielding his patrimony – the prior transfer of "all control of his affairs" to an adult, married son, the casuistic prenuptial terms he enforces – cannot deflect the potential for acrimonious property disputes in the next generation. The very existence of Hildirid and her sons undermines Brynjolf's ostensible command over the family fortunes: his father's loins – like Bjorn's when he refuses his father's commandment to live alongside Thora "as if she were ... your sister" (56: "sem hon væri ... systir þín," 84) – had contravened his authority, and the boys Bjorgolf and Hildirid produce now threaten to erode his birthright. No sooner does Bjorgolf go to his grave than Brynjolf unceremoniously kicks Hildirid and her sons out (11: 17).

The narrative ramifications of Bjorgolf's second marriage and of the resulting discord between his two lineages extend well beyond rending the peace of the kin group. Brynjolf's son, the gallant Bard, befriends Thorolf Kveldulfsson. When Bard falls in Harald Fair-hair's service, he leaves all his worldly goods to his companion Thorolf – another of the king's elite retainers. This generous bequest proves Thorolf's undoing, for it both invests him with greater wealth and power than the jealous king can tolerate and transfers onto him the enmity of the sons of Hildirid. As in the case of Bjorn's romantic entanglements, Bjorgolf's desire for Hildirid indirectly implicates the protagonist of his portion of the saga, an Egil avatar, in an epic clash with a powerful family of the Norwegian aristocracy, all too well connected to the reigning monarch. Harald's destruction of Thorolf, at the persistent instigation of Bjorgolf's younger sons, forms the climax of the saga's opening third; it propels Thorolf's brother Skallagrim – Egil's father – out to Iceland and it presages generations of enmity between his kindred and the Norwegian royal dynasty.

The author of *Egil's Saga*, a particularly ingenious artificer and lover of symmetries,[18] evidently spied a compelling narrative pattern in the complications stemming from widowers' poorly managed remarriages. He rings the changes on this motif to plot a subtle parallelism, providing an artful illustration of how the dynamics of widower (mis)conduct could be evoked in shaping the arc of dispute – the ultimate building block of all saga narrative (cf. Andersson 1967). The author puts into Thorolf's mouth, as he rebuffs the sons of Hildirid, almost precisely the same vocabulary that Berg-Onund will later turn against Egil: "I don't in the least consider that you have any birthright, … because I am told that your mother was ravished and taken as booty to your father's house. … Bard said you were sons of a concubine" (17: "Því síðr ætla ek ykkr arfborna, at mér er sagt móðir ykkur væri með valdi tekin ok hernumin heim hǫfð. … [Bárðr] kallaði ykkr frillusonu," 27, 26). Only in hindsight does the full force of these arguments strike the audience, as they witness the same assertions deployed now to uphold, now to undermine the protagonist's position. The author drew out the nuances of competing claims whose contrary logics could not ultimately be decided in any clear-cut fashion (cf. Magnúsdóttir 2001, 103). In so doing, he had to make certain assumptions about the cultural filters through which his audience would read or listen to the saga.

What, then, can an analysis of Bjorn's and Bjorgolf's remarriages and their consequences – coupled with Egil's dispassionately single widowerhood and the scattered evidence concerning some other Norse widowers[19] – teach the cultural historian about medieval Norsemen's world views? What do we learn of the range of possibilities available to a widower, and of Egil's place within such a context of potentialities?

First, we may conclude that the author of *Egil's Saga* and members of his society did have a firm, if perhaps not entirely sharply delineated, notion of "widower" as a distinct category. As a point both of gender history and of our understanding of Icelandic culture, this is hardly trivial: recall that the starting point for this investigation had been the resounding silence of the eloquent, self-centred Egil upon entering this status; it could be argued that Egil simply does not recognize widowerhood as a specific rubric of experience. Nor does the Old Norse lexicon, which denominated women bereft of their spouses as *ekkjur* (singular *ekkja*), contain a word to denote "widower" (neither did other medieval languages).[20] These points notwithstanding, close narrative homologies between Bjorn's and Bjorgolf's tales strongly suggest authorial attentiveness to their status specifically as men whose first wives had died. When we find further textual parallels, we may begin to suspect a literary topos,[21] but (setting aside the question of historical facticity) we can certainly affirm that, even without the requisite terminology, speakers of Old Norse would have known a widower when they saw one. We may indeed go farther and deduce from the contrast between Bjorgolf's troubles, on the one hand, and those experienced by *Ágrip*'s Harald, on the other, that Norse sensibilities tracked bereaved spouses not only by gender but also by age. Just as the predatory elderly hag gave rise to different literary stereotypes from the remarriageable young widow – contrast, say, the witch Katla of Holt with the no less dangerous, thrice-widowed Hallgerd Long-breeches – so also widowers old (Bjorgolf) and young (Harald) were sized up as beasts of different stripes.[22]

Second, the patterns emerging from *Egil's Saga* suggest a culture anxious about the consequences of a maladjusted widower's integration into society. The elaborate steps Bjorgolf takes upon the death of his wife clearly attest to such anxiety. They confirm that the retired widower seeking reinstatement into full social personhood was indeed an emic cultural category, substantial enough to have provoked sanctions and sentiments opposed to such men's remarriage. Unfortunately for Bjorgolf's various heirs, all of his present precautions crumble before future generations' determination to find pretexts for feud; as William Ian Miller clarifies (1990, 217), feuding culture affords its practitioners nearly unlimited latitude in redefining grievances retroactively to fuel current hostilities.

Third, it appears that questions of property distribution fuelled much of the Norse angst about widowers. Medieval Norsemen's sexual mores (including the customs of easy divorce and polygamy) provided plenty of opportunity for creating multiplex, confused ties of kinship, further exacerbated by such non-sexual modes of affiliation as fosterage and blood-brotherhood; one need only consider the plot of *Gisli Sursson's Saga* to realize how rife with potential conflict such complex kinship webs were. But serial monogamy seems to have aroused particular fears of intrafamilial squabbles over inheritance. Full-blooded heirs could, of course, also engage in disputes, and the sources sometimes portray them as doing so, but those who shared fewer genes – and who had, moreover, been backed into affinity through family-generating acts in which they had had no say – seem particularly inclined to do so and particularly vicious in pursuing their grievances. Bjorgolf and Bjorn offer two conspicuous examples of this pattern.[23]

A fourth and final point has to do with what the affairs of these now-wifeless men might reveal, through contrast with their still-married brethren, about the sagas' imaginary gendered order. It is well known that Norse texts often attribute social disruption to women, casting them in the thankless role of "whetters" who incite their husbands to parade virility by recourse to vengeance,[24] but the conduct of some widowers, at least, points to the possibility that, while still alive, their wives had acted as peace-weavers, curbing the latent ferocity of their husbands. The most explicit example of such contrast between the temperance exhibited by a married man and the same man's impetuosity once he becomes a widower occurs in *Svinfellinga saga* (ch. 6, 8, 9; in *Sturlunga Saga* 2.92, 95, 97). While alive, Steinunn Jonsdottir prevails on her husband

Ogmund Helgason to observe a truce with her nephews. Once he is widowed, this constraint is removed: two weeks after Steinunn's passing, Ogmund ambushes his two in-laws, takes them captive, denies them absolution, and puts them both to death. The saga is quite explicit about the ameliorative effect Steinunn has on her husband's temperament while she lives, as well as about the propensity of all hell to break loose once she is deceased. It is instructive to consider Egil in these terms, focusing on the final chapters of his saga.

Never a mild man, Egil had nonetheless maintained reasonably peaceable relations with his family throughout most of his life. We have already seen his measured responses to his brother Thorolf's besting him in the competition for Asgerd's affections. When his father, Skallagrim, in a fit of berserk rage kills two of the people dearest to him, his old nurse and a boyhood friend, Egil brains one of Skallagrim's subordinates; this is as far as Egil will go in expressing antagonism within the kin-group (69: 102).[25] In the intervening decades, moreover – at least since his marriage – Egil had lived in remarkable harmony with his family. Even his dislike of Thorstein, his least-favourite son – whom Egil goes so far as to accuse of treachery[26] – does not translate into action: at the moment of truth, Egil throws his weight behind Thorstein to repel foreign interlopers (192–6: 282–8).

With Asgerd gone, however, we may detect in Egil something of the unruly widower no longer restrained by a wife's firm tenderness. Just as when he had told his brother Thorolf that, if he could not join him and Asgerd on the trip to Norway, then perhaps neither man would get to go, so also now Egil's wretchedness in his widowed state manifests itself first and foremost in his striving to secure that his family share his unhappiness. As noted above, Egil (now in his eighties, blind, and barely ambulatory) has moved in with Thordis and her husband Grim. Yet Egil's affection for Thordis does not stop him from proposing a fantastic scheme: to scatter his wealth to the crowds at the Thing. The nastiness of this plan is two-pronged. On the surface, it targets society as a whole: by appealing to men's basest instincts ("I'll toss the silver at them and I'll be very much surprised if they all share it out fairly among themselves," 202: "ætla ek at sá silfrinu, ok þykki mér undrligt, ef allir skipta vel sín í milli," 297), Egil means to provoke a murderous brawl and thereby rend in an instant the delicate social fabric woven over a century of Icelandic settlement. Thordis, who like her half-sister Thorgerd knows something about humouring Egil's harebrained ideas, picks up on this grandiose political dimension in her sarcastic reply, echoing an idiom more typically used by advocates of social stability: "That sounds to me like a brilliant plan, and its fame will live *for as long as this country is inhabited*" (203: "Þetta þykkir mér þjóðráð, ok mun uppi *meðan landit er byggt*," 297, emphasis mine).[27] Appalled by Egil's scheme ("He must never be allowed to get away with such a monstrous act!," 203: "Þat skal aldri verða, at hann komi þessu fram, svá miklum firnum," 297), she and Grim find means of shielding Icelandic society at large from its impact.

But below the surface, Egil's design bubbles with corrosive rancour directed more specifically at his own kindred. For one thing, the money he means to toss about was not, in fact, his to disburse in the first place: the English King Athelstan, in whose service Egil's brother Thorolf had died, entrusted Egil with two chests of silver as reparation, specifying that these coffers were "filial compensation" intended for Skallagrim, to be kept distinct from the "fraternal compensation" he had offered Egil (101: "sonargjǫld ... bróðurgjǫld," 145). The silver never reaches Skallagrim, despite his explicit demand to receive it (120: 173). Egil had never intended to part with this wergild; now, in old age, he unapologetically speaks of it as his proprietary treasure. Moreover, once Egil's original project of weaponizing the coins has been thwarted, he buries the hoard in a secret location, effectively disinheriting his own children. Egil thus hangs on to Athelstan's silver even beyond the grave, denying those he holds dearest the usufruct of these ill-appropriated funds.

It is typical of the style of *Egil's Saga* that its author does not lift a finger to render this implication explicit, leaving it entirely up to the reader to piece it together from equivocal clues. Egil's unkind overture towards his beloved Thordis falls, I suggest, under the shadow of his relations with the two people, now dead, whom Thordis represents for Egil, Asgerd and Thorolf. "The saga is constructed in such a way," Bredsdorff (2001, 29) notes, "that the premises of a scene are first presented long after the scene." Egil's sequestration of Athelstan's coffers is an example of such postponed premises, glossing in retrospect his composure at Asgerd's death: in place of the funerary poem he had failed to compose for her, Egil expresses his grief for Asgerd (and indeed, for Thorolf, long since transubstantiated into English pennies) in the idiom of belligerent widowerhood. With no second wife to bear him a child of his old age, who might ruinously complicate inheritance matters in the manner of Hildirid's sons or Gunnhild Bjarnardottir, Egil manoeuvres to become his own heir.

Clearly, the concept of widowerhood was familiar to the author of *Egil's Saga*, who could deploy it effectively and aesthetically. Yet equally clearly, the lack of a native term for this class of men and the narratives' tendency to gloss over the deaths of wives altogether must also be given due weight. The unrealised **Konutorrek*, like other such silences, speaks loudly to the isolation of widowers' experience from the mainstream of the cultural discourse. Egil composed no requiem for Asgerd, then, because his culture supplied him with no tools for doing so. In medieval Norse poetics, the loss of a wife was not to be conceptualized as irreparable, a *torrek*; the *exemplum* of Harald Fair-hair served to remind Norsemen of the perversity of contravening this norm.[28] Unlike the premature death of a son (which Gregory the Great himself recognised as the summit of intolerable pain), a wife's decease ought to occasion no downpour of torrential grief. Egil had ample poetic resources for lauding a king whom he despised (*Hǫfuðlausn*), for honouring a comrade he held dear (*Arinbjarnarkviða*), or, as we have seen, for bewailing a beloved son (*Sonatorrek*), but none for seeing Asgerd off in verse. **Konutorrek* was not composed because it quite literally was not capable of being composed.

NOTES

1 Gregory the Great, lib. 3 ch. 21 (2.400, glossing Sir 34:24: "qui offert sacrifici[um] ex substantia pauper[um] quasi qui victimat filium in conspectu patris sui," in *Biblia*, 2.1072). Translations of the Sagas of Icelanders (except for *Egil's Saga*) are adapted from *The Complete Sagas of Icelanders*. Translations of *Egil's Saga* are based on Scudder with some modifications. Unless otherwise noted, other translations are mine. I owe an inestimable debt of gratitude to the editors, but especially to Russell Poole; the *cura editorialis* he practised with this essay far exceeds any author's rosiest hopes. Remaining errors and infelicities are, of course, mine. An extended version of this essay appears in *Viator* 45:3 (Autumn 2014): 59–88.

2 When the sagas identify a man as a widower, they typically do so only fleetingly, as, e.g., in *The Saga of the Ynglings* ch. 48 (in *Heimskringla*, ÍF 26: 79; King Gudrod). Often, the deceased wife does not even merit a proper name, as, e.g., in *Viglund's Saga* ch. 18 (ÍF 14: 96–7; Helgi). Sometimes, a widower's former spouse is not mentioned at all, and her existence may only be inferred from circumstantial evidence (what Clover, in another context, calls an "implied wi[fe]," 1988, 168), as, e.g., in *The Tale of Thorstein Staff-Struck* (ÍF 11: 69–79; Thorarin).

3 The model implicit throughout my analysis is that the sagas reveal to us the worldviews which the period of writing attributed to the Saga Age, not those of the historical figures who might or might not have served as models for saga characters. To speak of what Egil does, thinks, or feels is thus shorthand for speaking of what the saga author has the character Egil do, think, or feel.

4 Cf. Quinn 1997, esp. 64–8, 70. For appreciations of *Sonatorrek*, see, e.g., Helgason 1953, 137; Turville-Petre 1976, 24; Larrington 1992, 49. For further discussion see the essays by Margaret Clunies Ross and Guðrún Nordal in this volume.

5 On this verse, see further Harris 2006. I am indebted to Joseph Harris for making available to me a copy of this and other articles he has published on *Sonatorrek*.

6 See Finlay (1992, 34–5); Einarsson (in *Egil's Saga* 2003, 187); Bredsdorff (2001, 26–7).

7 Cf. older literature cited by Bredsdorff (2001, 34–5). Harris's comment on the scene in which Egil reveals his love, where the saga "masterfully … dallies with our expectations of genre and psychology" (1994, 195–6), similarly brings out the interlacing of Egil's sentiments towards his brother and his bride: Arinbjorn urges Egil to ease his grief for Thorolf by composing a poem in his honour, much as he later would for Bodvar, and "[t]hen Egill did speak a poem, but it was not an elegy for Þórólfr as we have been led to expect but his first love poem for Ásgerðr."

8 For further discussion of this episode, see Ármann Jakobsson's essay in this volume.

9 Þorvaldsson (1968, 21), in a reading that largely anticipates mine, rightly comments that Egil's attachment to Asgerd is treated with such subtlety that readers are prone to overlook it.

10 An apparent exception is the verse in memory of Helga Thorsteinsdottir – Egil's granddaughter – spoken by her husband in *The Saga of Gunnlaug Serpent-Tongue* (discussed by Einarsson 1961, 265). Arguably in this case, however, it is not widowerhood per se that constitutes the subject of lament but the man's inability to win his wife's heart throughout her life, now made permanent by her death. A close analogue occurs in *The Saga of Bjorn, Champion of the Hitardal People*; see references to both episodes in the next note.

11 For Helga, see *The Saga of Gunnlaug Serpent-Tongue* ch. 13 (ÍF 3: 106–7); for Oddny, *The Saga of Bjorn, Champion of the Hitardal People* ch. 33 (ÍF 3: 205–6); for Gudrun, *The Saga of the People of Laxardal* ch. 55–56 (ÍF 5: 168–9).

12 Examples include Thorstein the Black in *The Saga of the People of Laxardal* ch. 10 and the eponymous hero in *The Saga of Thorstein the White* ch. 1–2, 7 (ÍF 11: 5–6, 17); cf. also old Thorarin in *The Tale of Thorstein Staff-Struck* (ÍF 11: 69–79).

13 Examples occur in *Bard's Saga* chs. 2 and 10 (ÍF 13: 105, 136–7); *The Saga of Grettir the Strong* ch. 11 (ÍF 7: 25); *Kormak's Saga* ch. 7 (ÍF 8: 224–5); *Valla-Ljots Saga* ch. 1 (ÍF 9: 234–5); *The Saga of the People of Reykjadal and of Killer-Skuta* ch. 24 (ÍF 10: 227–8); *The Saga of Droplaug's Sons* ch. 4 (ÍF 11: 147); *Njal's Saga* ch. 159 (ÍF 12: 462–3); *Viglund's Saga* ch. 5 (ÍF 14: 70); *The Saga of the Ynglings* ch. 48 (in *Heimskringla*, ÍF 26: 79); *Sturlu saga* ch. 10 (in *Sturlunga saga* 1.76); and, more obliquely, *Eirik the Red's Saga* [*H*] ch. 6 (ÍF 4: 216) and *The Saga of the People of Fljotsdal* ch. 13 (ÍF 11: 249–51).

14 Nordal takes Bjorn's identification as a *hǫlðr*, "high-ranking yeoman," to imply that he is of lesser status than Thorir, a *hersir*, "count" (ÍF 2: 104n1); yet Bjorn, too, is the grandson (and, presumably, the son) of a *hersir* (ÍF 2: 83). On these titles, see Bøe (1961, 251); Foote and Wilson (1980, 84–5, 129).

15 We may recall Egil's, Thorstein the Black's, and Thorstein the White's reliance on their *married* children's householding skills.

16 Such a reading calls into question Magnúsdóttir's (2001, 102) contention that Bjorgolf's courtship of Hildirid may be read as "in many respects comical" ("på många sätt komiskt"). Although the old man infatuated with a young woman is a staple of commedia dell'arte (*inter alia*), there is to my mind nothing light-hearted about the treatment of this theme in *Egil's Saga*.

17 On the question of the price given for Hildirid and the general legality of the union, see Nordal's note (17n3). As far as I can determine, *lausabrullaup* is a *hapax legomenon*; see *ONP*'s Wordlist at http://dataonp.hum.ku.dk/index_e.html.

18 For detailed discussion, see the essay by Torfi H. Tulinius in this volume.

19 I explore these cases in greater detail in "Widowers' Might: Towards a History of Bereaved Husbands in the Norse Middle Ages" (unpublished manuscript).

20 In the various European languages, the "terminology of widowhood … is one of the rare cases where the male term, widower, derives from the female term" (Cavallo and Warner 1999b, 4); in English, *widower* is first attested at the end of the fourteenth century (Bremmer 1995, 58; *MED* s.v. *widwer*); similarly, *veuf* only appears in French in the sixteenth century (Roberts 1999, 25), and *ekkill* in this sense is first attested in Icelandic in the eighteenth century (Magnússon 1989, 149–50; cf. Sigfússon 1934, 128). The lack of a specific term for bereaved husbands may be bound up with such men's propensity to remarry swiftly. In the early modern period, when a terminology of widowerhood begins to take shape, it tends to refer not to "all men who had lost their wives, but rather to those about to marry for the second time. … Thus, widowers were such mainly for the fleeting period just before a second marriage" (Pelling 1999, 38–9).

21 The closest analogue I have found occurs in the opening chapters of *Guðmundar saga dýra* (ch. 1–3, in *Sturlunga saga* 1.160–6) and involves the widowed Gudmund Eyjolfsson, remarried to the Church.

22 For Katla, see *The Saga of the People of Eyri* ch. 15–16, 20 (ÍF 4: 28–9, 51–4); for Hallgerd, see *Njal's Saga* ch. 11–12, 16–17, 48, 77 (ÍF 12: 33–6, 48–51, 123–4, 189–90).

23 No less a celebrity than the great Snorri Sturluson himself might be adduced as a further example: shortly after the death of his long-time common-law wife, the normally canny Snorri became entangled in a property dispute with her sons by a previous marriage, one of whom took part in the raid which sealed Snorri's fate (see *Íslendinga saga* ch. 149–51 [153–6], in *Sturlunga Saga* 1.452–3).

24 There is extensive literature on this Norse tradition of *hvǫt*, "incitement." See, for instance, Gehl (1937, 34–7, 72–3); Heller (1958, 98–122); Clover (1986); Miller (1990, 212–14); Jesch (1991, 188–91); Meulengracht Sørensen (1993, 238–46); Jochens (1996, 162–203); Tolmie (2001, 1–7, 15–69); compare Meulengracht Sørensen (1983, esp. 21). In a different cultural context, compare Black-Michaud (1975, 14, 78–80).

25 For a detailed discussion of this episode, see Ármann Jakobsson's essay in this volume.

26 See v. 55 (186–7; 274), and cf. 171 (245) and the narrator's comment at 186 (274).

27 Cf. Njal's famous quip, "með lǫgum skal land várt byggja, en með ólǫgum eyða" ("our country shall be made habitable by law, but laid waste by lawlessness," *Njal's Saga* ch. 70, ÍF 12: 172).

28 The exemplary character of this anecdote is underscored by its use as refrain in the early thirteenth-century *Málsháttakvæði* (v. 11, 14, 17, 20; *Skj* B.2 pp. 138–45); cf. Frank (2004: 8–9). I am indebted to Russell Poole for pointing this out to me. See also an analogue in *Hrólfs saga Gautrekssonar* ch. 1 (in Jónsson 1954, 4.53).

BIBLIOGRAPHY

Ágrip af Nóregs konunga sǫgum. 1984. Ed. Bjarni Einarsson. Íslenzk fornrit 29. Reykjavík: Hið íslenzk fornritafélag.

Andersson, Theodore M. 1967. *The Icelandic Family Saga: An Analytic Reading*. Cambridge, MA: Harvard University Press.

– 1969. "Some Ambiguities in *Gísla saga*: A Balance Sheet." *BONIS* (1969 for 1968): 7–42.

Biblia Sacra iuxta Vulgatam Versionem. 1983. Ed. Robertus Weber. 2 vols. 3rd edn, rev. Bonifatius Fischer et al. Stuttgart: Deutsche Bibelgesellschaft.

Black-Michaud, Jacob. 1975. *Feuding Societies*. Foreword by E.L. Peters. Oxford: Basil Blackwell [also published as: *Cohesive Force: Feud in the Mediterranean and the Middle East*. New York: St Martin's Press.]

Bredsdorff, Thomas. 2001 [orig. 1971]. *Chaos and Love: The Philosophy of the Icelandic Family Sagas*. Trans. John Tucker. Copenhagen: Museum Tusculanum Press.

Bremmer, Rolf H., Jr. 1995. "Widows in Anglo-Saxon England." In *Between Poverty and the Pyre: Moments in the History of Widowhood*. Ed. Jan Bremmer and Lourens van den Bosch, 58–88. London and New York: Routledge.

Bøe, Arne. 1961. "Hauld." *Kulturhistorisk leksikon for nordisk middelalder, fra vikingetid til reformationstid*. 1956–78. 22 vols. Copenhagen: Rosenkilde & Bagger, vol. 6. 251–4.

Cavallo, Sandra, and Lyndan Warner, eds. 1999a. *Widowhood in Medieval and Early Modern Europe*. Women and Men in History. Eds. Patricia Skinner, Pamela Sharpe and Penny Summerfield. Harlow: Longman.

– 1999b. "Introduction." In Cavallo and Warner 1999a, 3–23.

Clover, Carol J. 1986. "Hildigunnr's Lament." *Structure and Meaning in Old Norse Literature: New Approaches to Textual Analysis and Literary Criticism*. Eds. John Lindow, Lars Lönnroth and Gerd Wolfgang Weber, 141–83. The Viking Collection 3. Odense: Odense University Press.

– 1988. "The Politics of Scarcity: Notes on the Sex Ratio in Early Scandinavia." *Scandinavian Studies* 60,2: 147–88.

The Complete Sagas of Icelanders (including 49 Tales). 1997. Ed. Viðar Hreinsson et al. 5 vols. Reykjavík: Leifur Eiríksson.

Egils saga. 2003. Ed. Bjarni Einarsson. London: Viking Society for Northern Research and University College London.

Einarsson, Bjarni. 1961. *Skáldasögur: Um uppruna og eðli ástaskáldasagnanna fornu*. Reykjavík: Bókútgáfa Menningarsjóðs.

Finlay, Alison. 1992. "*Egils saga* and Other Poets; Sagas." In Hines and Slay 1992, 33–48.

Foote, Peter, and David Wilson. 1980. *The Viking Achievement: The Society and Culture of Early Medieval Scandinavia*. Rev. edn. Great Civilizations. Ed. A.L. Basham and Christopher Brooke. London: Sidgwick & Jackson.

Frank, Roberta. 1985. "Skaldic Poetry." In *Old Norse-Icelandic Literature: A Critical Guide*. Ed. Carol J. Clover and John Lindow, 157–96. Islandica 45. Ithaca: Cornell University Press.

– 2004. *Sex, Lies and Málsháttakvæði: A Norse Poem from Medieval Orkney*. The Fell-Benedikz Lecture delivered in the University of Nottingham 22 May 2003. Occasional Papers of the Centre for the Study of the Viking Age 2. Nottingham: Centre for the Study of the Viking Age.

Gehl, Walther. 1937. *Ruhm und Ehre bei den Nordgermanen: Studien zum Lebensgefühl der isländischen Saga*. Neue deutsche Forschungen, Abteilung deutsche Philologie 121.3. Berlin: Junker und Dünnhaupt.

Gregory the Great. 1992. *Règle pastorale*. Ed. Bruno Judic and Floribert Rommel. Trans. Charles Morel, 381–2. 2 vols. Sources chrétiennes. Paris: Editions du Cerf.

Harris, Joseph. 1994. "Sacrifice and Guilt in *Sonatorrek*." In *Studien zum Altgermanischen: Festschrift für Heinrich Beck*. Ed. Heiko Uecker, 173–96. Ergänzungsbände zum Reallexikon der Germanischen Altertumskunde 11. Berlin and New York: Walter de Gruyter.

– 2006. "The Rune-Stone Ög 31 and an 'Elegiac' Trope in Sonatorrek." *Maal og Minne* 1: 3–14.

– 2007. "*Homo necans borealis*: Fatherhood and Sacrifice in *Sonatorrek*." In *Myth in Early Northwest Europe*. Ed. Stephen O. Glosecki, 153–73. Tempe: ACMRS.

Helgason, Jón. 1953. "Norges og Islands digtning." In *Litteraturhistorie B: Norge og Island*. Ed. Sigurður Nordal, 3–179. Nordisk kultur 8:B. Stockholm, Oslo, and Copenhagen: Albert Bonnier, H. Aschehoug & Co. and J.H. Schultz.

Heller, Rolf. 1958. *Die literarische Darstellung der Frau in den Isländersagas*. Saga: Untersuchungen zur nordischen Literatur- und Sprachgeshichte, 2. Halle [Saale]: Max Niemeyer Verlag.

Hines, John, and Desmond Slay (eds.). 1992. *Introductory Essays on Egils saga and Njáls saga*. London: Viking Society for Northern Research.

Jesch, Judith. 1991. *Women in the Viking Age*. Woodbridge: Boydell.

Jochens, Jenny. 1996. *Old Norse Images of Women*. Philadelphia: University of Pennsylvania Press.

Jónsson, Guðni, ed. 1954. *Fornaldar sögur Norðurlanda*. 4 vols. [Reykjavík:] Íslendingasagnaútgáfan.

Larrington, Carolyne. 1992. "Egill's Longer Poems: *Arinbjarnarkviða* and *Sonatorrek*." In Hines and Slay 1992, 49–63.

Magnússon, Ásgeir Blöndal. 1989. *Íslensk orðsifjabók*. Reykjavík: Orðabók Háskólans.

Magnúsdóttir, Auður. 2001. *Frillor och fruar: Politik och samlevnad på Island 1120–1400*. Avhandlingar från Historiska institutionen i Göteborg 29. Göteborg: Historiska institutionen i Göteborg.

MED = *Middle English Dictionary*. 1984–2003. Ed. Robert E. Lewis et al. Ann Arbor: University of Michigan Press.

Meulengracht Sørensen, Preben. 1983 [orig. 1980]. *The Unmanly Man: Concepts of Sexual Defamation in Early Northern Society*. Trans. Joan Turville-Petre. The Viking Collection 1. Odense: Odense University Press.

– 1993. *Fortælling og ære: Studier i islændingesagaerne*. Århus: Aarhus universitetsforlag.

Miller, William Ian. 1990. *Bloodtaking and Peacemaking: Feud, Law, and Society in Saga Iceland*. Chicago and London: University of Chicago Press.

ONP = *Ordbog over det norrøne prosasprog*. 1989–. Ed. Helle Degnbol et al. Copenhagen: Den arnamagnæanske kommission.

Pelling, Margaret. 1999. "Finding Widowers: Men without Women in English Towns before 1700." In Cavallo and Warner, 1999a, 37–54.

Quinn, Judy. 1997. "'ok er þetta upphaf' – First-Stanza Quotation in Old Norse Prosimetrum." *alvíssmál* 7: 61–80.

Roberts, Anna. 1999. "Helpful Widows, Virgins in Distress: Women's Friendship in French Romance of the Thirteenth and Fourteenth Centuries." In *Constructions of Widowhood and Virginity in the Middle Ages*. Ed. Cindy L. Carlson and Angela Jane Weisl, 25–47. The New Middle Ages. Ed. Bonnie Wheeler. New York: St Martin's Press.

Sigfússon, Björn. 1934. "Names of Sea-Kings (*Heiti sækonunga*)." *Modern Philology* 32,2: 125–42.

Sturlunga saga. 1946. Ed. Jón Jóhannesson, Magnús Finnbogason, and Kristján Eldjárn. 2 vols. Reykjavík: Sturlunguútgáfan.

Tolmie, Jane Marianna. 2001. *Persuasion: Blood-feud, Romance and the Disenfranchised*. PhD dissertation. Cambridge MA: Harvard University.

Turville-Petre, [E.O.]G. 1976. *Scaldic Poetry*. Oxford: Clarendon.

Þorvaldsson, Eysteinn. 1968. "Hugleiðingar um ástarsögu Egils." *Mímir* 7,2: 20–4.

9 Facebook for Vikings: Social Network Analysis and *Egil's Saga*[1]

TIMOTHY R. TANGHERLINI

On a snowy evening with the light of day quickly seeping from the sky and ominous steel grey clouds pressing down on a wooded path near Eideskog, a small group of travellers stops at a fork in the road. A nagging worry about the prospects for shelter creeps in at the edges of the men's thoughts as they consider their options. One of King Hakon's men turns to Egil and says:

> "The trail forks here. ... The farmer who lives beneath the ridge is named Arnald and he's a friend of ours. We will go and stay with him, and you should go up on the ridge. When you get there you'll soon see a big farm where you are sure of a place to stay. A very wealthy man named Armod Beard lives there. We will meet up again early tomorrow morning and go to Eideskog in the evening. A farmer lives there, a good man named Thorfinn." (154)

> ["Nú skiljask hér vegar, en hér fram undan hálsinum býr bóndi sá, er heitir Arnaldr, vinr várr; munu vér fǫrunautar fara þangat til gistingar, en þér skuluð fara hér upp á hálsinn, ok þá er þér komið þar, mun brátt verða fyrir yðr bœr mikill, ok er yðr þar vís gisting; þar býr stórauðigr maðr, er heitir Ármóðr skegg. En á morgin árdegis skulu vér hittask ok fara annat kveld til Eiðaskógs; þar býr góðr bóndi, er Þorfinnr heitir." (223)]

At first glance the suggestion appears to be a friendly one; since the group is large, they need to split up, each seeking shelter with friends. There is of course something slightly foreboding about the suggestion: Armod Beard is not only not a friend of Egil and his men but is in fact completely unknown to them, having been introduced into the saga at that very moment. The only thing recommending him is that he is very wealthy – he isn't even a distant relation of anyone in the group (or the saga for that matter). But the law of transitivity of friendship, which says that any friend of mine is a friend of yours, seems to be at work here.[2] This transitivity is certainly implicit in the suggestion made by the king's men, and Egil and his men have few other choices than to trust it, even though Egil can hardly count King Hakon among his friends. Arnald, after all, will clearly have his hands full with the other party, his Norwegian friends, for the night.

Unfortunately for Egil and his men, the suggestion to stay with Armod Beard is not a friendly gesture at all but instead one of barely concealed murderous intent, since the king's men believe that the treacherous pathway to Armod's door will spell Egil's demise. Their hasty retreat back to the king in Trondheim reveals that their friend Arnald and his alleged farm are fictitious: there is no farm down this other fork and there is no one there to "friend." Beyond tricking Egil and his men into a situation where the transitivity of friendship does not apply, King Hakon's men add another twist to their treachery: their refuge from the cold and snowy night is with a friend who resides on a different social network altogether, that of fictional characters.[3] They have no intention of staying with Arnald; their only intention is to abandon Egil and his group to the elements. "After all, the king hates [Egil] and would be pleased with our mission if we could arrange to have him killed" (153: "'er konungi'," sǫgðu þeir, 'allilla til hans, ok mun honum þykkja vár ferð allgóð, ef vér komum því til leiðar at hann sé drepinn'," 222).

Fortunately for his companions, Egil is a remarkably persistent Viking. When the directions to the farm turn out to be faulty, he forges a path through the snow and the dark, eventually leading his group to the farm. After they arrive, Armod's people express their dismay at the route they have taken. During the ensuing "feast," Armod conceals his overt hostility towards Egil under a guise of apparent hospitality while clearly devaluing Egil's status: he seats him on the lower benches of the hall and feeds him bowls of curds. This "performed hospitality" contrasts markedly with Armod's wife and daughter's more genuine welcome. Fortunately for Armod, his family's friendly gestures act as an insurance policy, based on the tit-for-tat nature of friendship that often applies in the saga, ultimately ensuring that Egil does not kill Armod in his bed.[4]

In this single day of fraught encounters lie several important discoveries. The first is the simple affirmation that Egil's initial suspicions about the treacherous nature of King Hakon's men were correct. The second is that the transitivity of friendship (and its inverse, enmity) as described by Structural Balance theory does not always apply evenly: a friend's friend is not always a friend, and a friend's enemy is not always an enemy. A third is that familial relationships can be included in this transitivity but only up to a point: if you are related to a friend, then you are also a friend, or at least worthy of friendly consideration, even if you have acted with hostility. An equally important realization is that siblings quickly complicate an assumption of friendliness across familial relationships when positions of unique status (e.g., kingship which can only be occupied by a single individual) are brought into the equation. How else to explain the enmity between King Hakon and his brother Eirik's sons who feel that they have an equally valid claim to the throne? A final discovery is that remarkable feats of physical derring-do can allow an individual to accrue a great deal of status, complicating other calculations of status based on criteria such as wealth, stature, articulateness, bravery, honour, origin, and family.

Basing relationships on evaluations of status is an important component of many sagas, and *Egil's Saga* is no exception. The status argument, as opposed to the balance argument, proposes that people like to become friends with those who have higher status. Indeed, some of the most vexing interpersonal problems arise in the sagas when allegiances or friendships based on the balanced nature of the transitivity of friendship clash with a desire to forge friendships based on the ever shifting and murky terrain of status.

Analysis that focuses on social groups, and the flow or the potential for the flow of resources within, between, and across groups is referred to as social network analysis (SNA) and has long been a staple of quantitative social sciences.[5] When applied to the Icelandic saga, this approach allows one to analyse the numerous interconnections between people and families that characterize the narratives (Mac Carron and Kenna 2013, 4–5). SNA also provides sophisticated algorithmic approaches for describing the distribution and change of different types of relationships within networks.[6] Exploring the structure and changing qualities of the social networks of saga characters offers a valuable interpretive window for understanding the sagas (Mac Carron and Kenna 2013). Richard Gaskins, for example, argues that an exploration of "weak ties" in the sagas might offer insight into the representation of alliance-building at the Althing (Gaskins 2005; Granovetter 1973), while Robin Dunbar explores the role that kinship plays in murder and revenge (Dunbar, Clark, and Hurst 1995). In the following pages, a social network is described that is built on the characters and events in *Egil's Saga* emphasizing (a) genealogical relationships and (b) acts of friendship and enmity.

Although designed for "real world" data, SNA methods can be applied to the world of the sagas. Unlike the data used by sociologists to model interpersonal relationships in organizations or communities, the saga social network is a meta-fictional representation of idealized interactions. Consequently, some of the conclusions drawn about human interactions in standard SNA do not necessarily apply to the analysis of the saga. Similarly, predictive models of behaviour on the network have little applicability to a story where the end is actually known.[7] Instead, one should interpret this similarity to "real world" social networks as a feature of the genre. Accordingly, one needs to exercise caution in reaching conclusions about the characteristics of social networks encoded in these and similar literary works. Simply because a network exhibits features similar to "real world" data sets, such as being small world, highly clustered, assortatively mixed by degree, and scale free, does not necessarily suggest the "historicity" of the narratives or events described in those narratives; instead, one should interpret this similarity between the saga networks and "real world" social networks as a feature of the genre (Mac Carron and Kenna 2012, 4).

Ultimately, the goal of this analysis is the discovery of patterns in *Egil's Saga* that are hard to discern from the perspective of close reading or philological analysis. Franco Moretti labels this type of analysis "distant reading," an approach that aligns well with structural approaches to the sagas (Andersson 1967; Clover 1982; Byock 1982; Lönnroth 2007). However, whereas most structural approaches to the saga focus on plot and plot development at the level of complete narrative (Andersson 1967), scene (Clover 1982), specific type of interaction (Byock 1982; Miller 1990), or multi-level analysis (Danielsson 1986), network analysis allows one to integrate several different views on the saga that include plot but are not overtly focused on events, sequences of events, or other syntagmatic features of structure.

On its most basic level, network analysis relies on graphs to describe the networks in the saga, including networks of character interactions, motifs and themes, places, interactions, and genealogic relationships.[8] These individual networks can be joined, allowing one to consider several of the graphs simultaneously. In the simplest analysis, the networks are presented as "end state" graphs, where all the relationships and interactions in the saga are considered as a complete representation of the saga. A more complex set of analyses considers the saga as a dynamic series of changing networks, where the differences between networks from one moment to the next can be explored. Unlike other structural approaches to the saga, network analysis allows one to assess simultaneously the impact on all the connections of a particular interaction, whether they are based on genealogy, action, or interaction. Consequently, one can address complex questions such as, "What happens to all the relations from each actor's perspective subsequent to an interaction between Arinbjorn and Eirik, given that, prior to the interaction, Arinbjorn likes Egil, Egil does not like Eirik, and Eirik is married to Gunnhild who does not like Egil?"[9] The approach also allows one to discover "roles" for characters and to search for similar patterns of interaction across the graph(s).[10]

Genealogy and Familial Relationships as a Network in *Egil's Saga*

Genealogies are a common aspect of the sagas of Icelanders and constitute one of the most accessible and easily extracted social networks. Although descent charts, or family trees, often accompany saga editions, these charts tend to be abbreviated so as to focus on one or two key figures in the saga and rarely, if ever, include all the connections between families that develop during the course of the saga (cf. Thorsson 2001, lxii–lxiii; Pálsson and Edwards 1976, 14–15). In a digital realm, a complete descent graph is relatively easy to extract from the saga and reveals connections that are otherwise difficult to discern or remember.[11] In *Egil's Saga*, the resulting graph has 320 nodes (characters) and 431 edges and provides a complete overview of family relationships.[12] Perhaps the most striking feature of this descent graph is the fact that the saga is not composed of a series of discrete, disconnected components, as one might expect, but is dominated by a single large connected component. Of the 320 characters in the saga, there is only one major descent component consisting of 151 connected nodes; this component includes not only Kveldulf and his descendants, but also Harald Fair-hair and his son Eirik Blood-axe. The next-largest connected component of the graph, with a scant five nodes, describes the family of Atli the Slender, earl in Gaular, who, along with his children, is introduced early in the saga. This family's only significant function in the saga is to reduce Olvir Hump from a marauding Viking into a poet pining for the love of Solveig. The graph also reveals ninety isolated characters for whom no descent information is included in the saga. That is not to say that they serve no purpose in the saga, as once interactions are included in the network analysis nearly all the nodes appear in a single connected component.[13]

The descent graph also reveals a relatively close connection between Egil's family and that of Eirik Blood-axe (see Figure 1). A "shortest path" algorithm shows that even on the very limited descent graph, Egil is only ten steps away from Eirik (making Skallagrim eight steps away from Harald Fair-hair). The connecting link on this path is high on the descent graph (two generations above Egil), running through Skallagrim's mother Salbjorg, the daughter of Kari from Berle and the sister of Eyvind Lamb. Eyvind's grandson Finn the Squinter is married to Gunnhild, the granddaughter of Harald Fair-hair through his daughter Ingibjorg. Ingibjorg and Gunnhild thus play important roles in the description of descent implicit in the saga, since both serve as critical links – or "cut points" – between these two segments of the graph (if either one were removed, the graph would split into two components). It is not clear if the saga audiences or the saga writer were aware of this role for Ingibjorg and Gunnhild, given the complexity of the genealogical relationships detailed in

Figure 1. Descent in *Egil's Saga*, with nodes on the shortest path between Egil and Eirik Blood-axe highlighted.

the saga. In light of the aggressive nature of women named "Gunnhild" in the saga, her position as a cut point on the descent graph between Kveldulf's side of the graph and Harald's side of the graph suggests that this connection may not have been accidental.[14]

The characteristics of the descent graph change in interesting ways when the ten foster relationships described in the saga are included in the analysis.[15] Fostering is a special case in the sagas, one that is based largely on friendship, much as spousal relationships are. Unlike spousal relationships, fostering outwardly assumes many of the characteristics of ties by consanguineous descent. Although these fosterings are mentioned almost in passing, implying that they are not of great importance, the changes to the descent graph caused by these relationships countermand that suggestion. Indeed, despite the fact that only ten additional edges are added to a relatively large graph, these additions have a significant impact on the shortest paths between many of the main saga characters, particularly across the antagonistic divide of Kveldulf, Skallagrim, and Egil on one side and Harald and Eirik on the other. In terms of the descent graph, the most important of these fosterings are the two involving Thorir Hroaldsson. Arinbjorn's fostering relationships, while important, gain far greater significance when the friendship/enmity graphs are taken into consideration. Thorir Hroaldsson's, in contrast, have a dramatic effect on the length of the shortest paths between the two main groups of antagonists on the genealogy network, reducing the distance between Skallagrim and Harald from eight steps to four, and also reducing the distance from Egil to Eirik even more markedly from ten steps to four (Figure 2):

Figure 2. Nodes along the shortest paths from Egil to Eirik and from Skallagrim to Harald are isolated in this figure; in A, the paths are without fosters, where Skallagrim and Harald lie on the line between Egil and Eirik. When fosters are included, the paths between Skallagrim and Harald (B) and Egil and Eirik (C) are notably shorter.

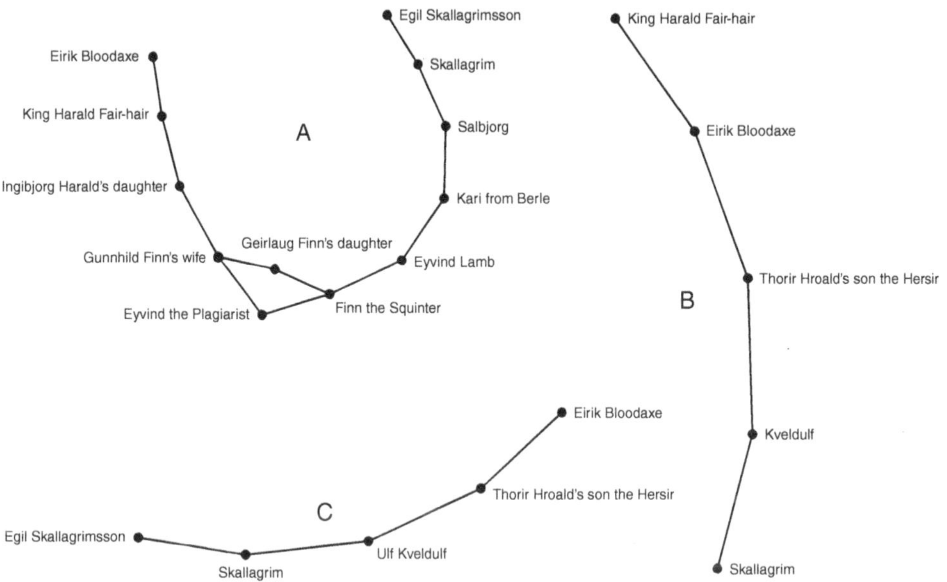

Even though weak ties might offer excellent prospects for potential alliances, as proposed by Gaskins (2005), weak ties are also clearly fraught with many negative and violent possibilities (Miller 1983).

Friendship and Enmity as an Interaction Network in *Egil's Saga*

In saga scholarship there is a natural emphasis on understanding enmity, with friendship acting as a powerful counter force (Byock 1982; Miller 1983 and 1990). Network analysis allows one to consider friendly interactions and antagonistic relationships both as individual features of the saga narrative and in concert with each other. For the following analysis, two graphs, one describing friendship and one describing enmity, were created. Each of these graphs is in turn based on several subgraphs. The friendship graph comprises all those interactions in the saga that could be coded as positive interactions between individuals or groups[16] and represents the union of eight different friendly action graphs, with each of these actions weighted differently according to how important the action is in establishing friendship (gift giving, for example, is a much "weightier" friendship interaction than simply indicating allegiance).[17] Such weighting is necessarily subjective and, as more saga networks are developed, it will be important to develop a consistent method for identifying, classifying, and weighting interactions.[18] The enmity interaction graph is easier to extract from the saga, and is based on all antagonistic interactions between individuals, individuals and groups, or separate groups. The two subgraphs that comprise the enmity graph are equally straightforward: one describes non-lethal antagonism (from unfriendly actions to insults to physical injury) and the other lethal antagonism (any interaction that ends in the death of one of the parties). The weights attached to these are negative, with non-lethal interactions weighted −4 (the inverse of gift giving) and lethal interactions weighted −8 (the inverse of inheritance or succession).

Considering friendship first, the union of all friendship graphs yields a total of 316 interactions, involving 190 characters, meaning that 130 characters do not engage in any friendly interactions throughout the saga. Since the number of characters whose only role is genealogical in the saga is large, if one corrects for these characters, the main group of saga "actants" (the number of active nodes on the union of the two interaction graphs, enmity and friendship) is 200. The friendship graph itself consists of one major connected component with 150 nodes and 18 smaller connected components, with an average size of 2.

Measures of "degree centrality" help identify characters that play pivotal roles in these interactions. Egil and Skallagrim occupy the two highest spots on the total degree centrality measure of the friendship graph, while Harald Fairhair and Arinbjorn occupy the next two positions.[19] Eirik Blood-axe and Thorir Hroaldsson have identical measures in fifth position. Another measure, known as "betweenness centrality," identifies individuals who lie along the shortest path between two nodes in the graph; the more often the individual appears on such a pathway, the more likely they are to play a central role in the friendship interactions. Predictably, four of the top five characters as ranked by betweenness centrality are the saga's main players: Egil, Skallagrim, Harald, and Eirik. The appearance of Grim Thorisson the Halagolander and Thorgils Boomer high on this ranked list suggests that they have a great deal of potential to broker deals between groups, a potential that is not exploited in any significant manner in the saga. If one considers the ratio of betweenness centrality to total degree centrality for these two characters, their position as possible "friendship brokers" becomes even more pronounced. This corrected measure indicates that, while these two have great potential to influence disparate groups given their position in the network, they are "not in the know" (have low total degree centrality), reflecting their relative inactivity in the saga (Carley 2008). Although purely a matter of speculation, it is interesting to consider why these characters' role as potential friendship brokers is not exploited.

Considering each friendship graph individually provides a more detailed view of the main figures for different types of friendly interactions. The graph with the largest number of nodes and links is the one describing "allegiance," with 98 characters interacting in 7 connected components. On this network, Arinbjorn and Beard Thorir occupy high rank positions on measures of betweenness centrality, identifying them as central players in many of the saga's allegiances. The gift giving graph, consisting of 43 nodes and 5 connected components, offers equally fascinating insights. For example, there are two three-person gift-giving cliques spanning four people (Skallagrim, Thorolf Skallagrimsson, Egil, and Eirik Blood-axe), with Skallagrim and Eirik as the shared members between these two cliques. Despite the enmity between Skallagrim and his sons on one side and Eirik on the other – or perhaps because of it – there is an equally intense friendship relationship signaled by gift giving. Of course, some of this gift giving within the clique is only mildly disguised enmity, the most notable instance being Egil's gift of *Hǫfuðlausn* to Eirik and the return gift of his head. Another fascinating feature of the gift-giving network is the emergence of star patterns describing the numerous gift-giving relationships of an individual. Egil, for example, is involved in 17 gift-giving interactions, far more than his father Skallagrim with 11 such interactions, Harald Fair-hair with 5, and Egil's brother Thorolf with 4. When the gift-giving graph is combined with the inheritance and command graphs, Athelstan emerges as another character engaged in numerous friendship exchanges of high value. A useful algorithm, CONCOR, searches for structural equivalence in a network graph; running this algorithm on the gift-giving graph reveals two structurally equivalent groups, as described in Table 1.[20] Future work could explore similar structurally equivalent groups in the saga.

The enmity graphs offer a competing view of interaction. The enmity union graph is significantly smaller than the friendship union graph, comprising 116 characters in 10 connected components. The largest single connected component consists of 83 characters. Here, the characters with the highest measures of betweenness centrality, which signal their importance in antagonistic relationships, include Thord Granason, who replaces Arinbjorn as one of the 5 highest ranked characters, reflecting not only his role in the very bloody series of confrontations in Egil's childhood that lead to his death at the hands of Skallagrim, but also underscoring Arinbjorn's role as a peace-maker as opposed to a trouble-maker.

Table 1. Results of running CONCOR structural equivalence on the gift-giving graph.

Group	Size	Members
1	18	Skallagrim, Thorir Hroald's son the Hersir, Ani (Skallagrim's man), Thorbjorn Hunchback, Thord Hobbler, Thorir the Giant, Thorgeir Earth-Long, Odd, Grim Thorisson the Halagolander, Sigmund, Egil.Skallagrimsson, Thorolf Skallagrimsson, Thord Brynjolfsson, Asgerd Bjornsdottir, Hakon the Good, Adils, Ulf, and Earl Hakon Sigurdarson
2	14	Eirik Bloodaxe, Arinbjorn Thorarson, Earl Arnfinn in Halland, Thorfinn the Strong, Athelstan the Victorious, Thordis Thorolf's daughter, Thord Thorgeir Lambason, Thorstein Eiriksson Thoruson, Bodvarr Egilsson, Gunnar Egilsson, Thorstein Egilsson, Alf the Wealthy, Grim Svertingsson, and Einar Helgason Skalaglam

Separating the two enmity graphs leads to a more nuanced view of hostility in the saga. The non-lethal enmity graph includes a greater number of actors and interactions than the lethal enmity graph, with 85 characters, engaged in 97 antagonistic interactions on 6 linked components. The lethal enmity graph, by way of contrast, includes 68 characters involved in 61 lethal interactions on more than a dozen linked components. This difference is attributable to the fact that one can interact with an antagonist in a non-lethal fashion many times, while one can interact with lethal consequences but once. Characters with high betweenness centrality on the non-lethal enmity graph are those at the focal points of some of the most important antagonisms in the saga. The top seven characters all have betweenness centrality measures that are very close, and significantly greater than those further down on the list. In order, they are Egil, Berg-Onund, Thora of the Embroidered Hand, Bjorn Brynjolfsson, King Harald Fair-hair, Eirik Blood-axe, and Gunnhild Ozurardottir; the betweenness centrality measure for non-lethal antagonism thus confirms quite readily the importance of Egil's inheritance claim that stems from Thora's kidnapping early in the saga, while also highlighting Gunnhild's role in perpetuating this antagonism.

On the lethal enmity graph, one finds that the characters with the highest degree centrality are Norwegian, with Kveldulf on Egil's side making an appearance within the group of Harald Fair-hair, Eirik Blood-axe, and Harald Eiriksson Greycloak. This finding reflects the general skew in *Egil's Saga* towards casting Norwegians, in particular their royalty, as ill-tempered, murderous louts. Interestingly, Egil and Bard are the two "closest" characters to these lethal interactions, where closeness is the inverse of the average distance on the network between a node (e.g., Bard) and all the other nodes. An enduring question, and one beyond the scope of the current study, is the impact that killings have on the relationships between people indirectly linked to the killer and the victim (degree greater than 2).

As noted, the union of the friendship and enmity graphs results in an interaction network over the friend/foe divide in the saga and includes nearly all the characters when the genealogical graph of descents and fosterings is included. Measures of the total degree centrality for nodes on this graph identify a core group of actors who not only have high betweenness centrality but also many links to many others in their networks – this group includes Egil, but also Thorir Hroald's son, Arinbjorn, and Thorstein Thoruson. These four are crucial players in the development of the saga action, given their control of information in the saga, irrespective of whether that information is antagonistic or conciliatory.

Another measure, hub centrality, can be used to identify characters that have many out-links to characters with many in-links; in the saga, these characters include the generally overlooked Moeid Hildisdottir, the wife of Vestar Haengsson, and Harald's maternal uncle, Guttorm Sigurdarson. Given Steven and Roy Johnson's suggestions about maternal uncles in the Icelandic sagas, coupled to William Miller's evaluation of their fraught position, it might be worthwhile to consider the impact that the death of Guttorm's sons has on the overall topology of friendship and enmity in *Egil's Saga* (Johnson and Johnson 1991; Miller 1983).

A final area that raises some interesting questions is the consideration of measures on one sub-graph in relation to the same measures on a different sub-graph. Previously, a measure has been used that identifies those characters with high betweenness centrality and low total degree centrality, who therefore occupy the role of potential boundary spanners for that network, perched as they are between groups. If one looks for such characters on both the enmity graph and the friendship graph, Eyvind Braggart and Gunnhild Ozurardottir leap out as the two most likely boundary spanners for both graphs, reflecting the role that they play in fostering both friendly relationships and antagonisms in the saga.

Ego-nets in *Egil's Saga*

Saga narratives tend to privilege the point of view of one or two central characters. In the case of *Egil's Saga*, it is generally accepted that the saga has two parts, the first focusing on Skallagrim's antagonistic relationship with Harald Fair-hair and the second on Egil's similarly antagonistic relationship with Eirik Blood-axe. Most structural approaches to the saga understandably focus on these main characters. Network analysis provides an opportunity to change this focus by considering the topology of the saga relations and interactions from the perspective of any character through the use of ego-nets (or "spheres of influence"). Granted, for a great many of the characters in *Egil's Saga*, the ego-net representation of the saga is very simple. Yet the approach reveals that quite complex views of the saga can emerge if one considers the relational and interactional perspective of secondary characters in the saga.

Gunnhild Ozurardottir, for instance, is rightfully considered to be a major antagonist in the saga, even though she only appears in a few scenes. In an ego-network for Gunnhild of radius 2 (where radius measures degree of separation), she is able to reach nearly 28 per cent of the characters in the saga (88 characters); shrinking the ego-network radius to 1, her sphere of direct influence is reduced to 14 characters (a decrease of 84 per cent). More interesting than the reach of her network is the role that she plays in the saga and, in particular, her membership in cliques. Gunnhild, it turns out, is a member of 5 cliques on the friendship graph and 4 cliques on the enmity graph, a very high rate of membership, highlighting her active role in influencing both.

Arinbjorn presents an interesting foil to Gunnhild, in many respects playing the role of peace-maker to Gunnhild's trouble-maker. His ego-net presents a different view of the saga. Unlike Gunnhild, who had considerable reach with second-degree neighbours, Arinbjorn can only reach a modest 8.5 per cent of the saga characters (27 characters) when his ego-network radius is set to 2. Reducing the radius of his sphere of influence to immediate neighbours (degree one) does not result in the same dramatic reduction as that for Gunnhild; instead Arinbjorn's immediate neighbourhood is reduced to 16 characters (a decrease of 40 per cent). Arinbjorn appears very high on total degree centrality and, as noted above, is one of the top-ranked hub characters on the friendly interaction union graph. Arinbjorn, like Gunnhild, also plays a role in a large number of cliques on the union of the friendship and enmity graphs, emphasizing his position of being in the thick of things when it comes to brokering the peace between Egil and his antagonists.

Structural Balance in *Egil's Saga*

Perhaps one of the most complicated aspects of social interaction considered in the sagas is the selection of friends and its inverse, the selection of enemies. In the 1940s, Fritz Heider proposed a theory of structural balance for social interactions that formalized the concept of friendship transitivity (Davis 1967, 185–6; Bott 1957; Rapoport 1963).

Figure 3. Triad solutions in structural balance theory. These are signed, undirected graphs (Leskovec, Huttenlocher, Kleinberg 2010, 2).

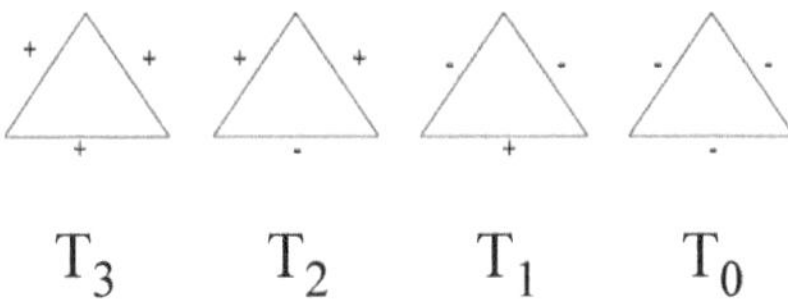

The theory considers the various ways that a triangular relationship of three people can be signed positively or negatively, with four possible solutions (Figure 3): A and B like each other, B and C like each other, A and C like each other (T_3); A and B do not like each other, B and C do not like each other, A and C like each other (T_1); A and B like each other, B and C like each other, A and C do not like each other (T_2); and A and B do not like each other, B and C do not like each other, A and C do not like each other (T_0). According to the theory of structured balance, solutions T_3 and T_1 are considered to be more plausible – and hence more prevalent in "real networks"– than the two remaining solutions. James Davis proposed a modification of strict structural balance, offering the notion of "weak structural balance," suggesting that triangles with three negative ties (T_3) were equally plausible, leaving only triangles with two negative ties and one positive tie (T_2) as "implausible" (Davis 1967, 186). He also noted that the selection of signed relationships in a real world social network leads to polarization, a situation described by Harary as "two highly cohesive cliques which dislike each other" (Davis 1967, 185; Harary 1955–6, 144). Concerning the "implausible" triangle, where two enemies have a common friend (T_2), Davis notes that "sociologically, such situations may be interpreted as ones where a pair's direct relationship is inconsistent with that implied by their relationships with a third party" (Davis 1967, 186). This observation has considerable currency in the context of the Icelandic sagas, where many of the interactions between firsts and seconds are in conflict with inconsistent relationships with thirds.

In his work Davis offers a series of terms to help understand the possible states of signed pair-wise relationships between individuals on an incomplete graph. Ultimately he suggests that "pairs are 'strained' if an edge exists on a cycle with one negative edge (T_2); reinforced if a reversal of the sign of the edge would lead to a cycle with one negative edge (T_3 or T_1); and free if the relationship is neither reinforced nor strained (T_0). Pairs that are not joined by edges have a latent relationship, with similar potentials" (Davis 1967, 186).

This approach can be applied to an interesting series of triangles which involve Gunnhild Ozurardottir and are related to the famous *Hǫfuðlausn* or head ransom episode near the end of the saga. One can reduce the complexity of this problem by considering the very limited subgraph of Egil, Arinbjorn, Eirik, and Gunnhild at the start and end of the episode. At the start of the episode, Egil decides to visit Athelstan in England. Bad weather forces him ashore at the mouth of the Humber River and effectively delivers him into the lap of King Eirik. Egil seeks out his good friend Arinbjorn, who has been characterized immediately prior to this as King Eirik's foster brother, foster father to his children, and as someone he greatly values: "King Eirik was fondest of him among all his landholders" (109: "hann var kærstr konungi af ǫllum lendum mǫnnum," 175–6). Given past interactions, the relationships between the characters on this subgraph can be summarized as follows in Figure 4. Here, the question marks denote relations that are not already determined or are in potential flux. By the end of the episode, several important events have happened, and the sign(s) along several of the edges have become fixed. At the start of the episode, one finds a series of competing evaluations for Egil's various relationships: on the first triangle (Egil-Eirik-Arinbjorn) his relationship with Eirik is strained (!), while on the third triangle (Egil-Eirik-Gunnhild) his negative relationship with Gunnhild reinforces his relationship with Eirik as negative. The two triangles on the right-hand side of the figure complicate matters, as they require a determination of a sign for the Arinbjorn-Gunnhild edge.

The episode is certainly one of the most suspenseful of the saga, and the outcome of it at times seems to be in question. Egil throws the poetic equivalent of a Hail Mary pass and saves his head at essentially the last moment. Although Eirik accepts the poem and grants Egil safe passage away from his territory, it is hard to give this interaction a positive sign. In the friendship graph's gift-giving subgraph, this act is the only negatively valued gift. Eirik, one should recall, accepts the poem saying, "You can be sure that this is not a reconciliation with me or my sons, nor any of my kinsmen who wants to seek justice" (132: "en vita skaltu þat til sanns, at þetta er engi sætt við mik né sonu mína ok enga frændr vára, þá sem réttar vilja reka," 193), an acceptance speech that hardly rises to the standard of what one would term friendly. Egil's poetic evaluation of the encounter similarly emphasizes his deep enmity for Eirik.

Nevertheless, for the sake of illustration, the end state of the relationships by the end of chapter 62 can be signed as below (Figure 5). In this case, the relationship between Egil and Eirik is signed as ~+ to indicate the very brief nature of this positive interaction. Another reading proposes negative signs for these edges (Figure 6). This latter signing of the graph is significantly easier to evaluate: Egil's negative relationship with both Eirik and Gunnhild is in a "reinforced" state, as is Egil's positive relationship with Arinbjorn, when seen in the context of their negative consideration of Gunnhild. The relationship becomes

Figure 4. Status of friendship / enmity triangles at the beginning of chapter 60.

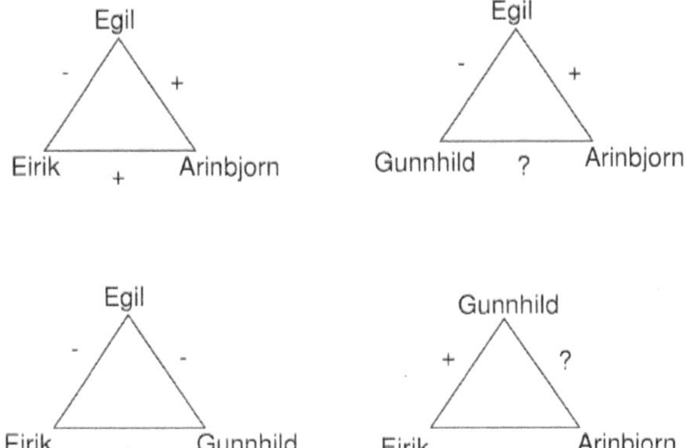

Figure 5. Status of friendship / enmity triangles at the end of chapter 62. ~+ indicates a temporary positively signed relationship.

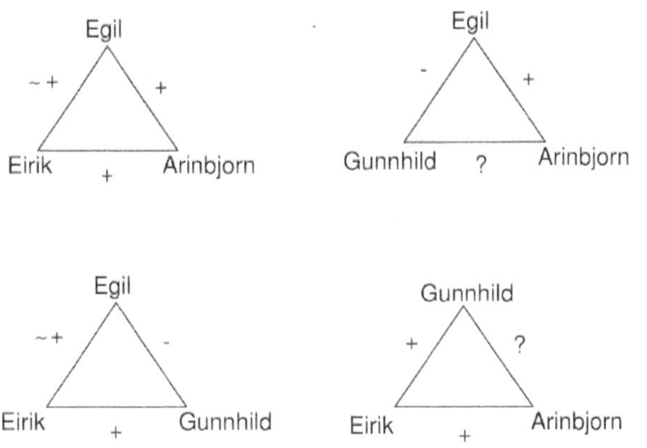

Figure 6. An alternative view of the signs on friendship / enmity triangles at the end of chapter 62.

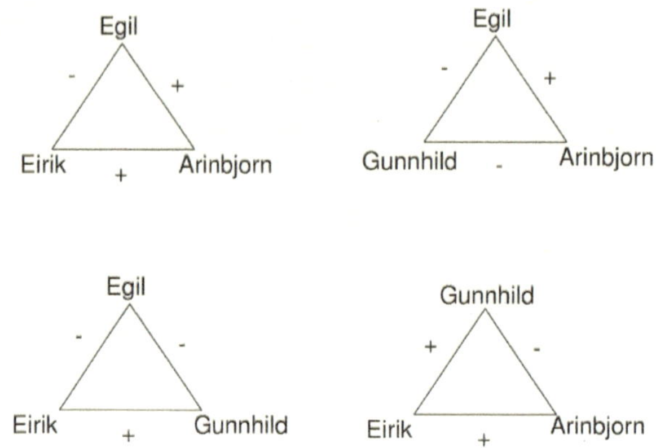

"strained" when seen on the graph that includes Eirik, an excellent evaluation of the end state of the episode.

Leskovec, Huttenlocher, and Kleinberg extend the consideration of structural balance in signed undirected networks to the consideration of likes and dislikes on a directed network graph, labelling their approach a "theory of status" (2010, 2; see also Marvel, Strogatz, and Kleinberg 2009). Changing from an undirected graph to a directed graph increases the number of possible signed triads to 16, a considerable complication but one that aligns better with the unreciprocated nature of many friendships in the sagas. In short, their theory holds that "a positive directed link … indicate[s] that the creator of the link views the recipient as having higher status; and a negative directed link indicates that the recipient is viewed as having lower status" (Leskovec, Huttenlocher, and Kleinberg 2010, 2). This theory thus supplants the concept of friendship/enmity transitivity with a calculation based on status. An analysis of friendship and enmity based on status is certainly worth exploring in the context of the Icelandic sagas, and *Egil's Saga* might be the prime candidate for such an analysis given the frequent discussions of people's status in the saga. In the episode under question here, Gunnhild attempts to egg Eirik on to execute Egil post-haste, offering a status argument and saying that "not long ago King Eirik would have seemed unlikely to lack the will and the character to take vengeance for what he has suffered from the likes of Egil" (127: "en fyrir skǫmmu mundi þat þykkja ekki líkligt, at Eiríkr konungr mundi eigi hafa til þess vilja ok atferð, at hefna harma sinna á hverjum manni slíkum sem Egill er," 184). Arinbjorn deflects this argument by giving Egil his own high-status endorsement.

At the start of the episode the open question is whether Eirik will allow Egil to keep his head – in short, whether Eirik will sign their relationship positively long enough for Egil to get out of town. The problem then stands as one related to predicting the sign of the link directed from Eirik to Egil. Gunnhild's role is one of influence, helping Eirik to decide what type of status valuation to ascribe Egil (and thus whether or not to spare him). Egil has to hope that Gunnhild's arguments about status are offset by Arinbjorn's equally forceful arguments not only about Egil's status but, more importantly, about his own status. In an interesting prefiguration of his status-gaining feat on the way to Armod Beard's farm, Egil's masterful poetic composition similarly throws a wrench in Gunnhild's otherwise well-oiled calculation of status. One can almost hear the gears turning in Eirik's mind as he works out the signs of the numerous directed subgraphs that feed his calculations as he ponders whether to accept Egil's poem.

The diagram below illustrates the "status" problem of these two triads at the start of the episode, with question marks marking links that are to be determined by status calculations over the course of the episode. Here, it is proposed that in the first graph Egil has linked positively to Arinbjorn, who has linked positively to Eirik; in the second graph, Egil has linked positively to Eirik in the sense that he has come to implore him for free passage (and thus recognizes Eirik's high status), and Gunnhild has also linked positively to Eirik (through marriage) (Figure 7). Given these status relations, the resulting signs on the question marks are resolved as negative. Gunnhild's negative evaluation of Egil thus reinforces Eirik's negative evaluation, and this can serve to influence his actions (Figure 8).

Despite these negative signs, Egil keeps his head. Apparently, while his status is low, it is not so low as to warrant death and, instead, the antagonism remains on the non-lethal enmity graph. In many regards, these newly signed triads capture the nuanced inflections of enmity in the episode, allowing Egil to escape with his life but keep his negative evaluation of Eirik and Gunnhild intact. As a consequence of Eirik's negative signing of the link between him and Egil, Egil can flip the sign of his evaluation of Eirik on the graph, which is indeed what happens.

The status considerations in this episode confirm that all interpersonal links in the saga should be considered as directed links and illustrates the role that status evaluation can play in deciding how to "sign" these links. Leskovec notes that the embedding of triads in larger networks can have a significant impact on the signing of links between nodes, concluding that the theory of

Figure 7. Triads signed according to status at the start of chapter 60.

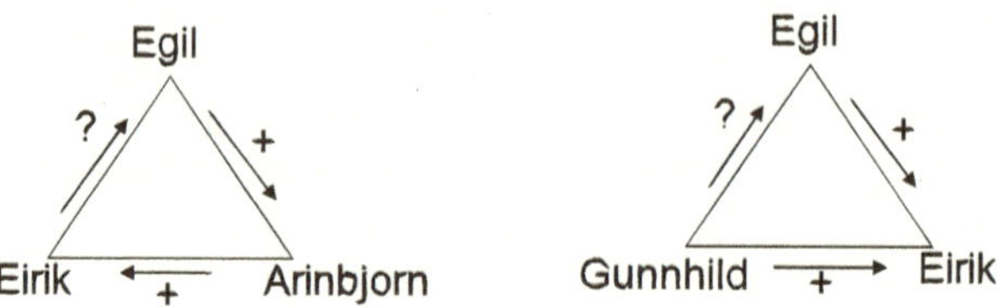

Figure 8. Triads signed according to status at the start of chapter 62.

status is more effective at explaining local patterns of signed links (Leskovec, Huttenlocher, and Kleinberg 2010, 3). The role of familial relationships – an integral form of social network embedding in the saga – emerges as an important part of any of these calculations. The focus on local patterns and the wider embedding of nodes in a greater network context means that this approach is likely to have significant applicability to the highly episodic Sagas of Icelanders, where considerations of status often clash with the demands of family.

Conclusion

The present study of *Egil's Saga* has highlighted how applying social network analysis can result in potential interpretive gains in regard to understanding the complexities of relationships among saga characters. There are countless other measures and refinements that could be added to the very cursory introduction presented here. These include the application of more sophisticated dynamic techniques, allowing one to explore change in relationships over the course of the entire saga narrative at varying levels of granularity and expanding the scope of the network to include multiple sagas. Similarly, consideration of more of the ego-networks in the saga might foster the development of a faceted view of the saga narrative – while the saga audience can readily conceptualize the saga from the perspective of the saga hero, ego-net approaches allow for the rapid conceptualization of the saga from the perspective of any saga character. Network analysis will not supplant existing interpretive methodologies but rather holds the potential to augment current approaches and to suggest new areas of inquiry into the complex relationships that animate the sagas. One cannot help but wonder whom Egil would have "friended" over the course of his life if Facebook had existed in his time, and whether Eirik would have surreptitiously unfriended Arinbjorn after Egil's performance of *Hǫfuðlausn*. Gunnhild would certainly have wanted that.

NOTES

1 Funding for the research for this article was generously provided by the American Council of Learned Societies. I learned many of the techniques employed in this article from my collaboration with colleagues at NSF's Institute for Pure and Applied Mathematics at UCLA and during an intensive summer school at UCLA funded by the NEH on "Network Analysis for the Humanities." In particular, I would like to thank Tina Eliassi-Rad, Jure Leskovec, Sofus Macskassy, Katy Börner, and Peter Broadwell for many productive discussions of network analysis and the study of literature. I would also like to thank Tamar Boyadjian for working on developing the edgelist for this saga, and for fruitful discussions with members of the Wildcat Canyon Advanced Seminars on the applicability of these approaches to Old Icelandic literature. I would like to dedicate this article to my niece Nastasia, who introduced me to Facebook.

2 The transitivity of friendship is a key feature of "Structural Balance Theory" developed by Fritz Heider in the 1940s and formalized mathematically by Dorwin Cartwright and Frank Harary (Cartwright and Harary 1956 and 1965). The other law at work here is the clear legal requirement that a wealthy farmer provide hospitality for a person on a royal mission.

3 Although often rooted in external historical sources, the realization of the saga characters is largely fictional and in many respects aligned with the representation of historical detail common to the legend genre (Tangherlini 1994; Sigurðsson 2004). Here, King Hakon's man invokes this same type of fiction to get out of accompanying Egil and, in his mind, setting Egil and his companions up for sure death.

4 A "tit for tat" strategy in deciding how to react in a social situation is one that is closely tied to the transitive nature of friendship and enmity.

5 Extending the analytical approach of SNA to include other aspects of narrative (where the nodes of the graph are not limited to characters) allows one to generalize the underlying approach to "network analysis." An obvious extension would be to shift the domain from a single saga to the entire saga corpus. Another

important extension would be to include the variant witnesses to the "standard editions" of the sagas, allowing one to consider variation in social relations across the different variants of the text. Still another extension would be to include a much finer-grained delineation of action in the saga, focusing on the sentence or phrase level of the saga texts. Finally, a word-level network for a saga text would allow one to explore the philological network of the story.

6 The development of the field of Social Network Analysis is described well in Freeman 2004. Three popular and accessible studies of network analysis can be found in Watts 2003, Barabási 2002, and Buchanan 2002. The most thorough introduction to the methods and theory of social network analysis can be found in Wasserman and Faust 1995 and a more recent overview including developments in the study of networks in Carrington, Scott, and Wasserman 2005. At the most fundamental level, a network consists of nodes and edges between these nodes. Nodes are usually characters or people; edges are produced by a relationship between these characters. The relationship can be either directed (A kills B) or undirected (A and B shake each other's hands); similarly, the relationships can be signed (A hates B is signed -, while B loves C is signed +) or otherwise valued or weighted (A likes B has less value than A presents B with half his kingdom). Finally, nodes can have attributes attached to them (A is male, B is female, C is a corporate actor such as "The Lapps").

7 It can be interesting to consider "what if" scenarios for literary works where substitutions or deletions in the network lead to significantly different pathways for positive or negative interaction.

8 For the purposes of computer analysis, these graphs are stored as "edgelists" or adjacency matrices. Each node is assigned a unique identifier and a label. A spreadsheet containing the various edgelists in csv format is available for download at http://www.purl.org/egilsaganetworks/examples.

9 The current network representation of *Egil's Saga* is not as tuned to aspects of plot as the structural analyses presented in Andersson 1967 and Clover 1982.

10 Several user-friendly software packages exist for the analysis of networks. Sci2, developed by Katy Börner's laboratory at Indiana University, provides a suite of clear analytical and visualization tools (Sci2 Team 2009). The ORA (Organizational Risk Assessment) tools developed by Kathleen Carley's group at CMU offer a series of easy to use methods for exploring networks (Carley 2008). Finally, Cytoscape, a system developed for the analysis of biological molecule interaction, can be repurposed particularly for genealogical charts (Shannon, Markiel, et al. 2003).

11 All familial relationships mentioned in the saga were catalogued and categorized as one of three possible types: consanguineous-descent, conjugal-spouse, and fosters. Directed edges point from children to their parents and from foster children to their foster parents.

12 For simplicity's sake in the analysis presented below, the graph is reduced to one that describes consanguineous descent.

13 The only exception to this consists of Bragi Boddason and King Bjorn of Sweden, whose appearance in the saga is used by Arinbjorn to draw an analogy to Egil's situation encouraging him to compose *Hǫfuðlausn*.

14 Private conversation with Carol Clover. Given the critical interest in women's roles in the sagas, it might be worthwhile to examine the metrics related to powerful or strong female figures in the social networks.

15 These ten foster relationships are as follows: Ketil Haeng and Baug are foster brothers, implying that Earl Thorkel, Ketil's father, fostered Baug; Thorir Hroaldsson is fostered by Kveldulf Bjalfason; Eirik Blood-axe is fostered by Thorir Hroaldsson; Egil is fostered by Thorgerd Brak; Athelstan the Victorious fosters Hakon the Good; Eirik Blood-axe fosters Frodi; Beard Thorir fosters Rognvald Eiriksson; and Arinbjorn fosters both Thorstein Thoruson and Harald Eiriksson Grey-cloak. Arinbjorn is in turn fostered by either Thorstein Thoruson or Harald Fine-hair, making him Eirik's foster brother.

16 Ambivalent interactions have not been included in any of the network graphs presented here, and represent a future refinement of the work. Other future extensions include attaching actual text from the sagas as features for each link between nodes enabling "drill-down" to the underlying texts.

17 In decreasing order of weight (provided in parentheses), they are: inheritance or succession (8), fostering (7), marriage (6), being placed in command (5), gift giving (4), pledge of allegiance or friendship (3), request or offer of assistance (2), providing or discovering information (1). Inheritance or succession is seen as a special case of gift giving, and therefore is given twice the weight of other gift giving.

18 One need only think of *Njal's Saga* to realize that not all gifts have the same "weight." An exploration of evaluating the value of gifts can be found in Tangherlini 1998.

19 In this and subsequent measures, the weight of the edge between two nodes is taken into consideration.

20 An excellent description of the CONCOR algorithm can be found in Hanneman and Riddle 2005.

BIBLIOGRAPHY

Andersson, Theodore M. 1967. *The Icelandic Family Saga: An analytic reading.* Cambridge, MA: Harvard University Press.

Barabási, Albert-László. 2002. *Linked: The New Science of Networks*. Cambridge, MA: Perseus Pub.

Bott, Elizabeth. 1957. *Family and Social Network: Roles, Norms, and External Relationships in Ordinary Urban Families*. London: Tavistock Publications.

Buchanan, Mark. 2002. *Nexus: Small Worlds and the Groundbreaking Science of Networks.* New York: Norton.

Byock, Jesse L. 1982. *Feud in the Icelandic Saga*. Berkeley: University of California Press.

Carley, Kathleen M., Dave Columbus, Matt DeReno, Jeff Reminga, and Il-Chul Moon. 2008. *ORA User's Guide*. Pittsburgh: Carnegie Mellon University, School of Computer Science, Institute for Software Research.

Carrington, Peter J., John Scott, and Stanley Wasserman. 2005. *Models and Methods in Social Network Analysis*. Structural Analysis in the Social Sciences 27. Cambridge: Cambridge University Press.

Clover, Carol J. 1982. *The Medieval Saga*. Ithaca, NY: Cornell University Press.

Cormack, Margaret. 2007. "Fact and Fiction in the Icelandic sagas." *History Compass* 5: 207–17.

Danielsson, Tommy. 1986. *Om den isländska släktsagans uppbyggnad*. Uppsala: Uppsala Universitet.

Davis, James A. 1967. "Clustering and Structural Balance on Graphs." *Human Relations* 20: 181–7.

Dunbar, Robin I.M., Amanda Clark, and Nicola L. Hurst. 1995. "Conflict and Cooperation among the Vikings: Contingent Behavioral Decisions." *Ethology and Social Biology* 16(3): 233–46.

Freeman, Linton C. 2004. *The Development of Social Network Analysis: A Study in the Sociology of Science*. Vancouver: Empirical Press.

Gaskins, Richard. 2005. "Network Dynamics in Saga and Society." *Scandinavian Studies* 77: 201–16.

Granovetter, Mark. 1973. "The Strength of Weak Ties." *The American Journal of Sociology* 78: 1360–80.

Hanneman, Robert A., and Mark Riddle. 2005. *Introduction to Social Network Methods.* Riverside, CA: University of California, Riverside. Online at http://faculty.ucr.edu/~hanneman/nettext/.

Harary, Frank. 1955–6. "On the Notion of Balance of a Signed Graph." *Michigan Mathematics Journal* 2: 143–6.

Harary, Frank, and Dorwin Cartwright. 1956. "Structural Balance: A Generalization of Heider's Theory." *Psychological Review* 63: 277–93.

Harary, Frank, Dorwin Cartwright, and Robert Z. Norman. 1965. *Structural Models: AnIintroduction to the Theory of Directed Graphs*. New York: Wiley.

Johnson, Steven B., and Ronald C. Johnson. 1991. "Support and Conflict of Kinsmen in Norse Earldoms, Icelandic Families, and the English Royalty." *Ethology and Social Biology* 12: 213–20.

Labov, William, and Joshua Waletzky. 1967. "Narrative Analysis." In *Essays on the verbal and visual arts*. Ed. June Helm, 12–44. Seattle: University of Washington Press.

Leskovec, Jure, Daniel Huttenlocher, and Jon M. Kleinberg. 2010. "Signed Networks in Social Media." In *CHI 2010*. Atlanta, GA: ACM.

Lönnroth, Lars. 2007. "Structuralist Approaches to Saga Literature." In *Learning and Understanding in the Old Norse World: Essays in Honour of Margaret Clunies Ross*. Ed. Judy Quinn, Kate Heslop, and Tarrin Wills, 63–74. Medieval Texts and Cultures of Northern Europe 18. Turnhout: Brepols.

Mac Carron, Pádraig, and Ralph Kenna. 2012. "Universal Properties of Mythical Networks." *Europhysics Letters* 99(2): 28002. doi:10.1209/0295-5075/99/28002

– 2013. "Network Analysis of the Íslendinga sögur – the Sagas of Icelanders." *The European Physical Journal* B 86(407): 1–9.

Marvel, Seth A., Steven Strogatz, and Jon M. Kleinberg. 2009. "The Energy Landscape of Social Balance." *Physical Review Letters* 103: 1–4.

Miller, William Ian. 1983. "Choosing the Avenger: Some Aspects of the Bloodfeud in Medieval Iceland and England." *Law and History Review* 1: 159–204.

– 1990. *Bloodtaking and Peacemaking: Feud, Law, and Society in Saga Iceland*. Chicago: University of Chicago Press.

Norrick, Neal R. 2005. "The Dark Side of Tellability." *Narrative Inquiry* 15: 323–44.

Pálsson, Hermann, and Paul Edwards. 1976. *Egil's saga*. Harmondsworth: Penguin.

Quinn, Judy, Kate Heslop, and Tarrin Wills. 2007. *Learning and Understanding in the Old Norse World: Essays in Honour of Margaret Clunies Ross*. Medieval Texts and Cultures of Northern Europe 18. Turnhout: Brepols.

Rapoport, Anatol. 1963. "Mathematical Models of Social Interaction." In *Handbook of Mathematical Psychology*. Vol. 2. Ed. R. Luce, E. Bush, and R. Galanter, 493–579. New York: Wiley.

Robinson, John A. 1981. "Personal narratives reconsidered." *The Journal of American Folklore* 94: 58–85.

Sacks, Harvey, and Gail Jefferson. 1992. *Lectures on Conversation*. 2 volumes. Oxford: Blackwell.

Sci^2 Team. 2009. *Science of Science (Sci^2) Tool*. Indiana University and SciTech Strategies, http://sci2.cns.iu.edu.

Scudder, Bernard. 2005. *Egil's Saga*. London: Penguin.

Shannon, P., A. Markiel, O. Ozier, N.S. Baliga, J.T. Wang, D. Ramage, N. Amin, B. Schwikowski, and T. Ideker. 2003. "Cytoscape: A Software Environment for Integrated Models of Biomolecular Interaction Networks." *Genome Research* 13: 2498–2504.

Sigurðsson, Gísli. 2004. *The Medieval Icelandic Saga and Oral Tradition: A Discourse on Method*. Publications of the Milman Parry Collection of Oral

Literature 2. Cambridge, MA: Milman Parry Collection of Oral Literature Harvard University, distributed by Harvard University Press.

Tangherlini, Timothy R. 1994. *Interpreting Legend: Danish Storytellers and Their Repertoires*. New York: Garland.

– 1998. "Barter and Games: Economics and the Supernatural in Danish Legendry." *Arv* 54: 41–62.

Thorsson, Örnólfur. 2001. "A Note on the Texts." In *The Sagas of Icelanders: A Selection.* New York: Penguin.

Wasserman, Stanley, and Katherine Faust. 1994. *Social Network Analysis: Methods and Applications*. Structural Analysis in the Social Sciences 8. Cambridge: Cambridge University Press.

Watts, Duncan J. 2003. *Six Degrees: The Science of a Connected Age*. New York: Norton.

Reception

10 Egil Strikes Again: Textual Variation and the Seventeenth-Century Reworkings of *Egil's Saga*

SVANHILDUR ÓSKARSDÓTTIR

1

The structural unity of *Egil's Saga* – or the lack of it – is a topic frequently addressed by scholars (cf. Tulinius 2004, 21–2). It is generally accepted that the saga's first part, which deals with the career of Thorolf Kveldulfsson, is tighter in structure than the second, much longer part, which follows Egil Skallagrimsson's exploits, but whether this significantly detracts from the aesthetic merits of the saga is a matter of dispute. Theodore Andersson for his part claims that "the central part of the saga ... is diluted and made bland by a quantity of episodic scatterings about the Norwegian court, the colonization of Iceland, and viking raids abroad" (Andersson 1967, 107), whereas Torfi H. Tulinius – partly in response to Andersson – sets out "to show that the second part of the saga is just as well constructed as the first and that every element of it is pertinent to its understanding as a whole" (Tulinius 2001, 206). In tune with this, there seems to be scholarly consensus which sees the death of Thorolf Kveldulfsson as the structural climax of the first part of the saga, whereas opinions differ on what constitutes the climax of the second part. For Andersson it is the episode at Gulathing where Egil's efforts to claim Asgerd's inheritance are thwarted (although Andersson laments that the scene does not represent a "true climax"), while Óskar Halldórsson defines Egil's meeting with Eirik in York as the pinnacle of the narrative (Halldórsson 1967, 6). Torfi H. Tulinius is more inclined to view the "Egil part" of the story as a continuum of sometimes seemingly disparate narratives which are nevertheless bound together by thematic developments (Tulinius 2004, 47–52).

For their discussions about the structure of *Egil's Saga*, scholars have relied on editions of the saga which give insufficient information about the manuscript tradition of the work, principally Sigurður Nordal's edition for Íslenzk fornrit. Nordal followed Finnur Jónsson in taking Möðruvallabók as his main text and produced his edition before Jón Helgason published his groundbreaking article on the manuscripts of *Egil's Saga* (1956, English translation 2005). As the work on the critical edition of the saga in the Editiones Arnamagnæanæ series progresses, we are gradually being placed in a better position to evaluate the variation in the texts, and that variation may put some of the structural issues concerning the saga into a new perspective.

The extant manuscripts of the saga fall into three branches (cf. Helgason 1956a/2005): A comprises the Möðruvallabók codex and its descendants as well as the very early θ-fragment and two other fragments. B is represented by the Wolfenbüttel codex together with six vellum fragments and some paper manuscripts – among them AM 463 4to and AM 560 d 4to, which preserve some B-text no longer extant in the older manuscripts. The main witnesses for the C-branch are Ketill Jörundsson's seventeenth-century paper copies plus the vellum fragments ε and α, which date from the fifteenth and the sixteenth centuries respectively.

How do these versions differ? Do they present a significantly diverse tradition? The short answer is no. The Egil of these three versions is essentially the same and his life and those of his ancestors are played out in much the same way, with the same sequence of episodes. There is variation, however, in the fullness of the narrative, which in its turn influences the style. This variation can also be detected between manuscripts of the same branch, as is seen in the case of Möðruvallabók which condenses the text compared with the older θ-fragment. Finnur Jónsson remarked, comparing Möðruvallabók and the Wolfenbüttel codex, that "W is shorter, as a rule, and this brevity is partly due to the fact that W leaves out clauses from sentences and even whole (shorter) sentences, and partly to a more condensed sentence structure than in M (and to a certain extent in K)" ("W i regelen er mere kort, og denne korthed består dels deri, at W udelader dele af sætninger og hele (mindre) sætninger, dels deri, at sætningerne gives i en mere sammentrængt form end i M (og tildels i K)," Jónsson 1886–8, xx). The C-version is closer to A in that respect but contains additions of its own (Helgason 1956a, 120; 2005, 16) and the language of the Ketilsbækur naturally reflects seventeenth-century usage. Gunnhild's reproach of King Eirik at the Gulathing provides a brief illustration of the differences.

Although Egil could be seen as essentially the same in all three versions of the saga, his characterization is affected by two variables: the amount of poetry each version contains and the way it portrays Egil in old age. For it is in these two respects that one finds significant material differences between the three versions, and these differences all occur in the last part of the saga, thus making for differences in the structural balance of the narrative.[1] Three long poems

A (AM 162 fol. θ – c. 1250)	B (W – c. 1350)	C (K[1] – 17th c.)
How peculiar of you, King, to let this big man Egil run circles around you. Would you even raise an objection if he claimed the throne out of your hands? You might refuse to make any ruling in Onund's favour, but I will not tolerate Egil trampling over my [our M] friends and wrongly taking this money from Onund. Where are you now, Alf Askmann? Take your men to where the court is sitting and prevent this injustice from coming to pass. (109) Þetta er undarligt konungr, hvernig þú lætr Egil þenna inn mikla vefja mál ǫll fyr þér. Eða hvárt myndir þú eigi móti honum mæla þótt hann kallaði til konungdómsins í hendr þér? En þótt þú vilir ǫnga órskurði veita þá er Ǫnundi sé lið at, þá skal ek þat eigi þola at Egill troði svá undir fótum vini mína [vini vora M] at hann taki með rangindi sín fé þetta af Ǫnundi. En hvar ertu Askmaðr? Far þú til með sveit þína þar sem dómendrnir eru ok lát eigi dœma rangindi þessi! (Speed-Kjeldsen 2005, 202; orthography normalized and punctuation added)	Why do you let this big man Egil run circles around you? Would you even raise an objection if he claimed the throne out of your hands? You might refuse to make any ruling in Onund's favour, but I will not do that. Where is Alf my brother? Take your men to where the court is sitting and break up the session! Hví lætr þú Egil þenna vefja mál ǫll fyrir þér, enda mundir þú eigi í móti mæla ef hann kallaði til konungdómsins í hendr þér? En þóttú vilir enga órskurði veita til liðs Berg-Ǫnundi þá skal ek þat eigi gøra. Hvar er Álfr bróðir minn? Farðu til með sveit þína ok hleyp upp dóminum! (Helgason 1956b, 45r; orthography normalized and punctuation added)	How peculiar of you, King, to let this big man Egil run circles around you. Would you even raise an objection if he claimed the throne out of your hands? You might refuse to make any ruling in Onund's favour, but I will not tolerate Egil trampling over my friends and wrongly taking this money from Onund. Where are my brothers, Alf and Eyvind? Go to where the court is sitting and prevent this injustice from coming to pass. (109) Þetta eru undr mikil, kóngr, hvǫrn veg þú lætr Egil þenna hinn mikla vefja fyrir þér ǫll mál, eður hvǫrt muntú ei í móti mæla þó hann kalli til kóngdóms í hendr þér? En þó þú viljir ǫngva úrskurði veita, þá er Ǫnundi sé lið að, þá skal eg það ei þola að Egill troði so undir fótum vini mína, að hann taki fé með rángindum af Ǫnundi, eður hvar eru Álfr og Eyvindr bræður mínir? Farið til þar sem dómar eru og látið ei dæma rángindi þessi! (Chesnutt 2006, 84–5; orthography slightly normalized and punctuation added)

attributed to Egil survive as part of his saga, but no version includes all of them. An additional three long poems are attributed to Egil in the A-version, which also gives their opening stanzas (see Clunies Ross 2010, 193–5 for an extensive discussion). *Höfuðlausn* is not a part of Möðruvallabók's account of the events in York although editors have added the poem to the text (128–32: 185–92). *Höfuðlausn* is included in the Wolfenbüttel codex, but not in other B-manuscripts, and it exists in a different version in C.[2] The other two poems, *Arinbjarnarkviða* and *Sonatorrek*, are printed in chapter 78 in the ÍF edition (246–56), but no manuscript includes them both in this one chapter. The B-version does not have *Arinbjarnarkviða* and only cites the first stanza of *Sonatorrek*. C contains *Sonatorrek* but not *Arinbjarnarkviða*. The A-version mentions both poems and cites their first stanzas within the narrative and *Arinbjarnarkviða* is then copied separately, after the saga, in Möðruvallabók. The remainder of chapter 78 is in A taken up by a further narrative about Einar Helgason Skalaglamm which includes three verses. This material is also in C, but shortened and with only one of the three verses. In B it is skipped entirely. Michael Chesnutt (2005, 234–43) takes this evidence to show that the A-version was expanded whereas B better reflects the original state of the text. (The expansion in A subsequently influenced the C-version.) Version A further distinguishes itself from the other two versions by including an episode about Iri, Thorstein Egilsson's worker in chapter 83, and augmenting the narrative about Egil's old age with the following additional material in chapter 85 (cf. Helgason 1956a, 120; 2005, 16):

- Short passage with verse. The cook at Mosfell complains that Egil is in their way in the kitchen (295: 201)
- Episode about Egil's plans to go to Althing and scatter his silver (from Athelstan) there (296–7: 202–3)
- A couple of lines with additional speculations on the whereabouts of Egil's silver (297.32–298.2: 203.31–4).

The A-version therefore reflects an interest in keeping in a series of anecdotes from the last part of Egil's life, often attached to a stanza (or indeed a poem as in the case of *Arinbjarnarkviða*). The structure of the narrative becomes looser, as a result, and it is easy to imagine rearrangement and variation in this part.[3] The end of the saga in the B-version is tighter in this respect whereas C hovers in between. The inclusion of passages such as those about Einar Skalaglamm and about Egil's plans to scatter his silver at the Althing means that the Egil of the A-version comes across as more temperamental, unpredictable, and vindictive than the Egil in the B-version, who saves his energy for the final showdown with Steinar and Onund. And the B-version relies less on the fame of Egil's poetry than do A and C, where more of it is reproduced.

2

Unbeknownst to many, the saga of Egil is preserved in yet another guise, a version produced in the seventeenth century. The Egil who emerges in that redaction turns out to be vastly different from his medieval counterpart – not least in the way he behaves towards the end of his life. It is to the post-medieval Egil that we now turn, and the area that fostered him: the districts around Breiðafjörður in Western Iceland.

Ketill Jörundsson (1603–70), Árni Magnússon's grandfather, was a crucial figure in the transmission history of *Egil's Saga.* He produced two copies of the saga which are now the main witnesses for the C-version. Michael Chesnutt has shown that Ketill's copies are descended from a sixteenth-century manuscript, the remnants of which are the α-fragment, and further argues (2006, xli) that the copies could have been made while Ketill was at Skálholt, i.e., before he became priest at Hvammur in the Dalir region in 1638. The possibility that Ketill wrote his copies at Hvammur, however, must also be considered. It is significant in this respect that α was in Northwest Iceland (at Lokinhamrar in Arnarfjörður) at the beginning of the eighteenth century, and other manuscripts descended from it were, like the two Ketilsbækur and its descendants, produced in the Breiðafjörður area. A copy of the C-version was also at hand when the saga was printed for the first time, at Hrappsey in Breiðafjörður in 1782, and used to supply the ending to the saga (Chesnutt 2006, xxii–xxviii).

The people of Breiðafjörður and Vestfirðir clearly had a taste for *Egil's Saga* that was not confined to the medieval tradition. In 1643 the poet Jón Guðmundsson of Rauðseyjar (or Russeyjar) in Breiðafjörður composed a set of forty *rímur* based on the C-version of the saga. The *rímur*, which remain unedited, are preserved in two known manuscripts, AM 610a 4to and an uncatalogued manuscript at the Héraðsskjalasafn Skagfirðinga in Sauðárkrókur. AM 610 was in all likelihood written by Þórður Jónsson at Strandseljar in Ísafjarðardjúp (Karlsson 1964, 7–8), but the book's subsequent owners were Magnús Björnsson at Bassastaðir in Steingrímsfjörður and then Gísli Jónsson at Mávahlíð in Snæfellsnes, from whom Árni procured the manuscript in 1709. The precise origins of the other manuscript are unknown, but the style of the decorated initials points to a provenance similar to that of 610. The *rímur* were composed at the behest of Eggert Björnsson (1612–81), sheriff at

Skarð in Skarðsströnd (almost "around the corner" from Ketill at Hvammur), whom the poet praises in the first *mansöngur,* a lyrical non-narrative introduction to each *ríma* (cf. Karlsson 1964, 8–9). That the *rímur* are based on a written text is made explicit in several places, for instance in the penultimate stanza of the fifth *ríma*:

Ulf began to age rapidly, so the book told us. Grim gained the powers of manhood and attended to the estate admirably.

[Úlfur tók að eldast frekt,
oss það bókin skýrði,
Grímur jók þá manndóms mekt
og mætum búskap stýrði. (AM 610a 4to, 20v)]

The *rímur* follow the plot of the saga and include all major episodes, although the narrative is necessarily reshaped and condensed to suit the new medium. There is nevertheless close correspondence in vocabulary, and the *rímur* include details which make it possible to determine that they are based on a manuscript of the C-version of *Egil's Saga*, as demonstrated by Stefán Karlsson (1964) and confirmed by Chesnutt (2006, lv–lvi). To give an idea of how the story progresses through the *rímur* it may be mentioned that *ríma* 6 ends after Thorolf Kveldulfsson is killed by King Harald; the brothers Thorolf and Egil are introduced in *ríma* 10; *ríma* 20 ends after Thorolf Skallagrimsson falls at Wen Heath and Egil receives his compensation from King Adalstein; *rímur* 25 and 26 describe events in York; *ríma* 35 begins with an account of Bodvar's death; and the last five *rímur* relate the dispute between Thorstein Egilsson and Steinar Sjonason before recounting the final phase of Egil's life.

3

Some time after Jón Guðmundsson composed his *Egils rímur* somebody wrote down a new prose version of *Egil's Saga*. This version is not well known but is usually referred to as *Vitlausa Egla* ("Silly Saga of Egil," henceforward in this essay referred to as "New Egil's Saga"). The derogatory name is a testament to views once current among philologists who did not assign any value to manuscripts which could not be classified as primary witnesses to the "original text." A seventeenth-century reworked prose version of a saga had no place in that philological universe, as is witnessed by Finnur Jónsson's remark on *Vitlausa Egla*: "a peculiar version, a complete but extraordinarily silly reworking of the saga" ("en særegen recension, en fuldstændig men overmåde tåbelig omarbejdelse af sagaen," Jónsson 1886–8, xxviii, my translation). This disdain is foreshadowed in a comment by Árni Magnússon in one of the manuscripts of this new version of the saga, where he supposes a certain Gísli Jónsson of Melrakkadalur could well be its author since, according to Árni, he was a "known impostor."[4]

The attribution to Gísli Jónsson must remain doubtful but the preserved manuscripts of "New Egil's Saga" point to origins in the Breiðafjörður region. There are four manuscripts extant:

AM 163 r fol, written by Þorleifur Kláusson (1627–99), priest at Útskálar, in southwest Iceland in the late seventeenth century. Interestingly, *Bandamanna saga* and *Gísla saga*, the latter in a considerably reworked version, are found in the same manuscript.[5]

Holm Papp fol nr. 15, written in Sweden by Jón Vigfússon (d. 1692) for Antikvitetskollegiet in the late seventeenth century.

AM 454 4to written by Gísli Guðmundsson at Rauðilækur at the beginning of the eighteenth century. According to Árni Magnússon's information, Gísli copied a book in folio which was written by Sigurður Jónsson (1633–1717) at Knör in Snæfellsnes and owned by the sheriff Ólafur Einarsson.

Oslo UB 313 fol from the eighteenth century, written in three hands and containing, in addition to "New Egil's Saga," the following: *Sverris saga*, *Hákonar saga Hákonarsonar*, *Víga-Glúms saga*, and the *Saga af Vémundi kögur og Víga-Skúta*. The book was owned by the sheriff Jón Árnason at Ingjaldshóll in Snæfellsnes, who died in 1777. His books were sold at an auction in Copenhagen two years later.

"New Egil's Saga" has never been edited and therefore remains almost completely unexamined. The only scholar who has paid it attention so far is Stefán Karlsson, who referred to it in his article on *Egils rímur* (1964). Stefán later gave Icelandic radio listeners a taste of this unfamiliar version of the Egil story and published a short article about it in 1995. Comparison of the saga with the *rímur* led Stefán to the conclusion that while the author of "New Egil's Saga" had based his text partly on the *rímur*, he had also drawn on the medieval saga, since "New Egil's Saga" includes material which Jón Guðmundsson had to leave out of his *rímur* (Karlsson 1995, 70; cf. Chesnutt 2006, lvii).

4

In this new version the saga is completely recast, using seventeenth-century idioms and vocabulary and exaggerating the characteristics and exploits of the protagonists. This is how Gunnhild's reproach at the Gulathing looks in "New Egil's Saga":

> Now Gunnhild started getting annoyed and said to the king, "You are hardly suited to be a lord because you are lenient in your temperament and want to do what pleases everyone, and you show quite extraordinary foolishness in wishing Egil to gain his legal rights when he has proved himself to be an overbearing man and antagonistic towards you and most people here. Whereas Onund is the best man in this country, our friend, and you let him incur a wrongful judgment because of false testimony from rhymesters and thugs and from this it's clear that you are tempting him to take shameful action." Now the queen was quite carried away and asked where her brothers were. They came to her straightaway and she leant over to their ears and told them to instigate a riot at the assembly and disrupt the hearing so that no conclusion could be made in the case.
>
> [Nú tók Gunnhildur ad ybba sig, og mælti til kóngs: "Varla hæfir þér herra að vera, því þú ert oflinur í lund þinni og vilt gjöra sem öllum líkar, og er þín heimska dæmalaus að þú vilt Egill þessi nái réttindum þar hann er sannreyndur níðingur og óvildarmaður þinn og flestra hér. En Önundur er besti maður innanlands, vinur okkar, og þú lætur á hann ganga rangan dóm fyrir lygiframburð skálda og bófa og er af þessu augljóst að þú hillir hann til skammarverka." Nú var drottning málóð og spyr hvar bræður sínir væri. Komu þeir til hennar skjótt og laut hún þeim í eyra og bað þá gjöra óspekt á þinginu og riðla í sundur dómi so ei yrði ályktan gjörð á málið.][6]

This example amply illustrates one characteristic of "New Egil's Saga," namely that conversations are wordier and prone to hyperbole (cf. "you let him incur a wrongful judgment because of false testimony from rhymesters and thugs"). The vocabulary is very different from the medieval version, and the syntax is characterized by long sentences with paratactic clauses connected by *og* ("and"). The narrative in this way gains its own special flavour but the sequence of events is usually preserved, as may be seen in the passage describing Thorolf Kveldulfsson's death:

> Let's leave these brothers for a while and recount that as soon as Hallvard and Sigtrygg had left, King Harald prepared his retinue. His temper was fierce and he made ready to leave with one ship and 360 men and set off in a vengeful, brutal

state of mind. He ordered all sails to be hoisted full-mast, never to be lowered no matter what, and this was done. They came late at night east to Hálogaland and docked at Sandnes where Thorolf lived. The King had his Viking-ship moored and ordered everyone to step ashore and take to arms. This was done immediately. The men saw a ship floating in the harbour complete with cargo and all the trappings, for Thorolf had planned to sail away, but he didn't know about the arrival of the King and sat with all his men drinking, leaving no one outside.

King Harald marched on the farm with his men; he had a white banner raised in the middle of his troops and ordered them to surround the farmhouse. Thorolf's men heard there was an army outside making loud noises and clinking weapons. They reached for their own weapons hastily, as did Thorolf himself, girdling his sword. Many of the King's men had gathered outside the men's entrance so no one dared nor was allowed to exit the building.

The King shouted to those inside and offered all women and children safe passage out of the house. Thorolf's wife heard this and came out, as did the other women. When she came round to the men's entrance she said to the King's retinue:

"Is Olvir Rough here with the King? I would like to speak with him."

Olvir heard this and came forward saying: "What is it you want to talk about?"

The lady said: "Take me to the King so I can present my case to him."

Olvir took her by the hand and led her to the King. She was in a sorrowful mood.

When the King saw her he said: "What is it you seek from us?"

She answered: "I would like to plead for mercy on behalf of Thorolf, my husband, so that your anger might be stilled and he would be spared."

The King said: "If Thorolf is prepared to come to me and ask for peace, acknowledging his overbearing actions against me and willing to be my faithful servant as long as he shall live, then he may keep his life as you ask."

Olvir went to the farmhouse and told Thorolf the terms laid down by the King.

Upon hearing those Thorolf said: "I will sooner drop dead to the ground than be his slave for the rest of my days. Tell the King that I seek his permission for my men and me to come out and fight. May he win whom Fate chooses. It is furthermore to be expected that the King would rather be victorious through bravery than through the cowardice of a villain."

Olvir relayed Thorolf's words to the King.

When the King heard this, he said that there was nothing to Thorolf but arrogance and ambition and he ordered his men to set fire to the farm immediately and burn it down "since it is obvious that should this evil Viking manage to get out he will deplete our ranks, for I am well acquainted with his great strength. If he finds the chance to get at us we will surely die."

All four walls of the farmhouse were made of wood and fire was therefore lit on all sides. Thorolf's men were in the main hall and Thorolf ordered them to break out through the west-facing gable. All able-bodied men struck at it together but it required great force before the gable collapsed and Thorolf stepped out together with Thorgils. They were followed by all able men. They were exhausted from the heat and smoke but were met by a great army of men. A fierce battle ensued with the King's men attacking them from outside but the fire seeking to destroy them from behind. Many of Thorolf's men were killed, as was to be expected. He had more than 80 men under arms. Many of the King's men fell as well. As Thorolf saw his men succumbing, his courage swelled; he struck equally fast on either side killing many a brave man. He slew one after the other so that no one was able to resist him. When Thorolf saw Thorgils, his companion, being struck down dead he was greatly upset and in a fury he broke through the ranks of the enemy all the way to where the King's standard was being carried. He attacked the standard-bearer and pierced him through his chest, so that the sword came out through his back, then sent him flying a long way off the sword. Thorolf was now exposed so the King's men attacked him and stabbed him as best they could; his own men were already slain, most of them. He was exhausted and wounded from fighting against the odds but he still wanted to get to the King. Harald saw it coming and attacked Thorolf with his spear. Thorolf was unable to counter the King's blow because he was being attacked by so many men that he was unable to fend everybody off. The spear passed through him and he dropped dead. The King was gladdened by this and offered truce to those who had survived. He ordered his men to go to the beach and set sails, "for we have won a precious victory, but Olvir Rough is to bury Thorolf's body and the bodies of his companions and see to the wounds of those who are alive."

The King embarked and said to his men: "Here lost his life the noblest man I know to have been in Norway – it is a great loss. I have yet to see a man who surpassed him in any field." King Harald sailed home to Trondheim and rested. People said his journey had been a great enterprise.

[Nú skal bíða um þessi bræður en hitt greina að Haraldur kóngur býr út sinn her strax sem þeir bræður burt voru. Var kóngur með grimmri lund og bjóst nú með þrjú hundruð manna og eitt skip og hélt nú af stað með einu skemmdarfullu skálksgeði, lét setja öll segl við hún en lægja aldrei hvað sem á gangi. Var nú so gjört sem kóngur bauð. Komu nú síð að kvöldi austur á Hálogaland og tóku höfn við Sandnes þar Þórúlfur byggði. Lét kóngur festa sinn dreka og bað nú allt fólk á land ganga og vopnast. Var þetta fljótt gjört. Nú sjá menn þar skip fyrir fljóta á höfninni með farmi og öllum tilbúnaði, því Þórúlfur hafði stefnu sett af landi að halda en vissi ei um ferðir kóngs heldur sat hann við drykkjuborð og menn hans allir so einginn var úti staddur.

Gekk nú Haraldur kóngur að bænum með fylktu liði og setti upp hvítt merki í miðjum hernum og lét nú slá hring um bæinn. Nú heyrðu menn Þórúlfs þetta, að herfólk er úti komið með háreysti og vopnaglamri. Hlupu nú menn til vopna sem hann og sjálfur, gyrti sig sverði. Var þröngt mjög fyrir karldyrum af mönnum kóngs so einginn þorði né fékk út að ganga.

Kóngur kallaði í bæinn og mælti að allar konur og börn mættu að frjálsu útganga ef vildu. Þetta heyrði húsfrú Þórúlfs og gekk út og allar hinar sem þar voru. Sem húsfreyja kom fyrir karldyrnar mælti hún til kóngs manna:

"Ef Ölvir hrjúfa er hér með kóngi vil eg tala við hann."

Nú heyrði Ölvir þetta og gekk til húsfreyju og mælti: "Hvað viltu tala við mig?"

Húsfreyja mælti: "Leið mig til kóngs að eg megi tjá hönum erendi mitt."

Tók nú Ölvir í hönd henni og leiddi fyrir kónginn. Nú var húsfreyja sorgandi.

Kóngur mælti er hann sá hana: "Hvörs viltu af oss óska?"

Hún mælti: "Það er mitt erendi að biðja þig griða fyrir Þórúlf bónda minn so þín reiði mætti stillast en hann feingi náð."

Kóngur mælti: "Vilji Þórúlfur ganga til mín og biðja friðar og ofgjört hafa öll sín stórræði við mig og vera minn þénari so leingi hann lifir með trú og staðfestu, má hann þá halda lífi sem þú biður."

Nú gekk Ölvir í bæinn og innir Þórúlfi kosti sem kóngur gjörði.

Sem Þórúlfur heyrði þetta mælti hann: "Fyrr skal eg dauður að velli hníga en vera þræll hans so leingi sem eg lifi. Og seig þú kóngi eg biðji hann leyfis að eg og mínir menn mættu útganga, og hafi sá sigur sem auðnan vill. Er og líklegt að kóngur vilji með frægð vinna en ei sem níðingur sá öngva manndáð hefur."

Nú innir Ölvir þetta aftur kóngi er Þórúlfur hafði mælt.

Sem kóngur þetta heyrði kvað hann Þórúlf fullan metnaðar og drambsemi og skipaði skjótt að bera eld að bænum og brenna á báli "því auðséð er það, komist þessi illi víkingur út er oss manntjón búið því ég þekki gjörla hans mikla afl. Megi hann því við koma er oss dauði búinn."

Var nú eldur borinn öllu megin að bænum því veggir voru allir af timbri. Voru menn Þórúlfs í stofunni og bað nú Þórúlfur menn sína að ganga á gaflþil stofunnar sem út horfði og brjóta það. Geingu nú að allir menn sem þrótt höfðu og var það aflraun stór, þar til allur gafl hrundi til jarðar og gekk Þórúlfur út fyrstur manna sinna og Þorgils, síðan hvör sem kunni. Voru þeir móðir mjög af eldi og svælu en var fyrir þeim her óvígur og tókst nú snarpur aðgangur því kóngs menn sóttu að utan en eldurinn sótti að þeim á bak til. Féll margur af Þórúlfi sem von var til. Voru með honum meir en 80 vopnfærir. Féllu nú margir kóngs menn líka. Nú sér Þórúlfur að menn hans falla; þrútnaði nú af móði og hjó á tvær hendur sér og hné nú margur að velli þó karskur færi. Hjó hann nú hvörn að öðrum so enginn kunni í móti að standa. Nú sér Þórúlfur að Þorgils maður hans hné dauður niður og eirði því illa og reiddist ákaflega og rauf alla fylking kóngs að merki og hitti nú þann merkið bar og lagði til hans inn um brjóst og út um bakið og snaraði honum langan veg af sverðsoddi. Nú var hann hlífarlaus og hjuggu nú kóngsmenn Þórúlf og lögðu sem hvör kunni, voru og fallnir flestir hans menn. Var nú bæði móður og sár við slíkt ofurefli en þó vildi Þórúlfur hitta kónginn. Sér nú Haraldur þetta og lagði til Þórúlfs sínu spjóti. Kunni Þórúlfur ei kóngi að mæta því so margir sóttu að honum að hann kunni ei öllum mæta. Gekk spjótið í gegnum hann og féll hann dauður niður. Gladdist kóngur við þetta og bauð öllum grið sem eftir stóðu. Kóngur bauð nú sínum mönnum ofan til strandar ganga og halda burt þaðan, "því vér höfum náð dýrum sigri, en Ölvir hrjúfa skal greftra líki Þórúlfs og hinna er með hönum voru en græða þá lífs eru."

Gekk nú kóngur á skip og mælti til manna sinna: "Hér hefur fallið hinn frægsti maður er eg veit nú í Noregi var og skaði stór var að slíkum manni og ei hef eg séð þann er neinar listir af hönum bar." Hélt nú Haraldur heim í Þrándheim og tók náðir. Þótti mönnum ferð hans rausnarmikil orðið hafa. (AM 454 4to, 13v–15v)]

This account is on the whole faithful to the medieval story: King Harald sails to Sandnes in a hurry and arrives in the evening. Thorolf has prepared his ship for departure and all his men are inside drinking. The king surrounds the homestead but allows women and children out. Sigrid seeks to intervene with the help of Olvir but Thorolf is defiant. The king orders the homestead to be burnt down and Thorolf and his men manage to break out. In the ensuing battle Thorolf tries to get to the king but is killed (by the king) before he reaches him. The main thread of the narrative is thus firmly in place but we also see here clearly some of the main characteristics of this version.

The author has for instance little sense of the geography of Norway as is evident in the wording "east to Halogaland" ("austur til Hálogalands"). This is repeated often in the saga, where pretty much every place seems to be in the East. "New Egil's Saga" also exhibits odd versions of names; in the passage above the nickname of Olvir Hump (*hnúfa)* is Rough (*hrjúfa*), elsewhere Ketil Haeng is called Hring, Earl Adils acquires the name of the heretic Arius, and the nickname of Thorgeir Thorn-foot (*þyrnifótr*) becomes Thunder-bolt (*þrumhnöttur)*. Some of these changes suggest a misreading of a manuscript. The conversation between the king, Olvir, Sigrid, and Thorolf is wordier than in the medieval version and the vocabulary more charged. The king refers to Thorolf as "evil Viking" ("illur víkingur," 14v11) and the narrator uses the words "in a vengeful, brutal state of mind" ("með skemmdarfullu skálksgeði," 13v9–10) to describe the king's mood. The judgment of characters is therefore much more pronounced than in the medieval *Egil's Saga* and is expressed both through the words of other characters and through the narrator's voice. Throughout "New Egil's Saga" one senses the author's love of battle descriptions, to which the passage above is no exception. These battle scenes are, however, quite standardized and clichéed; they serve to showcase the hero (or heroes) whose prowess is measured by how far he can throw the corpses of victims from his spear or by the number of men he butchers.

Just as the author of "New Egil's Saga" is unconcerned about Norwegian topography, he is equally reluctant to introduce into his tale any more characters than are absolutely necessary. He therefore skips genealogies for the most part and does not dwell on prehistory in Norway or the lineage of the settlers of Iceland. He also lacks an instinct for crucial scenes and memorable one-liners. In the passage quoted above we do not hear Thorolf utter the words: "I took three steps too few here" (36: "Nú gekk ek þremr fótum til skammt," 54), nor is it mentioned that Thorolf falls on his chest after the king kills him. In the medieval *Egil's Saga* Kveldulf interprets this fact as foretelling that Thorolf will be revenged, but Kveldulf's remark is omitted from "New Egil's Saga" as well. Subtle hints are thus often suppressed. But sometimes the reverse happens: information is made explicit, and this is done by the narrator of the story, not the characters. The narrator also describes the feelings of the characters, such as: "Rage for vengeance now entered Grim's breast" ("Kom nú heiftar reiði í brjóst Grími," 20r17–18).

Because the author of "New Egil's Saga" is reluctant to complicate the story and overcrowd his cast of characters, he fails to appreciate how intricately the plot is woven in the medieval saga. He skips for example the episode about Bjorgolf in Torgar and his forced marriage to Hildirid. They are the parents of Hildirid's sons and the history of the marriage has a crucial bearing on the story for two reasons. First, it explains the animosity of Hildirid's sons towards Thorolf, since in their view he denies them what they see as their rightful inheritance. Second, the inheritance dispute between the brothers and Thorolf serves as a parallel to Egil's fight for Asgerd's inheritance later in the story. The mechanisms that drive the plot in the medieval saga are thus often absent in "New Egil's Saga," which relies for its effect more on exuberant descriptions of plundering and combat.

Another omission in "New Egil's Saga" robs readers of the psychologically charged description of Egil's reaction to his brother's marriage to Asgerd (105–14: 71–8; cf. Helgason 1992). Egil doesn't go to the wedding, feigning illness, but then goes to Atley where memorable scenes of drinking and vomiting ensue before he ends up killing Bard, King Eirik's and Gunnhild's man. In "New Egil's Saga" the visit to Atley is conflated with Egil's (and Thorolf's) raiding in Courland, leaving out the grotesque scenes at Bard's. The reason for this significant omission is unclear; the Atley episode is recounted in the *rímur*, but since it is likely that the author of "New Egil's Saga" was also working from a manuscript of the saga it is possible that some leaves were simply missing from it at this point. Another reason might be a distaste for the Atley episode, but such an explanation is undermined by the fact that the author of "New Egil's Saga" does not seem to shrink from indelicate scenes elsewhere. Indeed, he even adds to the harrowing account of the "scorn-pole" (119: *níðstöng*, 171) the detail that it was the head of Rognvald, the king's son, that Egil mounted on the pole:[7]

> Egil climbed a hill called Smálsarhorn. There he erected a pole, put the prince's head upon it and carved runes all over the pole with scornful remarks about King Eirik and Queen Gunnhild, expressing the wish that their unhappiness and bad luck should increase bringing the direst ill fortune, that ignominy and derision should come their way with destitution and death, and that all Gunnhild's curses should be turned against herself and the King and their offspring. And Egil composed a drápa about this with spells and ancient evil sayings and he conjured all the elements, trolls, and all evil spirits to make it come to pass and stated that the poem related to Queen Gunnhild and King Eirik. When Egil had carved everything he wanted on the pole the head on the pole began to gape and blow ill wind in the direction where the King and Queen were, and the pole shook with rage.
>
> [Gekk Egill á eitt berg sem Smálsarhorn heitir. Þar reisti hann upp stöng og setti höfuð kóngssonar á hana ofan og risti rúnastafi um alla stöngina með illum ummælum yfir Eireki kóngi og Gunnhildi, að öll óhamingja skyldi þeim aukast og lukkuleysi með þeim verstu ókjörum og til þeirra hverfa alls kyns smán og fyrirlitning með ráni og dauða, og skyldi öll ill orð Gunnhildar á henni hrína og kóngi sjálfum og þeirra niðjum. Og hér um orti Egill drápu með særingum og ljótum fornyrðum og særði það við öll element, við tröll og allar illar kindur, og kvað hróðurinn heyra til Gunnhildi drottningu og Eireki kóngi. Sem Egill hafði nú þetta mjög á stöngina rist sem honum sýndist, tók höfuðið á stönginni að sperra upp kjaftinn og illum anda að blása í þá átt sem Eirekur kóngur og drottning var, en stöngin hristist með æði. (59v–60r)]

6

Let us now turn to the ending in "New Egil's Saga." It will hardly come as a surprise, knowing what we do about the variation between the medieval versions, that the final part of "New Egil's Saga" diverges considerably from the older texts. In the new version the feud between Thorstein Egilsson and Steinar Sjonason is prolonged, with added emphasis on battles. It is also interesting that children are given more prominence here, as can be seen in the account of the killing of Grim, Thorstein's son. There is a longer build-up to this event in "New Egil's Saga," including this delightful scene between father and son after the feast at Alftanes:

> In the morning on that same day Thorstein Egilsson set off from Alftanes and thanked Audun for his hospitality. He mounted his horse and Grim, his son, accompanied him. When they had travelled for quite a while Thorstein said to his son: "I don't know what's going on, one minute I am shaking all over but the next I am far too warm."
>
> The boy answered: "There is no need to feel surprise, this must be due to the ale and the copious drinking you engaged in with Farmer Audun."
>
> Thorstein said: "That is possible, but I suspect otherwise. If I had enemies or adversaries it would seem to me that they were somewhere near and their animosity is making itself felt. Should I happen to be right about this, we must react bravely, you shall stand behind my back and try to hinder anyone from injuring me. But I'll counter all blows and defend you as long as I endure and you must never leave the position where I have ordered you to be but follow me so that we are never parted."
>
> Thorstein took his shield on his arm and loosened his sword in the scabbard. He gave the boy a big axe, one ell wide across the blade, which King Eirik had sent to Skallagrim as was told before.
>
> [Þennan sama dag að morgni reið Þorsteinn Egilsson burt frá Álftanesi og þakkaði Auðuni greiða sinn. Sté nú á sinn hest og Grímur son hans fylgdi hönum. Og sem þeir hafa langan tíma riðið mælti Þorsteinn til sveinsins: "Ei veit eg hvörju það gegnir að eg þykist allur skjálfa, en aðra stund er mér öllum ofheitt sem ofbjóði."
>
> Sveinninn mælti: "Það mun ei nema af öli og kófdrykkju er þú hefur lengi haft með Auðun bónda og lát þig ei slíkt undra."
>
> Þorsteinn mælti: "Vera má að so sé, en annað segir mér hugur um þetta. Hefði eg átt ófriðarmenn eður óvini nálæga mundi mér þykja líkast þeir væri okkur ei fjærri, og mun þeirra heiftar hugur bíta mig, og mætti so til bera sem eg sagt hefi skulum við verða við vasklega, og skaltu standa að baki mínu, og sjá um ef getur að enginn kunni mig særa. En eg vil taka við öllum slögum og verja þig so lengi sem líf endist en far þú hvörgi þaðan sem eg skikka þér heldur láttu berast eftir mér so við skiljum alldrei."

Nú armaði Þorsteinn sinn skjöld og losaði sitt sverð í slíðrum. En piltinum fékk hann öxi stóra sem alin var fyrir munnann. Þá öxi hafði Eirekur kóngur blóðöxi sent áður Skallagrími sem fyrr greinir. (101v–102r)]

The emphasis is, as before, on courage in battle and the passage also exhibits fascination with weapons and their history. Grim participates valiantly in the ensuing encounter with Steinar and his men (which is described at length and includes a wordy diatribe between Steinar and Thorstein) and he manages to kill one of Steinar's men before being mortally wounded. In the medieval versions Grim is found wounded next to the body of Steinar's dead son but does not participate in the battle between the adults. The death of Grim then leads to Þorstein issuing an ultimatum to Steinar, who moves his farm to Snaefellsnes. In "New Egil's Saga" a new twist is added to the story, in which Thorstein rides to see his father at Mosfell after burying Grim. When Egil hears of Thorstein's dealings with Steinar he remarks:

"One thing has always hampered you, my son, you have never harboured the same manly courage that your forefathers had. You are such a great man when it comes to valour and masculinity, but your mind is placid and slow to react and it is most peculiar how long you are prepared to wait before you take your revenge on Steinar who has violated your trust and broken the agreement the two of you had reached, caused you injuries, and killed your son to boot. Had I been near I would have engaged in the game with you two even though I am getting old. Would you like me to ride west to Snaefellsnes with you and redress your rights on your behalf?"

["Ætíð hefur einn hlutur skaðað þinn hag, Þorsteinn sonur minn, sem er að þú hefur aldrei haft það rétta karlmannsgeð sem forfeður þínir áður, so mikill maður sem þú ert til hreysti og karlmennsku, en hugur þinn er seinn og ófljótur til aðgjörða og er það hin mestu undur að þú lætur þetta lengi óhefnt á Steinar er hann sveik þig í tryggðum ofan á búna sátt og skilmála áður gjörðan í milli ykkar og drap þar á ofan son þinn en særði þig og hefða eg nær þér verið skyldi eg hafa komið í leik með ykkur þó eg nú gamall gjörist. Eða viltu nú son minn eg ríði vestur með þér og rétti hluta þinn?" (106r–v)]

Thorstein declines this generous offer and incurs further accusations of cowardice in return. The author, however, desires to see Egil once more "in the game" ("í leik"), so he has Steinar arrange an attack on Mosfell. The story has already introduced the young Thorolf, son of Grim and Thordis at Mosfell, a boy of fifteen whom, the narrator tells us, Egil "loved dearly" ("unni mikið").

Steinar and his men plan to arrive at Mosfell by stealth, but their discussion is overheard by a shepherd from Mosfell, who divulges everything to Egil (Grim, the head of the household, happens to be away). Egil, Thorolf, and the rest of the household prepare for battle, which is Egil's last chance to show his mettle and also an initiation for young Thorolf. Naturally they emerge victorious, although Steinar escapes with his life, and Thorolf has proven to Egil that he is a real man. Soon after this Egil also learns that his son Thorstein has stepped up to the challenge and killed Steinar, prompting this remark from Egil:

> It was never any surprise for me that my son Thorstein should prove himself a match for any man in Iceland in terms of valour and masculinity, but he is so slow to react that it is as if he were sleepwalking.
>
> [Aldrei kom mér það óvart að Þorsteinn sonur minn væri nógu gildur fyrir hvörn einn á Íslandi til hreysti og karlmennsku, en hann er seinn til aðgjörða sem hann dreymi. (122v)]

The machismo that is so prominent a theme in the portrayal of Egil and his descendants in "New Egil's Saga" is subsequently underlined in a chapter in which Egil's grandchildren are paraded before him. He finds Thorstein's sons Bodvar and Helgi adequate but not likely to match their ancestors in prowess. When Thorgerd Egilsdottir presents her two older sons Egil suspects them of harbouring "a woman's mind in a man's breast" ("konuhug í karlmannsbrjósti," 124v5). She then presents her youngest, Kjartan Olafsson, who gets full marks from his grandfather and the sword Dragvandill to boot.

The final episode in "New Egil's Saga" shows a blind old man, as do the medieval versions, but in a very different situation:

> One day in the Spring, when all the men at Mosfell had left the farm on their errands, it happened that a horse had died and lay in front of the doors blocking the entrance and causing the women to complain bitterly that they couldn't shift it. When Egil heard this he got up – he was completely blind by this time – and the women led him to where the horse lay. He grabbed the hind legs of the horse and yanked it from the doors so forcefully that the intestines burst out of the carcass. There was a river by the homestead. In the middle of the river was an islet covered in scrub.
>
> Egil said: "Is the coast clear?"
>
> The women confirmed that it was. Egil then took the horse by the hind legs and threw it across the river so that it landed on the bank.
>
> Egil asked: "Where did it end up?"

The women said it was on the other bank of the river.

Egil said: "I aimed for the scrub."

Egil went to his bed and lived not long thereafter. He died at Mosfell and was buried there. We do not have more to say about him than what is recorded here and so ends the saga of Egil Skallagrimsson.

[Það var einn tíma um vorið að allir karlmenn voru heiman farnir frá Mosfelli til erinda sinna, að hestur einn lá í bænum að Mosfelli um þverar dyr dauður, so ei var hægt að ganga hjá, en konum varð mjög að orðum um það þær kæmi honum ei í burt. Sem Egill þetta heyrði gekk hann á fætur, og var hann þá allsendis blindur, og leiddu konur hann þangað sem hesturinn lá dauður, og tók hann um afturfætur hestsins og rykkti honum í einu út á hlað svo út gengu garnir. Á rann ein fyrir neðan túnið. Hólmi var í miðri ánni og víðir í hólmanum.

Egill mælti: "Er nú ei neitt fyrir?"

En konur kváðu svo vera. Egill tók nú í afturfætur hestsins og kastaði honum svo hann kom yfir alla ána og í bakkann hinumegin.

Egill mælti: "Hvar kom hann niður?"

En konur kváðu hann komið hafa í bakkann hinumegin hólmans.

Egill mælti: "Í víðirinn ætlaði eg honum."

Gekk Egill til rekkju sinnar og lifði ei lengi úr því. Dó hann að Mosfelli, og var hann þar heygður. Ei höfum vér meira af honum að segja en hér er skrifað og ljúkum so þessari sögu af Egli Skallagrímssyni. (125r–v)]

Whereas in the medieval A-version Egil is told off by the cook at Mosfell for being in her way in the kitchen, here it is a dead horse that gets in the women's way and Egil himself who sees to their problem. "New Egil's Saga" contains none of the anecdotes about Egil's old age that are found (varyingly) in other versions, and which the writer must have known from the *rímur*. His final stanzas are not here (in fact "New Egil's Saga" leaves out all the poetry attributed to Egil), no mention is made of the silver, and there is no account of the church-building at Mosfell and the resurfacing of the old man's skull and bones. The final chapter about Egil's descendants is also left out, which is very much in tune with the disregard for his ancestors in the first part of the saga.

The "looseness" at the end of *Egil's Saga* that is already apparent in the medieval tradition is therefore very much in evidence here. It seems to me likely that various anecdotes about Egil must have circulated, sometimes attached to a stanza attributed to him. These anecdotes would most naturally be set in Iceland and would therefore fit best into the last part of the saga, after Egil's career abroad as a Viking had finished and his disputes in Norway had been settled. People who were recreating the story, whether orally or in writing, could thus pick and choose to a certain extent, stringing episodes together as best suited them or their audience. The last part of *Egil's Saga* is in this way not very different from saints' lives, with miracles that could be amplified or abridged as need dictated. The medieval versions of *Egil's Saga* even include one "miracle *post mortem*" in the scene when Egil's bones are exhumed. It is left out of "New Egil's Saga," as already mentioned, but in the Oslo manuscript, there is an addition: the tale of a woman at Borg in the days of Bishop Arni Thorlaksson, who is visited in her dream by a young man who leads her into a mound where a feast is under way. One man at the feast is larger than all the others. He is the father of the young man and recites a verse. When the woman wakes up she remembers the verse and recites it to Bishop Arni, who recognizes in it the poetic language of Egil Skallagrimsson. The annalist and scribe Björn Jónsson á Skarðsá (1574–1655) included the story in his copy of *Árna saga biskups* ("Saga of Bishop Árni") with this remark: "The following is in old books of lore a short addendum to the story of Egil Skallagrimsson, although we record it here" ("Þetta eftirfylgjandi úr gömlum fræðibókum viðbætirskorn sögunnar Eiglu Skallagrímssonar þó hér sé sett," Grímsdóttir 1998, 210).[8] Egil Skallagrimsson clearly continued to inspire stories from beyond the grave.

7

What are we to make of Egil's afterlife in the seventeenth century? What was the appeal of this text? Who read it? If we look at the geographical origins of the *rímur* and the likely provenance of "New Egil's Saga," it is the district around Breiðafjörður that comes into focus. Interestingly, this is also the area where Ketill Jörundsson lived and where the first edition of *Egil's Saga* was printed in the late eighteenth century. Ketill, and other scribes of his ilk, often priests, followed in the footsteps of the humanist Arngrímur Jónsson lærði and were keen to preserve early sources for the history of Iceland. Copies of the medieval *Egil's Saga* were obviously in circulation around Breiðafjörður in the seventeenth century, as the manuscript tradition of the C-version shows. Are we then to think of the *rímur* and "New Egil's Saga" as some sort of vulgarization of the old tradition, texts produced for people of less good taste, for the common man perhaps? Making such assumptions would be barking up the wrong tree, however, as is evident if one considers the patrons behind the production and dissemination of *Egils rímur* and "New Egil's Saga." They were people from the upper classes. The *rímur* were composed for one of the wealthiest men in Iceland at the time, the sheriff Eggert Björnsson, and the AM manuscript which contains them passed from its scribe through the hands of a lawman, Magnús Björnsson, and the son of a bishop, Gísli Jónsson, before Árni Magnússon acquired it. The manuscripts of "New Egil's Saga" had a similar journey: the Oslo manuscript was owned by the sheriff Jón Árnason at Ingjaldshóll on Snæfellsnes, whereas AM 454 4to was copied from a manuscript which was written by Sigurður Jónsson (1633–1717), lawman in Snæfellsnes, and owned by yet another sheriff, Ólafur Einarsson at Þykkvibær in the south of Iceland.[9]

It is therefore easy to imagine that "New Egil's Saga" owed its birth to an antiquarian interest in Old Icelandic sources that blossomed in the seventeenth century and drew the sagas into the limelight again. Their readers, however, wanted literature that was more to their taste and hence had the old story of Egil recast, first as *rímur*, then in the mould of late pre-modern heroic sagas (*kappasögur*), with copious battles, ringing swords, and flying corpses. At the centre of all the versions is the indomitable figure of Egil Skallagrimsson who manages to bring unity to these works, however tenuous it sometimes may seem.[10]

NOTES

1 On this topic see also Finlay's essay in this volume.

2 For a comparison of the two versions, see Poole 1993.

3 In his statistical analysis of *Egil's Saga* Ralph West found the style of the last part of the saga to deviate from the rest (West 1980, 191). I thank Vésteinn Ólason for pointing this out to me.

4 The full text of the note runs: "I recollect that I have [a note?] somewhere, according to the account of Sigurður of Knór, that he wrote this saga of Egil following the learned Gísli of Melrakkadalur, and consequently Gísli is the undoubted author of the book. Gísli was certainly a blatant impostor. But Sigurður was a honest man" ("Mig minner, eg hafi einhversstadar, epter sógu Sigurdar ä Knór, ad hann þessa Egilssógu ritad hafi epter hendi lærda Gisla i Melrackadal, og er þä Gisle, öefad author bokarinar. Gisle var ad vïsu sannreyndr impostor. Enn Sigurdur var frömur madr," AM 454 4to, on a slip bound with the ms.).

5 I am grateful to Þórður Ingi Guðjónsson for pointing this out to me. The shelfmarks for the *Bandamanna saga* part and the *Gisla saga* parts are AM 162 o fol. and AM 162 p fol. respectively.

6 AM 454 4to, 55r–v, subsequent quotations are from this manuscript.

7 This makes Egil's attack against the head of state explicit, even *ofljóst*; cf. Kristjánsdóttir 1997, 87.

8 The story was also recorded by Jón Guðmundsson lærði in his Tíðfordríf (AM 727 4to, 16v–17r). I am indebted to Einar G. Pétursson for this information.

9 It is interesting to note in this respect that among the few details about minor characters in the saga that are retained in "New Egil's Saga" are those about men who became law-speakers.

10 I would like to thank M.J. Driscoll, Guðvarður Már Gunnlaugsson, Þórður Tómasson, Guðný Valberg, and Unnar Ingvarsson for their help in tracking down material for this study, and Margrét Eggertsdóttir for her constructive reading of the article and the many conversations we have had about scribal culture in the seventeenth century. I have had the opportunity to present some of this material at seminars at the Russian Academy of Sciences in Moscow, the Centre for Medieval Studies at the University of Bergen, and at Stofnun Árna Magnússonar í íslenskum fræðum as well as at the conference *The Hyperborean Muse* in Verona, and I am grateful to the organizers of these gatherings and to the participants for their comments.

BIBLIOGRAPHY

Manuscripts

AM 454 4to (Stofnun Árna Magnússonar, Reykjavík)
AM 610 a 4to (Stofnun Árna Magnússonar, Reykjavík)

Printed sources

Andersson, Theodore. 1967. *The Icelandic Family Saga: An Analytic Reading.* Cambridge, MA: Harvard University Press.

Chesnutt, Michael. 2005. "Tekstkritiske bemærkninger til C-redaktionen af Egils saga." *Opuscula* XII. 228–62. Copenhagen: Reitzel.

– ed. 2006. *Egils saga Skallagrímssonar. Bind III. C-redaktionen.* Editiones Arnamagnæanæ Series A, vol. 21. Copenhagen: Reitzel.

Clunies Ross, Margaret. 2010. "Verse and Prose in *Egils saga Skallagrímssonar*." In *Creating the Medieval Saga: Versions, Variability and Editorial Interpretations of Old Norse Saga Literature*. Ed. Judy Quinn and Emily Lethbridge, 191–211. The Viking Collection 18. Odense: University Press of Southern Denmark.

Grímsdóttir, Guðrún Ása, ed. 1998. *Biskupa sögur III.* Íslenzk fornrit XVII. Reykjavík: Hið íslenzka fornritafélag.

Halldórsson, Óskar, ed. 1967. *Egils saga.* Reykjavík: Skálholt.

Helgason, Jón. 1956a. "Athuganir um nokkur handrit Egils sögu." In *Nordæla. Afmæliskveðja til Sigurðar Nordals.* Reykjavík. 110–48. [English translation 2005:

"Observations on Some Manuscripts of Egils saga." Transl. Michael Chesnutt, 3–47. *Opuscula* XII. Copenhagen: Reitzel.]

– ed. 1956b. *The Saga Manuscript 9. 10. Aug. 4to in the Herzog August Library Wolfenbüttel.* Manuscripta Islandica III. Copenhagen: Munksgaard.

Helgason, Jón Karl. 1992. "'Rjóðum spjöll í dreyra.' Óhugnaður, úrkast og erótík í *Egils sögu.*" *Skáldskaparmál* 2: 60–76.

Jónsson, Finnur, ed. 1886–8. *Egils saga Skallagrímssonar tilligemed Egils större kvad.* STUAGNL. Copenhagen: Møller.

Karlsson, Stefán. 1964. "Gömul hljóðdvöl í ungum rímum." *Íslenzk tunga* 5: 7–27.

– 1995. "Af Agli í ellinni." In *Vöruvoð ofin Helga Þorlákssyni fimmtugum 8. ágúst 1995.* 70–2. Reykjavík: Menningar- og minningarsjóður Mette Magnussen.

Kristjánsdóttir, Bergljót S. 1997. "Primum caput: Um höfuð Egils Skalla-Grímssonar, John frá Salisbury o.fl." *Skáldskaparmál* 4: 74–96.

Kristjánsson, Jónas. 1967. *Skrá um íslenzk handrit í Noregi.* Reykjavík: Handritastofnun Íslands. [Typescript.]

Poole, Russell G. 1993. "Variants and Variability in the Text of Egill's Hǫfuðlausn." *The Politics of Editing Medieval Texts.* Ed. Roberta Frank, 65–105. New York: AMS Press.

Tulinius, Torfi H. 2001. "The Prosimetrum Form 2: Verses as the Basis for Saga Composition and Interpretation." *Skaldsagas. Text, Vocation, and Desire in the Icelandic Sagas of Poets.* Ed. Russell Poole, 191–217. Berlin: De Gruyter.

– 2004. *Skáldið í skriftinni. Snorri Sturluson og Egils saga.* Reykjavík: Hið íslenska bókmenntafélag/Reykjavíkur Akademían.

Speed-Kjeldsen, Alex, ed. 2005. "AM 162 A Θ fol (Reykjavík)." *Opuscula* XII. 183–208. Copenhagen: Reitzel.

West, Ralph. 1980. "Snorri Sturluson and *Egils saga*: Statistics of Style." *Scandinavian Studies* 52/2: 163–93.

11 Bloody Runes: The Transgressive Poetics of *Egil's Saga*[1]

JÓN KARL HELGASON

Poetry leads to the same place as all forms of eroticism – to the blending and fusion of separate objects. It leads us to eternity, it leads us to death, and through death to continuity.

Georges Bataille

Have you ever wondered how the drink of poetry really tastes? According to Snorri Sturluson's *Prose Edda*, it was initially a mixture of spittle of the Æsir-gods and the Vanir. A man named Kvasir was made from this liquid, and after he was killed mead was brewed from his blood and honey. Odin later drank the mead and spewed it out again. He also sent "some of the mead backwards, … the rhymester's share" (Sturluson 1987, 64: "sendi aptr suman mjǫðinn, … skáldfífla *hlut," Sturluson 1998, 1:79), but the better part of it would still have gone through the stages of spittle, blood, and vomit before skilled poets could complete the process of brewing by delivering their wonderful poems.

It has been argued that Snorri shaped this narrative in accordance with his own taste and purposes when he made it a part of the *Edda* (cf. Frank 1981). All the same, his account is an interesting description of the nature of poetic language, crossing the borders between what is pure and impure, creative and destructive. From that perspective, the tale of the poetic mead may have inspired another Icelandic medieval text, that of *Egil's Saga*, which also contains repeated images of blood, mead, and vomit. The goal of this paper is to examine the transgressive poetics of the saga and the impact that it may have on its audience.

The topic suggested itself to me when I heard of a young Icelandic college student who felt sick and had to be excused from class after having heard her teacher read a chapter from the saga. I had not had this experience. On the contrary, I felt that *Egil's Saga* was an intriguing and masterfully constructed narrative. These different responses puzzled me for some time. How could the same literary text be a source of pleasure for one person and completely repulsive for another? In an attempt to deal with that question, I appropriate ideas from the works of Sigmund Freud, Julia Kristeva, and Georges Bataille. It seems that all of them could have agreed that the scenes of *Egil's Saga* were designed to make a strong and sometimes conflicting impact on the minds and even the bodies of its readers. But most probably they would have disagreed on what images and emotions are in play.

I

In his article "Das Unheimliche" (1919) Sigmund Freud defines *the uncanny* as that domain of the horrific which can be traced to the past: "An uncanny experience occurs either when repressed infantile complexes have been revived by some impressions, or when the primitive beliefs we have surmounted seem once more to be confirmed" (Freud 1966, 55). At the outset, Freud discusses the paradoxical sense of the German concept *das Heimliche*, which refers at the same time to that which is familiar and foreign, mysterious and horrific, even something that has been revealed but should have been hidden. He refers to various examples from the world of fiction to illustrate his point, making a note of the fact, however, that "in the first place a great deal that is not uncanny in fiction would be so if it happened in real life; and in the second place that there are many more means of creating uncanny effects in fiction than there are in real life" (1966, 56). The reason for this, Freud explains, is that through their unusual access to our minds as readers, writers are capable of manipulating our emotions with various descriptions of the uncanny.

The uncanny examples Freud refers to are of various natures, quite a few of which are relevant to *Egil's Saga*. Descriptions of blinded eyes, amputation, and decapitation are all likely to trigger uncanny emotions, in particular if a hand is cut close to the wrist or when amputated limbs show signs of life (1966, 49–50). In *Egil's Saga* we are told that Egil gouged out with his finger one of Armod Beard's eyes, "leaving it hanging on his cheek" (158: "svá at úti lá á kinninni," 228). Egil also chopped off the leg of Ljot the Pale in a duel on the island of Valdero (205: 141) and the leg of another adversary on the island of Saudoy (112; 76–7). He almost decapitated Berg-Onund (168: 116) and in one of his many skaldic verses he boasted: "we made bloody bodies / slump dead by city gates" (84: "létum blóðga búka / í borghliðum sœfask," 121). Early in the narrative, when Egil's uncle Thorolf was raiding a farm in Norway, a man named Thorgeir ran to a wooden fence surrounding the farm, grabbed one of the posts, and vaulted over it. One of Thorolf's men who was standing nearby, "swung his sword at Thorgeir and chopped off the hand that was holding onto the post" (32: "sveiflaði til sverðinu eptir Þorgeiri, ok kom á hǫndina og tók af við garðstaurinn," 48). The one-handed Thorgeir was still able to escape into the woods. Last but not least, the dispersal of the human body is celebrated in a verse that Skallagrim, Egil's father, speaks after he and his father Kveldulf have killed Hallvard Travel-hard and fifty of his crew: "Hallvard's corpse flew / in pieces into the sea" (47: "flugu hǫggvin hræ / Hallvarðs á sæ," 70).

Another uncanny element that can be applied to *Egil's Saga* is the idea of a double reality. In his article, Freud discusses the literary tradition of the *Doppelgänger* as well as the effect that repetitions of the same circumstances, characteristics, or even the same names in successive generations can have on us as readers (1966, 39–40). In the saga we come across the characterizations of Thorolf, the son of Kveldulf, on the one hand, and of Thorolf, the son of Skallagrim, on the other. The former is introduced on the first page of the first chapter:

> Thorolf was an attractive and highly accomplished man. He took after his mother's side of the family, a cheerful, generous man, energetic and very eager to prove his worth. He was popular with everyone. (4)
>
> [Var Þórólfr manna vænstr ok gørviligastr; hann var líkr móðurfrændum sínum, gleðimaðr mikill, ǫrr ok ákafamaðr mikill í ǫllu ok hinn mesti kappsmaðr; var hann vinsæll af ǫllum mǫnnum. (5)]

His brother's son and namesake is introduced later in the saga:

> He was big and handsome from an early age, and everyone said he most resembled Kveldulf's son Thorolf, after whom he had been named. Thorolf far excelled boys of his age in strength, and when he grew up he became accomplished in most of the skills that it was customary for gifted men to practice. He was a cheerful character and so powerful in his youth that he was considered just as able-bodied as any grown man. He was popular with everyone. (54)
>
> [En er hann fœddisk upp, þá var hann snimma mikill vexti ok inn vænsti sýnum; var þat allra manna mál, at hann myndi vera inn líkasti Þórólfi Kveld-Úlfssyni, er hann var eptir heitinn. Þórólfr var langt um fram jafnaldra sína at afli; en er hann óx upp, gerðisk hann íþróttamaðr um flesta þá hluti, er þá var mǫnnum títt að

fremja, þeim er vel váru at sér gǫrvir. Þórólfr var gleðimaðr mikill; snimma var hann svá fullkominn at afli, at hann þótti vel liðfœrr með ǫðrum mǫnnum, varð hann brátt vinsæll af alþýðu. (80)]

In this context, one may also recall the similarities between Skallagrim and Egil. They share the role of the ugly brother who is raised in the shadow of the accomplished Thorolf and outlives him. The impact of these two doubles is intensified by the repeated occurrences of the same names throughout the narrative.[2] In addition to Skallagrim, eight characters called Grim appear in *Egil's Saga*, variously related to the family of Egil. The description of the sword given to Egil by Arinbjorn is a case in point. "Arinbjorn had been given it by Egil's brother Thorolf. Before him, Skallagrim had been given it by Egil's uncle Thorolf, who had received it from Grim Hairy-cheeks, the son of Ketil Haeng. Ketil had owned the sword and used it in duels" (133: "Þat hafði gefit Arinbirni Þórólfr Skalla-Grimsson, en áðr hafði Skalla-Grímr þegit af Þórólfi, bróður sínum, en Þórólfi gaf sverðit Grímr loðinkinni, sonr Ketils hœngs; þat sverð hafði átt Ketill hængr ok haft í hólmgǫngum," 195). If we leave out Arinbjorn's ownership, the sword is passed on from father to son, from one brother to another, from Grim to Thorolf or Thorolf to Grim. A different side of this double reality, inherent in the saga, can be seen in the metamorphosis of Kveldulf, Skallagrim, and Egil, who all have an animalistic or even werewolf nature that can take over their human personality under certain circumstances (cf. Holtsmark 1968).

Finally, it should be noted that *Egil's Saga* contains numerous repeated motifs. Baldur Hafstað (1990) claims, for instance, that friendship is one of the main themes of the saga, in which the friendship of equal partners is contrasted with the duties of a courtier to his king. Torfi H. Tulinius (2004, 219–33), on the other hand, sees fratricide as one of the saga's central themes. From a more general perspective, X kills Y is probably the most common narrative element in *Egil's Saga*, with one killing-scene frequently resembling another. A few examples will suffice to illustrate this. Thorolf, the son of Kveldulf, "thrust his sword through the standard-bearer" (36: "lagði hann sverði í gegnum þann mann, er merkit bar," 53–4) of King Harald before the king himself delivered Thorolf the mortal blow. Thorolf, the son of Skallagrim, was more successful when he found himself in a similar situation, as he first killed the standard-bearer of Earl Hring and then "drove the spear through the earl's coat of mail, into his chest and through his body so that it came out between his shoulder blades, lifted him up on it above his head and thrust the end into the ground" (96: "lagði hann spjótinu fyrir brjóst jarlinum, í gegnum brynjuna ok búkinn, svá at út gekk um herðarar, ok hóf hann upp á kesjunni yfir hǫfuð sér ok skaut niðr spjótshalanum í jǫrðina," 138). However, Egil's brother was subjected to the same destiny as his uncle and namesake: "Thorolf was stabbed with many spears at once and died there beside the forest" (98: "brugðu þegar mǫrgum kesjum senn á Þórólfi, ok fell hann þar við skóginn," 140). In his youth, Egil drove an axe into the head of eleven-year-old Grim, one of his father's namesakes, "right through to the brain" (68: "svá at þegar stóð í heila," 100). At the age of twelve, he also killed his father's favourite workhand (102: 69). Once in Norway, when Egil's boat passed the ship of King Eirik Blood-axe, he threw a spear, "striking the helmsman, Ketil the Slayer, through the middle" (112: "ok kom á þann miðjan, er við stýrit sat, en þar var Ketill hǫðr," 161). Later, Egil killed Frodi, a foster-son of the king, in a similar way: "He lunged at Frodi with his halberd, piercing his shield and plunging so deep into his chest that the point came out through his back" (117: "hann skaut kesjunni at Fróða ok í gegnum skjǫld hans ok í brjóstit, svá at yddi um bakit," 168).

It is possible to use other examples from "The 'Uncanny'" to illustrate the plot of *Egil's Saga* but it is time to turn our attention to the way in which Freud explains the impact of the uncanny. First of all, he suggests that the uncanniness of dismembered limbs, a severed head, and a hand cut off at the wrist "springs from its association with the castration-complex" (Freud 1966, 49–50). Second, he suggests that the image of the double can be traced to the narcissistic stage in our youth – and in primitive man – when the mirror image seems to confirm our immortality. As we mature, the *Doppelgänger* turns into "the ghastly harbinger of death" (1966, 40). But the double may also be a remainder from that period in our youth when the subject starts to divide itself into id, ego, and super-ego. The *Doppelgänger* could then be representative of the super-ego – our conscience or the voice of civilization – seeing us from the outside while still being a part of ourselves. Furthermore, Freud suggests that the

> quality of uncanniness can only come from the circumstances of the "double" being a creation dating back to a very early mental stage, long since left behind, and one, no doubt, in which it wore a more friendly aspect. The "double" has become a vision of terror, just as after the fall of their religion the gods took on daemonic shapes. (1966, 41–2)

This last explanation can be applied to the double nature of Kveldulf, Skallagrim, and Egil. Their animalistic tendencies may be seen as representative of those primitive desires that are suppressed in our subconscious and might break out at any moment.

As far as recurrence of the same situations, things, and events is concerned, Freud relates an interesting story about his own experience when he got lost in a provincial town in Italy. His repeated attempts to find his way led him back to the same narrow street where "painted women were to be seen at the windows of the small houses" (1966, 42). He found this uncanny, but that experience and other similar ones led him to believe that already in childhood we have a powerful repetition impulse that may contradict our basic desire for pleasure.[3] The same pattern can be found in the behaviour of people with mental disorders, who in their sleep (and even when awake) re-experience certain traumas from their past. Freud suggests that the aim of the child may be to gain control over a difficult experience by acting it out, but he believes that the repetition compulsion of the mentally disturbed is completely involuntary. The patient is the prey of painful memories, destined to relive the past as an eternally repeated present.

With reference to these ideas, it is tempting to speculate whether the experience we have when we read *Egil's Saga* is parallel to Freud's uncanny walk in the Italian city. Again and again, we come across similar descriptions which are likely to get mixed up in our confused minds as we continue to read. Do we, for instance, make a clear distinction between the deaths of the older and the younger Thorolf, between events leading up to the moment when the latter drives his spear through Earl Hring's coat of mail and those leading to the moment when Egil drives a spear through Frodi or Ketil the Slayer? In my view, the contradictory impact of the saga stems partially from the fact that the author repeats the same narrative functions with such a compulsive insistence that the plot becomes dreamlike (cf. Sigurjónsson and Jørgensen 1987), mesmerizing, and uncanny.

II

In her book *Pouvoirs de l'horreur* (1980), Julia Kristeva tries to define the effects of the horror that images of *the abject* can have on us. Like Freud in his discussion of the uncanny, Kristeva believes that various things that we experience in our youth continue to haunt us throughout our lives, but in particular she focuses on the first month of the child's existence when it starts to experience its separation from the mother but has not yet formed an independent identity. At this point, the child feels that it is an *abject*, a term Kristeva coins with reference to the words *subject* and *object*. According to her, the emotions of the child are in turmoil at this stage. It desires to be reunited with the mother but at the same time it is afraid of termination. As a result, the child may enter into a period of complete denial of the outer world, throwing away the things that are around it and vomiting everything that it has eaten (Kristeva 1980, 5–6).

Kristeva claims that food and various kinds of waste, excrement, and garbage are among the things that can trigger the horror of the abject later in our lives. She thus describes her own reaction when "the eyes see or the lips touch that skin on the surface of milk – harmless, thin as a sheet of cigarette paper, pitiful as a nail paring – I experience a gagging sensation and, still farther down, spasm in the stomach, the belly; and all the organs shrivel up in the body, provoke tears and bile, increase heartbeat, cause forehead and hands to perspire" (1980, 2–3). Most of us have shown such reactions, at least in our youth, to one kind of food or another. According to Kristeva, the juices of the body – spittle, blood, urine, sweat, and tears – can cause a similar reaction, as they all have an ambiguous status. These liquids are marginal things, transgressing the boundaries of the body, being both a part of me (subject) and something other (object) (1980, 69). Vomit can be added to this list, as it is on the border between nourishment and excrement.

When we start to look for images of this nature in *Egil's Saga* the scene describing the dealings of Egil and Armod brings itself to our attention. As host at his farm, Armod first treated Egil and his fellow travellers with large bowls of curds and later offered them strong brew. Egil took copious draughts of the ale but at a certain point he

> started to feel that he would not be able to go on like this. He stood up and walked across the floor where Armod was sitting, seized him by the shoulders, and thrust him up against a wall-post. Then Egil spewed a torrent of vomit that gushed all over Armod's face, filling his eyes and nostrils and mouth and pouring down his chest. Armod was close to choking, and when he managed to let out his breath, a jet of vomit gushed out with it. (156)
>
> [fann þá, at honum myndi eigi svá búit eira; stóð hann þá upp ok gekk um gólf þvert, þangat er Ármóðr sat, hann tók hǫndum í axlir honum ok kneikði hann upp að stǫfum. Síðan þeysti Egill upp ór sér spýju mikla, ok gaus í andlit Ármóði, í augun og nasarnar ok í munninn; rann svá ofan um bringuna, en Ármóði varð við andhlaup, ok er hann fekk ǫndinni frá sér hrundit, þá gaus upp spýja. (225–6)]

Incompatible drinks, curds and ale, cause Egil to spew. The nausea originates from within the body. In the second instance, it is Egil's vomit that causes Armod to spew. The nausea is caused by an external perception. But is there an end to this domino effect? We as readers experience this scene as it gushes all over our face, so to speak, and it may cause a powerful physical reaction.

Another side of the abject can be seen in the beastly nature of Egil, Skallagrim, and Kveldulf. The abject confronts us "with those fragile states where man strays on the territories of animal. Thus, by way of abjection, primitive societies have marked out a precise area of their culture in order to remove it from the threatening world of animal and animalism, which were imagined as representatives of sex and murder" (Kristeva 1980, 12–13). It is interesting to recall the fight of Egil and Atli the Short from this perspective. When Egil realizes that his opponent cannot be killed with a sword, he tries alternative measures:

> Egil saw that this was pointless, because his own shield was splitting through by then as well. He threw down his sword and shield, ran for Atli and grabbed him with his hands. By his great strength, Egil pushed Atli over backwards, then sprawled over him and bit through his throat. Atli died on the spot. Egil rushed to his feet and ran over to the sacrificial bull, took it by the nostrils with one hand and by the horns with the other, and swung it over onto its back, breaking its neck. (144)

> [Sér þá Egill, at eigi mun hlýða svá búit, því at skjǫldr hans gerðisk þá ónýtr; þá lét Egill laust sverðit ok skjǫldinn ok hljóp at Atla ok greip hann hǫndum. Kenndi þá aflsmunar, ok fell Atli á bak aptr, en Egill greyfðisk at niðr ok beit í sundr í honum barkann; lét Atli þar líf sitt. Egil hljóp upp skjótt ok þar til, er blótnautit stóð, ok snaraði svá, at fœtr vissu upp, en í sundr hálsbeinit; (209–10)]

It is striking how the killing of a human being and the sacrifice of an animal go hand in hand here. The method of killing is similar in both instances: Egil pushes Atli backwards and flips the bull on to its back. The difference lies in the fact that he bites through Atli's throat but breaks the neck of the bull. Kristeva suggests that the history of religion depicts the various ways humanity has tried to purify the abject and develop acceptable ways to stage it (e.g., through sacrifices). Art, in particular the art of literature, has in many ways taken over this role of purification (1980, 17). From this perspective, one may speculate whether the text that depicts Egil's double killing may serve the same purpose as an actual sacrifice. The "animalistic" impulses of the audience are being recognized and momentarily we are relieved of our humanity.

The corpse is one more example of the abject that Kristeva discusses. Faced with a lifeless being, she claims, we feel that the borders of our existence are being erased. Human refuse and corpses, she writes, "show me what I permanently thrust aside in order to live" (1980, 3). As already suggested, there are plenty of corpses in *Egil's Saga*, but one of the most memorable descriptions in this respect occurs in the scene where Skallagrim dies of old age:

At daybreak next morning, when everybody was getting dressed, Skallagrim was sitting on the edge of his bed, dead, and so stiff that they could neither straighten him out nor lift him no matter how they tried. A horse was saddled quickly and the rider set off at full pelt all the way to Lambastadir. He went straight to see Egil and told him the news. Egil took his weapons and clothes and rode back to Borg that evening. He dismounted, entered the house and went to an alcove in the fire-room where there was a door through to the benches where people slept and sat. Egil went through the bench, took Skallagrim by the shoulders and tugged him backwards. He laid him down on the bench and closed his nostrils, eyes and mouth. (120–1)

[En um morgininn, er lýsti ok menn klæddusk, þá sat Skalla-Grímr fram á stokk ok var þá andaðr ok svá stirðr, at menn fengu hvergi rétt hann né hafit, ok var alls við leitat. Þá var hesti skotit undir einn mann; hleypði sá sem ákafligast, til þess er hann kom á Lambastaði; gekk hann þegar á fund Egils ok segir honum þessi tíðendi. Þá tók Egill vápn sín ok klæði ok reið heim til Borgar um kveldit, ok þegar hann hafði af baki stigit, gekk hann inn ok í skot, er var um eldahúsit, en dyrr váru fram ór skotinu at setum innanverðum. Gekk Egill fram í setit ok tók í herðar Skalla-Grími ok kneikði hann aptr á bak, lagði hann niðr í setit ok veitti honum nábjargir. (174)]

Egil's behaviour most certainly is affected by traditional folk-belief in the potential evil powers of the dead, but with reference to Kristeva's ideas it can be suggested that this detailed description of the stiffness of Skallagrim's body reminds us of the borders of nonexistence that close tighter around us day by day.

Finally, these three different examples of the abject – horrific foods, beastly humans, and lifeless bodies – merge into one in many of the verses of the saga. Human beings kill one another and ravens, eagles, and wolves gobble the corpses. It is possible to distinguish between three stages in these descriptions. At the first stage, a sharp distinction is made between the killer and the beast of prey. The killer is often described as a host, even a steward, who invites the animal to dinner. The following example, characterizing King Eirik Blood-axe's achievements, is taken from Egil's poem "Head-Ransom":

Eirik fed flesh
to the wolf afresh. (131)

[bauð ulfum hræ
Eiríkr of sæ.] (190)

At the second stage, the difference between the human fighter and the beast is blurred. The example here is from a verse Egil composes after his brother dies:

Hring entered the weapon-fray
and the ravens did not starve. (99)

[helt, né hrafnar sultu,
Hringr á vápna þingi.] (142)

Instead of the chain of events of the first stage – a man kills another and thereby supplies food for beasts – the actions of man and animal are simply parallel. Finally, at the third stage, a description of the way in which the animals prey on the body replaces the actual killing scene. The following example is from "Head-Ransom":

Battle-cranes swooped
over heaps of dead,
wound-birds did not want
for blood to gulp.
The wolf gobbled flesh,
the raven daubed
the prow of its beak
in waves of red. (130)

[Flugu hjaldrs tranar
á hræs lanar,
órut blóðs vanar
benmós granar,
sleit und freki,
en oddbreki
gnúði hrafni
á hǫfuðstafni.] (189)

Here, the warrior and the beast of prey have merged into one entity. One cannot be sure if Egil is describing the activities of humans or animals, a fight or a feast, someone who is eating or sailing (in the original the beak of the raven is characterized as "the prow of the head" [*hǫfuðstafn*]). We are certainly faced with images of our imminent destruction, but the text itself also deconstructs some of the principal oppositions which underpin our system of signification.

The corpse is at the same time a symbol of death and nourishment; the killing is both a destruction and creation; the subject is concurrently a man, an animal, and an object (a ship). The experience of the abject, as defined by Kristeva, is reflected in the very language of the saga.

III

It may seem that Freud and Kristeva reach far into childhood experience to explain the uncanny emotions and horrors that haunt us, but Georges Bataille reaches even further back in his book *L'Erotisme* (1957) to explain the fears he believes we have of our erotic impulses. His argument is partially based on the difference between the asexual reproduction in elementary organisms and sexual reproduction in more complex ones. Eroticism, he claims, "unlike simple sexual activity is a psychological quest independent of the natural goal: reproduction and the desire for children"; it certainly is "an exuberance of life" but at the same time "this psychological quest is not alien to death" (Bataille 1957, 11). He explains this paradox with reference to the way in which two nuclei are formed from a single cell. Asexual reproduction means that the original cell ceases to exist but still experiences a continuity of being. "The same continuity cannot occur in the death of sexual creatures, where reproduction is in theory independent of death and disappearance" (1957, 14). Here two individuals create the third one, confirming their destinies as discontinuous beings.

According to Bataille, we desire to create something in death, just as the single-celled organism does at the point of reproduction. This is erotic desire, a desire tormented by fear of self-annihilation. Primarily, Bataille discusses three types of eroticism: physical, emotional, and religious. His aim "is to show that with all of them the concern is to substitute for the individual isolated discontinuity a feeling of profound continuity" (1957, 15). Hence, love-making and sacrifice, ecstasy and death, are all related in his view. Discussing the impact of human sacrifice on its audience, he writes: "In sacrifice, the victim is divested not only of clothes but of life (or is destroyed in some way if it is an inanimate object). … A violent death disrupts the creature's discontinuity; what remains, what the tense onlookers experience in the succeeding silence, is the continuity of all existence with which the victim is now one" (1957, 22).

We have already observed the scene in *Egil's Saga* where Egil kills Atli the Short and then sacrifices a bull. Another interesting scene from the saga involving bulls is inspired by an axe that King Eirik Blood-axe asks Thorolf to give to Skallagrim:

> Skallagrim took the axe, held it up and inspected it for a while without speaking, then hung it up above his bed.
>
> At Borg one day in the autumn, Skallagrim had a large number of oxen driven to his farm to be slaughtered. He had two of them tethered up against the wall, with their heads together, and took a large slab of rock and placed it under their necks. Then he went up to them with his axe "King's Gift" and struck at both oxen with it in one blow. It chopped off the oxen's heads, but when it went right through and struck the stone the mount broke completely and the blade shattered. Skallagrim inspected the edge without saying a word, then went into the fire-room, climbed up on a bench and put the axe on the rafters above the door, where it was left that winter. (65)
>
> [Skalla-Grímr tók við øxinni, helt upp ok sá á um hríð ok rœddi ekki um; festi upp hjá rúmi sínu. Þat var um haustit einn hvern dag at Borg, at Skalla-Grímr lét reka heim yxn mjǫg marga, er hann ætlaði til hǫggs; hann lét leiða tvá yxn saman undir húsvegg ok leiða á víxl; hann tók hellustein vel mikinn ok skaut niðr undir hálsana. Síðan gekk hann til með øxina konungsnaut ok hjó yxnina báða senn, svá at hǫfuðit tók af hvárumtveggja, en øxin hljóp niðr í steininn, svá at muðrinn brast ór allr ok rifnaði upp í gegnum herðuna. Skalla-Grímr sá í eggina ok rœddi ekki um; gekk síðan inn í eldahús ok steig síðan á stokk upp ok skaut øxinni upp á hurðása; lá hon þar um vetrinn. (95–6)]

Even if this is, in the context of the saga, a description of butchering, it may serve the same purpose for the reader as a sacrifice. We see how the animals are destroyed, like inanimate objects. This is emphasized by the fact that an inanimate object, King Eirik's gift to Skallagrim, is also destroyed at the same time. In addition, Skallagrim's method of beheading the two bulls in one blow resembles a rite. We are faced with two headless animals staggering on their feet for a moment or two before falling to either side. In the ensuing silence of this description we should be able to experience the continuity of all existence, as Bataille puts it.[4]

In his discussion of sexual intercourse, Bataille suggests that it is an act of transgression of various social constraints. In that context, he compares a lover to a blood-stained priest, stripping his victim of her identity. Even though *Egil's Saga* has many facets, its author does not show explicit interest in depicting people in a sexual act. We are, for instance, told only that Thorolf, son of Skallagrim, and Gunnhild, wife of King Eirik, struck up "a close friendship" (64: "[k]ærleikar miklir," 94). Similarly, it is reported that Egil and the daughter of Earl Arnfinn sat next to each other on her bed for a whole night, drinking "and got on well together" (84: "ok váru allkát," 121). A little later, when Thorolf marries Egil's foster-sister Asgerd, the author is completely silent about their first night together. In fact, the point of view in this part of the saga sticks to Egil, who fell ill at the farm of Thorolf's friend Thorir, and was unable to join his brother at the feast.[5]

Does this mean that there is no sexual eroticism in the saga? Not quite. Interestingly, Egil recovered soon after Thorolf had said goodbye to him, and instead of going to the wedding he went with Olvir, one of Thorir's farmhands, to another feast. It is reported that Thorolf and his men sailed on "a large, well-equipped longship" (72: "langskip eitt mikit," 105) to the farm of Asgerd's father in Sognefjord, but Egil and Olvir and twelve other men went in "a row-boat" (72: *róðrarferju*, 106) towards Atley. At this point, the narrative forks into two separate paths. One is visible and consists of images of violence and destruction. The other is concealed, but one can imagine it to consist of images of love and unity. Together, these two narrative paths make one "erotic" plot.

In order to prepare the reader for the subsequent interpretation, I want to shift the focus momentarily to Pushkin's "The Queen of Spades." In an article primarily dealing with the moral subtext of this celebrated tale, Richard Gregg devotes some pages to a "pattern of erotic mystification" within the narrative (Gregg 2000, 616). The keystone to this pattern is a bedroom scene in which Hermann, a young engineer in the Russian army, encounters Countess Anna Fedorovna. He has discovered that this 87-year-old woman knows a secret that enables her to name three winning cards in succession at a gambling table. He has persuaded her young and beautiful ward, Lisaveta Ivanovna, to let him into the Countess's house one night while the two women are away at a ball. Lisaveta, who thinks that Herman is in love with her, has explained how he can find the Countess's bedchamber and go from there, through a corridor and a narrow winding staircase, to her own bedroom. Instead, he waits in a study next to the old woman's bedroom and when she returns from the ball, he watches her disrobe, witnessing "all the loathsome mysteries of her dress" (Pushkin 1966, 292). When she has put on her gown and night-cap, he finally reveals himself and asks her to tell him her secret. He even goes down to his knees, entreating her not to deny his request, but when the Countess remains silent he stands up saying that he will force her to answer:

> With these words he drew a pistol from his pocket. At the sight of the pistol, the Countess, for the second time, exhibited signs of strong emotion. She shook her head and raising her hand as though to shield herself from the shot, she rolled over on her back and remained motionless.

> "Stop this childish behaviour now," Hermann said, taking her hand. "I ask you for the last time: will you name your three cards or won't you?"
> The Countess made no reply. Hermann saw that she was dead. (1966, 294)

In simplified terms, Hermann can choose between two different paths once he has entered the house; one leading to young Lisaveta and possibly also to love, the other one leading to the old Countess and potential fortune. Gregg remarks that even as Hermann takes the second path, the critical bedroom scene "may be viewed as both climax and caricature: at once replete with erotic innuendo but wholly devoid of erotic content":

> Specifically: the bedroom itself, the nocturnal hour, the handsome young male intruder, the woman's disrobing before his eyes; her "inexplicable" excitement on perceiving him; his kneeling pleas; his exposed *pistol*, her *supine* position. Whereupon, recalling the Elizabethan meaning of the word, the woman *dies*. In sum, what we are offered here is a caricatural pantomime of lovemaking, as empty of erotic substance as the bulletless pistol, which the hero brandishes, is empty of murderous purpose. (2000, 616–17)

Now we can go back to the scene of *Egil's Saga* that takes place in Atley. Instead of reading about the marriage of Thorolf and Asgerd, we follow Egil, Olvir, and their fellow travellers approaching a large farm on this island owned by King Eirik and run by his good steward Bard. When the visitors met Bard, he led them "into a fire-room which stood away from the other buildings" (72–3: "til eldahúss nǫkkurs; var þat brott frá ǫðrum húsum," 106). There they could dry their clothes. When they had dressed again, a table was laid "and they were given bread and butter, and large bowls of curds" (73: "ok gefinn þeim matr, brauð ok smjǫr, ok settir fram skyraskar stórir," 107) as twice Bard has stated he had no ale in his house for his visitors. The chapter ends by suggesting that the whole band of men have gone to rest: "There were plenty of mattresses in the room and he invited them to lie down and go to sleep" (73: "Hálm skorti þar eigi inni; bað hann þar þá niðr leggjask til svefns," 107). Until this point, one can assume that the two narrative paths run parallel, except that the food in Bard's fire-room is probably not as fancy as in the wedding feast in Sognefjord.

In the beginning of the next chapter the point of view is no longer with Egil but in the main room of the farm in Atley, where King Eirik and his wife Gunnhild were taking part in a feast "because a sacrifice was being made to the *disir*. It was a splendid feast, with plenty to drink" (73: "ok skyldi þar vera dísablót, ok var þar veizla in bezta ok drykkja mikil inni í stofunni," 107). Eirik asked where Bard had gone and when he was told that his steward was attending to Olvir and his men in the fire-room, the king ordered someone to fetch them all right away. When they entered the main room they were immediately served ale, and as the night wore on "many of Olvir's companions became incapacitated; some of them vomited inside the main room, while others made it out through the door" (73–4: "þá kom svá, at fǫrunautar Ǫlvis gerðusk margir ófœrir; sumir spjó þar inni í stofunni, en sumir kómusk út fyrir dyrr," 108). It is not reported that Egil vomited. In fact, he drank heavily from Olvir's drinking-horn and then delivered a verse suggesting that Bard had deceived them by saying he was short of feast-drink. Unlike his companions, Egil spewed poetry instead of vomit. Bard was by no means happy to be called a liar and he got Queen Gunnhild to assist him in mixing poison into Egil's draught, intending to put an end to the spewing of words from his mouth.

> Egil took out his knife and stabbed the palm of his hand with it, then took the drinking-horn, carved runes on it and smeared them with blood. He spoke a verse:
>
> I carve runes on this horn,
> redden words with my blood,
> I choose words for the trees
> of the wild beast's ear-roots;
> drink as we wish this mead
> brought by merry servants,
> let us find out how we fare
> from the ale that Bard blessed.
>
> The horn shattered and the drink spilled onto the straw. (74)
>
> [Egill brá þá knífi sínum ok stakk í lófa sér; hann tók við horninu ok reist á rúnar ok reið á blóðinu. Hann kvað:
>
> Rístum rún á horni,
> rjóðum spjǫll í dreyra,
> þau velk orð til eyrna
> óðs dýrs viðar róta;
> drekkum veig sem viljum
> vel glýjaðra þýja,
> vitum, hvé oss of eiri
> ǫl, þats Bárøðr signdi.
>
> Hornit sprakk í sundr, en drykkrinn fór niðr í hálm.] (109)

The uncanny power of the runes possibly saved Egil's life here, but at the same time the drinking-horn can be seen as a *mise en abyme* of the saga as a whole, which is all reddened with blood (cf. de Looze 1989). But even though the drinking-horn was shattered, the feast continued, to the point when Egil finally was ready to leave.

> Olvir was on the verge of passing out, so Egil got up and led him over to the door. He swung his cloak over his shoulders and gripped his sword underneath it. When they reached the door, Bard went after them with a full horn and asked Olvir to drink a farewell toast. Egil stood in the doorway and spoke this verse:
>
> I'm feeling drunk, and the ale
> has left Olvir pale in the gills,
> I let the spray of ox-spears
> foam over my beard.
> Your wits have gone, inviter
> of showers onto shields;
> now the rain of the high god
> starts pouring upon you.
>
> Egil tossed away the horn, grabbed hold of his sword and drew it. It was dark in the doorway; he thrust the sword so deep into Bard's stomach that the point came out through his back. Bard fell down dead, blood pouring from the wound. Then Olvir dropped to the floor, spewing vomit. Egil ran out of the room. It was pitch dark outside, and he dashed from the farm.
>
> People left the room and saw Bard and Olvir lying on the floor together, and imagined at first that they had killed each other. Because it was dark, the king had a light brought over, and they could see that Olvir was lying unconscious in his vomit, but Bard had been killed, and the floor was awash with his blood. (74–5)
>
> [Þá tók at líða at Qlvi; stóð þá Egill upp ok leiddi Qlvi útar til duranna ok helt á sverði sínu. En er þeir koma at durunum, þá kom Bárðr eptir þeim ok bað Qlvi drekka brautfararminni sitt. Egill tók við ok drakk ok kvað vísu:
>
> Qlvar mik, því́t Qlvi
> ǫl gervir nú fǫlvan,
> atgeira lætk ýrar
> ýrings of grǫn skýra;
> ǫllungis kannt illa,
> oddskýs, fyr þér nýsa,

rigna getr at regni,
regnbjóðr, Hávars þegna.

> Egill kastar horninu, en greip sverðit ok brá; myrkt var í forstofunni; hann lagði sverðinu á Bárði miðjum, svá at blóðrefillinn hljóp út um bakit; fell hann dauðr niðr, en blóð hljóp ór undinni. Þá fell Ǫlvir, ok gaus spýja ór honum. Egill hljóp þá út ór stofunni; þá var niðamyrkr úti; tók Egill þegar rás af bœnum. En inni í forstofunni sá menn, at þeir váru báðri fallnir, Bárðr ok Ǫlvir; kom þá konungr til ok lét bera at ljós; sá menn þá, hvat títt var, at Ǫlvir lá þar vitlauss, en Bárðr var veginn, ok flaut í blóði hans gólfit allt. (110–11)]

The text enveloping this verse echoes in various ways what has already taken place at the farm. Bard's body is shattered by Egil's sword, just like the drinking-horn that Egil had shattered earlier with the aid of poetry, blood, and runes. Instead of the poisonous drink that was spilled onto the mattresses, Bard's blood is now pouring out. Facing Bard, like a mirror reflection, Olvir lies in his own vomit; they look so similar that people first believe that they are both dead. This mirror-image within the visible path of the narrative can furthermore be seen as a travesty of the unity which is supposedly taking place during this very night in Sognefjord.

In the scene at Atloy, the focus is on Egil's drinking-horn. It is a vessel for a liquid – ale – which can be nourishing but can also cause nausea, or even death. In their original function, horns are the deadly weapons of animals – Egil referred to them as "ox-spears" (75: "ýrar atgeira," 110) in the verse quoted above. When he prepared to slay Bard, he tossed away the horn and grabbed hold of another weapon, his sword, which he has kept under his cloak. Echoing the scenes where Thorolf killed Earl Hring and Egil killed Ketil and Frodi, "he thrust the sword so deep into Bard's stomach that the point came out through his back" (75: "lagði sverðinu á Bárði miðjum, svá at blóðrefillinn hljóp út um bakit," 110). The violence can hardly be more graphic. Bard is turned into an inanimate object, resembling at the same time a shattered drinking-horn and the lovers at the moment of sexual satisfaction (*la petite mort*, as the French say). The narrative seems to be "replete with erotic innuendo" (Gregg 2000, 616).

IV

In this paper, I have highlighted certain mentally and even physically disturbing aspects of *Egil's Saga* with reference to the writings of Sigmund Freud, Julia Kristeva, and Georges Bataille. If these three theorists are to be trusted, the narrative and the imagery of this medieval saga are in some sense uncanny, contain variations of the abject, and also belong in the sphere of the erotic. I opened my analysis with reference to the myth about the mead of poetry, as it is presented in the *Prose Edda*. That myth has indeed many of the same elements I have identified in *Egil's Saga*: amputation (nine slaves cut each other's heads off), metamorphosis (Odin turns himself into a snake and an eagle), and repetitions (in particular recurring killings). The poetic mead itself is a multiple abject (spittle, blood, vomit). Even the scene in which Odin, in the shape of a snake, crawls into an auger-hole and the giant Baugi tries to stab him with an auger erotically foreshadows Odin's three nights with the giantess Gunnlod (cf. Kress 1990, 284–5). Together these two texts encourage further speculations about the nature of poetic language and its impact. To what degree, for instance, is our reading experience an emotional and even a carnal experience? Irrespective of the answers to this and other equally challenging questions, we have to agree that *Egil's Saga* is a complex tissue of powerful impressions. It is indeed one of these classical and excessive narratives that takes us to the edge of a precipice and tempts us to jump.

NOTES

1 A revised version of Jón Karl Helgason, "Rjóðum spjöll í dreyra: Óhugnaður, úrkast og erótík í Egils sögu." *Skáldskaparmál* 2 (1992): 60–76.

2 For a complementary discussion of recurring names in the saga, see Tulinius's essay in this volume.

3 Freud addresses this paradox directly in his article "Jenseits der Lustprinzips" (1920), where he describes how small children sometimes repeat a painful and difficult experience, such as separation from their parents.

4 It is worth noting how the axe as a signifier has two different signifieds. The bloody blade of the axe, which Skallagrim inspected at the end of the sacrifice, may have reflected the face of Eirik Blood-axe. The axe is a symbol of the king, Skallagrim's abuse of it reveals his hatred of Eirik. Additionally, the author refers to the axe as *konungsnaut*, playing on the ambiguity of the words *nautr* ("gift") and *naut* ("bull"). Ambiguity of this kind is not only common in *Egil's Saga* but is also one of the main characteristics of poetic use of language, according to Bataille.

5 For further discussion of this episode, see Oren Falk's essay in this volume.

WORKS CITED

Bataille, Georges. 1987. *Eroticism. Death and Sensuality*. Trans. Mary Dalwood. London and New York: Marion Boyars.

de Looze, Laurence. 1989. "Poet, Poem and Poetic Process in *Egils Saga Skalla-Grimssonar.*" *Arkiv för nordisk filologi* 104: 123–42.

Egils saga Skalla-Grímssonar. 1933. Ed. Sigurður Nordal. Íslenzk fornrit 2. Reykjavík: Hið íslenzka fornritafélag.

Egil's Saga. 1997. Trans. Bernard Scudder. London: Penguin.

Frank, Roberta. 1981. "Snorri and the Mead of Poetry." In *Speculum Norroenum: Norse Studies in Memory of Gabriel Turville-Petre.* Ed. Ursula Dronke, Guðrún P. Helgadóttir, Gerd Wolfgang Weber, and Hans Bekker-Nielsen, 155–70. Odense: Odense University Press.

Freud, Sigmund. 1966. "The 'Uncanny'." In *Studies in Parapsychology.* Trans. Alix Strachey. Ed. Philip Rieff, 19–60. New York: Collier Books.

Gregg, Richard. 2000. "Germann the Confessor and the Stony, Seated Countess: The Moral Subtext of Pushkin's 'The Queen of Spades'." *The Slavonic and East European Review* 78.4: 612–24.

Hafstað, Baldur. 1990. "Konungsmenn í kreppu og vinátta í *Egils sögu.*" *Skáldskaparmál* 1: 89–99.

Holtsmark, Anne. 1968. "On the Werewolf Motif in *Egil's Saga Skallagrimssonar.*" *Scientia Islandica – Science in Iceland* I: 7–9.

Kress, Helga. 1990. "The Apocalypse of a Culture: *Völuspá* and the Myth of the Sources/Sorceress in Old Icelandic Literature." In *Poetry in the Scandinavian Middle Ages: The Seventh International Saga Conference. Atti del 12° Congresso internazionale di studi sull'Alto Medioevo, Spoleto 4–10 settembre 1988.* 279–302. Spoleto: Presso la Sede del Centro Studi.

Kristeva, Julia. 1982. *Powers of Horror: An Essay on Abjection.* Trans. Leon S. Roudiez. New York: Columbia University Press.

Pushkin, Alexandr Sergeyevitch. 1966. "The Queen of Spades." In *The Complete Prose Tales of Alexandr Sergeyevitch Pushkin.* Trans. Gillon R. Aitken, 273–305. New York: Norton.

Sigurjónsson, Árni, and Keld Gall Jørgensen. 1987. "Saga og tegn. Udkast til en semiotisk sagalæsning." *Nordica* 4: 167–88.

Sturluson, Snorri. 1998. *Edda. Skáldskaparmál,* ed. Anthony Faulkes. 2 vols. London: Viking Society for Northern Research and University College London.

– 1987. *Edda.* Trans. Anthony Faulkes. London: Dent.

Tulinius, Torfi H. 2004. *Skáldið í skriftinni. Snorri Sturluson og* Egils saga. Reykjavík: Hið íslenska bókmenntafélag og Reykjavíkur Akademían.

12 A Selected Bibliography from the Online Annotated Bibliography of *Egil's Saga*

ÁLFDÍS ÞORLEIFSDÓTTIR, KATELIN PARSONS, AND JANE APPLETON

The online bibliography of *Egil's Saga* (https://wikisaga.hi.is), launched in March 2012, currently contains close to five hundred articles, books, and book chapters dealing with the saga, its memorable cast of characters, and its famously knotty fits of skaldic word-play. The database, WikiSaga, is designed as a resource for researchers, students, and other readers of the Icelandic medieval narrative. In addition to bibliographic resources, the site includes the full text of the saga in Bergljót Kristjánsdóttir's and Svanhildur Óskarsdóttir's 1992 Icelandic edition and in William Charles Green's 1893 English translation. Many of these bibliographic entries are annotated (in English and Icelandic), and in some instances the entry is linked to relevant chapters within the saga, enabling users to focus their research on specific verses and scenes.

Long the bridesmaid to *Njal's Saga* (even Green ranks it as coming in a close second to *The Story of Burnt Njal*), *Egil's Saga* has the honour of becoming the first Icelandic saga to be made available online in such a scholarly format. It is our hope that the online bibliography will continue to thrive and grow and that WikiSaga can be expanded in the future to include other saga literature.

The project took off in the summer of 2007, when Álfdís Þorleifsdóttir, under the supervision of Jón Karl Helgason, began gathering material for the bibliography, organizing articles, and defining keywords. While the bibliography was initially conceived as a resource for the saga's Icelandic-speaking readership only, the decision was reached at an early stage to develop the bibliography into a bilingual Icelandic-English research tool encompassing the entire corpus of international scholarship on *Egil's Saga*. The following summer, two additional students at the University of Iceland – Katelin Parsons and Jane Appleton – joined Þorleifsdóttir in collecting and annotating entries, working in both languages and often translating abstracts for each other. In 2010, Þorleifsdóttir and Parsons continued to add and annotate entries. Jón

Karl Helgason and Svanhildur Óskarsdóttir steered the project, jointly supervising the students' work and later editing and uploading the entries to the WikiSaga website.[1]

The sheer volume of scholarship unearthed in the project represents an interesting finding in its own right, but has also posed certain unforeseen problems. While the bibliography's digital format essentially freed it from conventional constrictions of space, time constraints continued to be an issue. Thus, while initial plans were to annotate all the entries, this did not prove feasible within the project's limited time frame. Instead, the focus of the project shifted somewhat to place greater emphasis on tracking down the "long tail" of scholarship on *Egil's Saga* – in particular older research that has less of a presence on the Internet than recent publications, the bibliographic details of which are generally easier to track down in an online search. Increasingly, however, both old and new research is being made available online, and one important feature of the database is that entries can be linked to digital versions of these texts where possible. WikiSaga itself is not designed as a repository for research articles, but anyone publishing in open-access journals or otherwise involved in a project making Egil-related scholarship available online should contact the editors through the WikiSaga site (https://wikisaga.hi.is).

Older printed bibliographies on scholarly research on *Egil's Saga* and other Icelandic sagas exist and were highly useful in preparing the online bibliography. For those looking for a basic introduction to seminal literature on *Egil's Saga*, John Hines's bibliographical guide to *Egil's Saga* and *Njal's Saga* (1992) is an excellent reference. The present project, on the other hand, is unique in that it links an annotated bibliography directly to the saga text itself.

Advances in digital technologies and in the potential of the Internet in recent years have opened up new possibilities for mediating classical literature and related research. There are some excellent information databases for many key works of world literature, but this project is, as mentioned earlier, the first of its kind for the Icelandic sagas. Until now, digital versions of the sagas have been limited to versions of the printed text and its translations (mainly those that are out of copyright). A growing number of the manuscripts preserving these sagas can be viewed online on the Handrit.is website, a digital manuscript catalogue, but this site does not link these primary sources to the secondary sources dealing with them. By contrast, the online bibliography for *Egil's Saga* links passages of the saga text to relevant quotations by scholars and other commentators, which link in turn to individual entries within the bibliographic database. A considerable number of the bibliographical entries in the database are annotated.

As with all online bibliographies, the database in its present form will require regular maintenance if it is to remain a useful research tool. To this end, there are plans to incorporate its development into the project work of students at the University of Iceland and other university institutions. Anyone interested in contributing to the site is welcome to contact Jón Karl Helgason.

For inclusion in the online bibliography, a work need not deal exclusively with *Egil's Saga*: for example, commentary on a stanza of *Sonatorrek* may be found in a broader discussion of skaldic poetry. Where they can be linked directly to the saga, these "peripheral" bibliographical entries can provide useful information to readers. Criteria for inclusion in the selected bibliography are more stringent. Only published articles, books, and book chapters in which *Egil's Saga* forms either the central focus or a very substantial part of the discussion have been printed here. This includes a large body of scholarship on the poetics of *Egil's Saga*; the most specialized of these entries have been omitted here, however, as they relate to interpretation of specific verses and will be of minimal interest for the majority of this bibliography's users.

Introductions to editions of *Egil's Saga* were omitted, as these are fairly self-evident sources of information on the saga. The list is nevertheless a lengthy one, and in the interest of saving space annotations appear only in the digital version of the bibliography. Here and in the online bibliography, entries are organized alphabetically by author, with the difference that Icelandic authors are listed by patronymic or surname in this chapter but by given name in the online version (as is Icelandic convention). A number of papers on *Egil's Saga* have been published more than once or are available in more than one platform; in these cases, only a single publication has been noted here. Several translations of scholarly articles into English or Icelandic from other languages have, however, been included.

A final aim of the project is to bridge the linguistic and material gap between Icelandic students and scholars of *Egil's Saga* and those based in other countries. The bulk of the scholarship on *Egil's Saga* available to researchers in Iceland is written in Icelandic, and many non-Icelandic publications remain unavailable in Icelandic libraries, despite efforts on the part of the National Library to obtain copies of all saga-related writings. Conversely, many of the Icelandic titles in this bibliography have very limited distribution outside Iceland. Lack of access is not the only obstacle in creating a functional bibliographic database for an Icelandic saga, however. Translations and student editions have opened up *Egil's Saga* to a much wider readership than the saga enjoyed at the time when the oldest items in this bibliography were published. For many readers, deciphering articles in modern Icelandic may be more challenging than the saga itself, while Icelandic-speaking students often find it easier to focus their attention on books and articles in Icelandic than to tackle a foreign-language discussion of paleopathology or character delineation. By including bilingual entries in the online bibliography, with summaries in both English and Icelandic, we hope to aid readers in finding scholarship and commentary of interest regardless of the language in which it has been written.

NOTE

1 The project's progression in stages reflects the availability of funding. In 2007, a grant from the Ministry of Education funded preliminary work. In 2008, the project was supported by a grant from the Icelandic Research Fund, which financed a combined total of three months' work at the Árni Magnússon Institute for Icelandic Studies. In 2010, a grant from the Icelandic Student Innovation Fund (Nýsköpunarsjóður) financed another two months' work, again at the Árni Magnússon Institute. Credit also needs to be given to the multimedia company Anok margmiðlun, run by Anna Melsteð (designer) and Pétur Björnsson (programmer), which developed and hosted the database between 2007 and 2011, and Olga Holownia, who developed the database in the MediaWiki environment.

SELECTED BIBLIOGRAPHY

Aðalsteinsson, Jón Hnefill. "Religious Ideas in *Sonatorrek*." *Saga-book* 25.2 (1999): 159–78.

– "Synpunkter på *Sonatorrek*." In *Nordisk hedendom: et symposium*. Ed. Gro Steinsland. Odense: Odense Universitetsforlag, 1991. 9–16.

– *Trúarhugmyndir í Sonatorreki*. Studia Islandica 57. Reykjavík: Háskólaútgáfan, 2001.

Albertsson, Kristján. "Egill Skallagrímsson í Jórvík." *Skírnir* 150 (1976): 88–98.

Almqvist, Bo. "Er konungsgarðr rúmr inngangs, en þrǫngr brottfarar. Ett fornisländskt ordspråk och dess iriska motstycke." *Arv* 22 (1966): 173–93.

Árnason, Kristján. "Hrynjandi höfuðlausnar og rímkvæðið fornenska." *Sagnaþing helgað Jónasi Kristjánssyni sjötugum*. Vol. 2. Reykjavík: Hið íslenska bókmenntafélag, 1994. 505–13.

Battaglia, Marco. "Brunanburh nella *Saga di Egill Skallagrímsson*? Quando la letteratura registra la storia." *Linguistica e Filologia* 23 (2006): 151–85.

Beck, Heinrich. "Erzählhaltung und Quellenberufung in der Egils saga." *Skandinavistik* 3.2 (1973): 89–103.

Bell, L. Michael. "A Computer Concordance to *Egils saga Skalla-Grímssonar*." In *Studies for Einar Haugen. Presented by Friends and Colleagues*. Ed. Evelyn Scherabon Firchow, Kaaren Grimstad, Nils Hasselmo, and Wayne A. O'Neil. Janua

Linguarum: Studia Memoriae Nicolai van Wijk Dedicata, Series Maior 59. The Hague: Mouton, 1972. 58–68.

– "Fighting Words in *Egils saga*: Lexical Pattern as Standard-Bearer." *Arkiv för nordisk filologi* 95 (1980): 89–112.

– "Oral Allusion in *Egils saga Skalla-Grímssonar*: A Computer-Aided Approach." *Arkiv för nordisk filologi* 91 (1976): 51–65.

Benediktsson, Pétur. "Hvers vegna orti Egill Höfuðlausn?" *Helgafell* 5 (1965): 3–29.

Bergsveinsson, Sveinn. "Tveir höfundar Egils sögu." *Skírnir* 157 (1983): 99–116.

Berman, Melissa A. "*Egils saga* and *Heimskringla*." *Scandinavian Studies* 54.1 (1982): 21–50.

Blaney, Benjamin. "The Narrative Technique of Character Delineation in *Egils saga Skalla-Grimssonar*." *Les Sagas de Chevaliers (Riddarasögur): Actes de la Ve Conférence Internationale sur les Sagas Présentés par Régis Boyer (Toulon. Juillet 1982)*. [Toulon]: [Presses de l'Université Paris-Sorbonne], [1985]. 343–53.

Bley, A. *Eigla-Studien*. Recueil de travaux 39. Gand: Librairie Scientifique Van Goethem & Cie, 1909.

Brekkan, Fr[iðrik] Ásmundsson. "Lidt om Egil Skallagrimssons Personlighed. En hjælp ved læsningen af Egils-saga." *Årbog Dansk-islandsk Samfund* 1 (1928): 94–119.

Byock, Jesse. "Egill Skalla-Grímsson. The Dark Figure as Survivor in an Icelandic Saga." In *The Dark Figure in Medieval German and Germanic Literature*. Ed. Edward R. Haynes and Stephanie Cain Van D'Elden. Göppinger Arbeiten zur Germanistik 448. Göppingen: Kümmerle, 1986. 151–63.

– "Egil's Bones." *Scientific American* 272.1 (1995): 82–7.

– "Egilssaga og samfélagsminni." *Íslenska söguþingið 28.–31. maí 1997.* Ráðstefnurit I. Ed. Guðmundur J. Guðmundsson and Eiríkur K. Björnsson. Reykjavík: Sagnfræðistofnun Háskóla Íslands, 1998. 379–89.

– "Hauskúpan og beinin í Egils sögu." Trans. Magnús Snædal. *Skírnir* 168.1 (1994): 73–108.

– "Some Thoughts on *Egils saga* and Social Memory." In *Vöruvoð ofin Helga Þorlákssyni fimmtugum 8. ágúst 1995*. Ed. Sigurgeir Steingrímsson. Reykjavík: Menningar- og minningarsjóður Mette Magnussen, 1995. 13–14.

– "The Skull and Bones in *Egils saga*: A Viking, a Grave, and Paget's Disease." *Viator: Medieval and Renaissance Studies* 24 (1993): 23–50.

Chesnutt, Michael. "Tekstkritiske bemærkninger til C-redaktionen af Egils saga." *Opuscula* 12 (2005): 228–62.

– "To fragmenter af Egils saga. AM 162 A fol. (R) fragm. β og ι." *Opuscula* 13 (2010): 173–96.

Clunies Ross, Margaret. "The Art of Poetry and the Figure of the Poet in *Egils Saga*." In *Sagas of the Icelanders: A Book of Essays*. Ed. John Tucker. Garland Reference Library of the Humanities 758. New York: Garland Publishing, 1989. 126–45.

– "Conjectural Emendation in Skaldic Editing Practice, with Reference to *Egils saga*." *Journal of English and Germanic Philology* 104.1 (2005): 12–30.
– "*Hǫfuðlausn* and *Egils saga*." *Notes and Queries* New Series 51.2 (2004): 114–18.
– "A Tale of Two Poets: Egill Skallagrímsson and Einarr skálaglamm." *Arkiv för nordisk filologi* 120 (2005): 69–82.
– "Verse and Prose in *Egils saga Skallagrímssonar*." In *Creating the Medieval Saga: Versions, Variability and Editorial Interpretations of Old Norse Saga Literature* Ed. Judy Quinn and Emily Lethbridge. [Odense]: University Press of Southern Denmark, 2010. 191–211.

Cormack, Margaret. "*Egils saga*, *Heimskringla*, and the Daughter of Eiríkr blóðøx." *alvíssmál* 10 (2001): 61–8.

De Looze, Laurence. "Poet, Poem and Poetic Process in *Egils Saga Skalla-Grímssonar*." *Arkiv för nordisk filologi* 104 (1989): 123–42.

Detter, F. *Die Lausavísur der Egilssaga. Beiträge zu ihrer Erklärung*. Halle: Max Niemeyer, 1898.

Dillmann, François-Xavier. "La fureur de Grímr … et la grandeur de sa servante." In *Grímsævintýri sögð Grími M. Helgasyni sextugum 2. september 1987. Fyrri bindi.* Reykjavík: n.p., 1987. 22–4.

Djupedal, Reidar. "Egill Skallagrimsson i pudderparryk. Nokre ord om ei omsetjing av Egilssaga." *Danica. Studier i dansk sprog. Til Aage Hansen 3.9.1964*. Aarhus: Universitetsforlaget, 1964. 89–104.

Einarsdóttir, Ólafía. "Om Eiglas traditionsbærere og forfatter." In *The Audience of the Sagas. The Eighth International Saga Conference. s. II: Authors L-W*. Gothenburg: Gothenburg University, 1991. 170–3.

Einarsson, Bjarni. "Andlitsmynd Egils í Möðruvallabók." In *Sólhvarfasumbl saman borið handa Þorleifi Haukssyni fimmtugum 21. desember 1991*. Reykjavík: Menningar- og minningarsjóður Mette Magnussen, 1992. 7–8.
– "Brákarsund." In *Mælt mál og forn fræði. Safn ritgerða eftir Bjarna Einarsson gefið út á sjötugsafmæli hans 11. apríl 1987*. Reykjavík: Stofnun Árna Magnússonar, 1987. 32–4.
– "Egill Skalla-Grímsson." In *Medieval Scandinavia: An Encyclopedia*. Ed. Phillip Pulsiano et al. Garland Reference Library of the Humanities 934. Garland Encyclopedias of the Middle Ages 1. New York: Garland Publishing, 1993. 153–4.
– "Egils saga Skalla-Grímssonar." *Medieval Scandinavia: An Encyclopedia*. Ed. Phillip Pulsiano et al. Garland Reference Library of the Humanities 934. Garland Encyclopedias of the Middle Ages 1. New York: Garland Publishing, 1993. 155–7.
– "Fólgið fé á Mosfelli." In *Sjötíu ritgerðir helgaðar Jakobi Benediktssyni 20. júlí 1977. Fyrri hluti.* Ed. Einar G. Pétursson and Jónas Kristjánsson. Reykjavík: Stofnun Árna Magnússonar, 1977. 100–6.

– "Hörð höfuðbein." In *Mælt mál og forn fræði. Safn ritgerða eftir Bjarna Einarsson gefið út á sjötugsafmæli hans 11. apríl 1987*. Reykjavík: Stofnun Árna Magnússonar, 1987. 107–14.
– *Litterære forudsætninger for Egils saga*. Reykjavík: Stofnun Árna Magnússonar á Íslandi, 1975.
– "Om den Arnamagnæanske kommissions udgave af *Egils saga Skallagrímssonar* (1809)." *Gripla* 21 (2010): 7–17.
– "Um Eglutexta Möðruvallabókar í 17du aldar eftirritum." *Gripla* 8 (1994): 7–53.
– "Um fáein harmræn atriði í Völsunga sögu og Egils sögu." In *Grímsævintýri sögð Grími M. Helgasyni sextugum 2. september 1987. Fyrra hefti*. Reykjavík: n.p., 1987. 10–11.
Einarsson, Stefán. "The Origin of Egill Skallagrímsson's Runhenda." In *Scandinavica et Fenno-Ugrica. Studier tillägnade Björn Collinder den 22. Juli 1954*. Stockholm: Almqvist och Wiksell, 1955. 54–60.
– "The Poetry of Egill Skalla-Grímsson." *Tímarit Þjóðræknisfélags Íslendinga í Vesturheimi* 49 (1967): 36–47.
Eldjárn, Kristján. "Kistur Aðalsteins konungs." In *Gengið á reka. Tólf fornleifaþættir*, Akureyri: Bókaútgáfan Norðri, 1948. 96–106.
Falk, Hjalmar. "Bemerkungen zu den Lausavísur der Egilssaga." *Beiträge zur Geschichte der deutschen Sprache und Literatur* 13 (1888): 359–66.
Fichtner, Edward G. "The Narrative Structure of *Egils saga*." In *Les Sagas de Chevaliers (Riddarasögur): Actes de la Vᵉ Conférence Internationale sur les Sagas Présentés par Régis Boyer (Toulon. Juillet 1982)*. [Toulon]: [Presses de l'Université Paris-Sorbonne], [1985]. 355–69.
Finlay, Alison. "*Egils saga* and Other Poets' Sagas." In *Introductory Essays on Egils saga and Njáls saga*. Ed. John Hines and Desmond Slay. London: Viking Society for Northern Research, 1992. 33–48.
Finnbogason, Guðmundur. "Egill Skallagrímsson." *Skírnir* 79 (1905): 119–33.
– "Hvers vegna orti Egill Höfuðlausn?" *Skírnir* 107 (1933): 194–7.
– "Um nokkrar vísur Egils Skallagrímssonar." *Skírnir* 99 (1925): 161–5.
Fix, Hans. "*Egils saga* Fragment Θ (AM 162 A fol. Θ) und Finnur Jónssons Edition." In *Jenseits von Index und Konkordanz: Beiträge zur Auswertung maschinenlesbarer altnordischer Texte*. Ed. Hans Fix. Texte und Untersuchungen zur Germanistik und Skandinavistik 9. Frankfurt am Main: Verlag Peter Lang, 1984. 135–41.
Fjalldal, Magnús. "A Farmer in the Court of King Athelstan: Historical and Literary Considerations in the Vínheiðr Episode of *Egils Saga*." *English Studies 77* (1996): 15–31.
Franz, L. "Egils 'Sonatorrek' und die Inschrift von Rök. Das Schicksal zweier Väter." *Mitteilungen der Islandfreunde* 11.1–2 (1923): 3–5.
Genzmer, Felix. "Die Geheimrunen der Egilssaga." *Arkiv för nordisk filologi* 67 (1952): 39–47.

Gjessing, G.A. "Egils-saga's Forhold til Kongesagaen." *Arkiv för nordisk filologi* 2 (1885): 289–318.

Gordon, E.V. "The Date of Hǫfuðlausn." *Proceedings of the Leeds Philosophical and Literary Society. Literary and Historical Section* 1.1 (1925): 12–14.

Grimstad, Kaaren. "The Giant as a Heroic Model: The Case of Egill and Starkaðr." *Scandinavian Studies* 48.3 (1976): 284–98.

Grímsson, Magnús. "Athugasemdir við Egilssögu Skallagrímssonar." *Safn til sögu Íslands og íslenzkra bókmennta.* Vol. 2. Copenhagen: Hið íslenzka Bókmenntafélag, 1886. 251–76.

Guðmundsson, Böðvar. "Jarðbundin gamansemi bóndamanns." *Mímir* 5.1 (1966): 36–7.

Guðmundsson, Finnbogi. *Gamansemi Egluhöfundar.* Reykjavík: Almenna bókaforlagið, 1967.

– "Hugstóran biðk heyra." In *Grímsævintýri sögð Grími M. Helgasyni sextugum 2. september 1987. Fyrra hefti.* Reykjavík: n.p., 1987. 28–30.

Gunnarsson, Karl. "Er kista Kveldúlfs fundin?" *Lesbók Morgunblaðsins* 5 Nov. 1994: 1–3.

– "Skoll og Hati í Egils sögu." *Lesbók Morgunblaðsins* 18 March 1995: 4–5.

Hafstað, Baldur. "*Egils saga, Njáls saga,* and the Shadow of *Landnáma.*" In *Sagnaheimur: Studies in Honour of Hermann Pálsson on his 80th Birthday, 26th May 2001.* Ed. Ásdís Egilsdóttir and Rudolf Simek. Trans. Allan Rettedal. Studia Medievalia Septentrionalia 6. Vienna: Fassbaender, 2001. 21–37.

– "Egils saga og Snorres Edda: Nogle spørgsmål vedrørende Snorres arbejdsmetoder og indflydelse." In *Snorres Edda i europeisk og islandsk kultur.* Ed. Jon Gunnar Jørgensen. Reykholt: Snorrastofa, 2009. 29–35.

– *Die Egils saga und ihr Verhältnis zu anderen Werken des nordischen Mittelalters.* Reykjavík: Rannsóknarstofnun Kennaraháskóla Íslands, 1995.

– "Er Arinbjarnarkviða ungt kvæði?" In *Sagnaþing helgað Jónasi Kristjánssyni sjötugum 10. apríl 1994.* Ed. Gísli Sigurðsson, Guðrún Kvaran, and Sigurgeir Steingrímsson. Vol. 1. Reykjavík: Hið íslenska bókmenntafélag, 1994. 19–31.

– "HSk, Landnáma og Egils saga og vinnuaðferðir höfunda til forna." In *Helgispjöll framin Helga Skúla Kjartanssyni fimmtugum, 1. febrúar 1999.* Ed. Baldur Hafstað and Baldur Sigurðsson. Reykjavík: Meistaraútgáfan, 1999. 29–35.

– "Konungsmenn í kreppu og vinátta í Egils sögu." *Skáldskaparmál* 1 (1990): 89–99.

– "Sighvatur Þórðarsson og Egils saga." *Skáldskaparmál* 3 (1994): 108–18.

Hallberg, Peter. *Snorri Sturluson och Egils saga Skallagrímssonar. Ett försök till språklig författarbestämning.* Studia Islandica 20. Reykjavík: Bókaútgáfa Menningarsjóðs, 1962.

– "Snorri Sturluson och Egils saga Skalla-Grímssonar. Kommentarer till en recension." In *Maal og minne* 1964 (1–2): 12–20.

Halldórsson, Halldór. *Egluskýringar handa skólum.* Akureyri: Bókaforlag Þorsteins M. Jónssonar, 1950.

Halldórsson, Ólafur. "Þél hreggi höggvin." In *Afmælisrit Björns Sigfússonar.* Reykjavík: Sögufélag, 1975. 189–93.

Hannesson, Pálmi. "Ef et betra telk." In *Íslenzkar úrvalsgreinar*. Reykjavík: Bókaútgáfa Menningarsjóðs og Þjóðvinafélagsins, 1976. 81–90.

Haraldsdóttir, Kolbrún. "Hvenær var Egils saga rituð?" In *Yfir Íslandsála. Afmælisrit til heiðurs Magnúsi Stefánssyni.* Reykjavík: Sögufræðslusjóður, 1991. 131–45.

Harðarson, Þórður. "Sjúkdómur Egils Skallagrímssonar." *Skírnir* 158 (1984): 244–8.

Harðarson, Þórður, and Elísabet Snorradóttir. "Egil's or Paget's Disease." *British Medical Journal* (International Edition) 313.7072 (1996): 1613–14.

Harris, Joseph. "'Goðsögn sem hjálp til að lífa af' í Sonatorreki." In *Heiðin minni: Greinar um fornar bókmenntir*. Ed. Haraldur Bessason and Baldur Hafstað. Reykjavík: Heimskringla, 1999, 47–70.

– "Sacrifice and Guilt in *Sonatorrek*." In *Studien zum Altgermanischen. Festschrift für Heinrich Beck.* Ed. Heiko Uecker. Ergänzungsbände zum Reallexikon der Germanischen Altertumskunde 11. Berlin: De Gruyter, 1994. 173–96.

Heide, Eldar. "Auga til Egil: Ei nytolkning av ein tekststad i Egilssoga." *Arkiv för nordisk filologi* 115 (2000): 119–24.

Heinrichs, Anne. "Gunnhild Ǫzurardóttir und Egil Skalla-Grímsson im Kampf um Leben und Tod." In *Studien zur Isländersaga. Festschrift für Rolf Heller.* Ed. Heinrich Beck and Else Ebel. Ergänzungsbände zum Reallexikon der Germanischen Altertumskunde 24. Berlin: De Gruyter, 2000. 72–108.

Helgason, Jón. "Athuganir um nokkur handrit Egils sögu." In *Nordæla. Afmæliskveðja til Sigurðar Nordals sjötugs 14. september 1956*. Reykjavík: Helgafell, 1956. 110–48.

– "Observations on Some Manuscripts of *Egils saga*." Trans. Michael Chesnutt. *Opuscula* 12 (2005): 3–47.

– "Höfuðlausnarhjal." In *Einarsbók. Afmæliskveðja til Einars Ól. Sveinssonar 12. desember 1969*. Ed. Bjarni Guðnason, Halldór Halldórsson, and Jónas Kristjánsson. Reykjavík: Nokkrir vinir, 1969. 156–76.

Helgason, Jón Karl. "Rjóðum spjöll í dreyra: Óhugnaður, úrkast og erótík í Egils sögu." *Skáldskaparmál* 2 (1992): 60–76.

Heslop, K.S. "'Gab mir ein Gott zu sagen, was ich leide': *Sonatorrek* and the Myth of Skaldic Lyric." In *Old Norse Myths, Literature and Society. Proceedings of the 11th International Saga Conference 2–7 July 2000, University of Sydney.* Ed. Geraldine Barnes and Margaret Clunies Ross. Sydney, Australia: Centre for Medieval Studies, University of Sydney, 2000. 152–64.

Hines, John. "Egill's *Hǫfuðlausn* in Time and Place." *Saga-Book* 24.2–3 (1995): 83–104.

– "*Egils saga* and *Njáls saga*: Bibliographical Guides." In *Introductory Essays on Egils saga and Njáls saga*. Ed. John Hines and Desmond Slay. London: Viking Society for Northern Research, 1992. 140–51.

– "Kingship in *Egils saga*." In *Introductory Essays on Egils saga and Njáls saga*. Ed. John Hines and Desmond Slay. London: Viking Society for Northern Research, 1992. 15–32.

Holtsmark, Anne. "On the Werewolf Motif in *Egil's saga Skallagrímssonar*." *Scientia Islandica* 1 (1968): 7–9.

– "Skallagrims Heimamenn." *Maal og minne* 1971 (3–4): 97–105.

Hovstad, Johan. "Tradisjon og dikting i Egils saga." *Syn og Segn* 52.2 (1946): 83–96.

Ingvarsdóttir, Auður. "Hin 'upphaflega Landnáma' og innskotin. Hugmyndir Björns M. Ólsens um Egils sögu og Landnámu." *Þriðja íslenska söguþingið 18.-21. maí 2006*. Ed. Benedikt Eyþórsson and Hrafnkell Lárusson. Reykjavík: Sagnfræðingafélag Íslands, 2007. 344–52.

Jakobsen, Alfred. "Om parallellepisoder i Egils saga." *Edda* 5 (1985): 315–18.

Jakobsson, Ármann. "Á ég að gæta bróður míns? Innlifunin og Þórólfur Skalla-Grímsson." *Skíma* 28.2 (2005): 35–41.

– "Beast and Man: Realism and the Occult in *Egils saga*." *Scandinavian Studies* 83.1 (2011): 29–44.

– "*Egils saga* and Empathy: Emotions and Moral Issues in a Dysfunctional Saga Family." *Scandinavian Studies* 80.1 (2008): 1–18.

Jesch, Judith. "Skaldic verse in Scandinavian England." In *Vikings and the Danelaw: Select Papers from the Proceedings of the Thirteenth Viking Congress*. Ed. James Graham-Campbell, Richard Hall, Judith Jesch, and David N. Parsons. Oxford: Oxbow Books, 2001. 313–25.

Jessen, E. "Glaubwürdigkeit der Egils-Saga und anderer Isländer-Saga's." *Historiche Zeitschrift* 28.1 (1872): 61–100.

Jochumsson, Matthías. "Enn um Höfuðlausn Egils." *Óðinn* 9.6 (1913): 46–8.

Jones, Gwyn. "The Angry Old Men." *Scandinavian Studies* 37 (1965): 54–62.

– "Egill Skallagrímsson in England. Sir Israel Gollancz Memorial Lecture. Read 19 November 1952." *Proceedings of the British Academy* 38 (1952): 127–44.

Jónasson, Jakob. "Aftur í aldir." *Morgunblaðið* 1 April 1984: 26–9.

Jónsson, Finnur. "Egil Skallagrimsson og Erik Blodøkse. Hǫfuðlausn." In *Oversigt over det kgl. danske videnskabernes selskabs forhandlinger* 3 (1903): 295–312.

Jónsson, Jón. "Eiríkr blóðöx í Jórvík." *Arkiv för nordisk filologi* 33 (1917): 314–19.

– "Um Eirík blóðöx." *Tímarit Hins íslenska bókmenntafélags* 16 (1894): 176–203.

Karlsson, Stefán. "Af Agli í ellinni." In *Vöruvoð ofin Helga Þorlákssyni fimmtugum 8. ágúst 1995*. Ed. Sigurgeir Steingrímsson. Reykjavík: Menningar- og minningarsjóður Mette Magnussen, 1995. 70–2.

Kristjánsdóttir, Bergljót S. "Primum caput: Um höfuð Egils Skalla-Grímssonar, John frá Salisbury o.fl." *Skáldskaparmál* 4 (1997): 74–96.

Kristjánsson, Jónas. "Egilssaga og Konungasögur." In *Sjötíu ritgerðir helgaðar Jakobi Benediktssyni*. Vol. 2. Ed. Einar G. Pétursson and Jónas Kristjánsson. Reykjavík: Stofnun Árna Magnússonar, 1977. 449–72.

– "Er Egilssaga 'Norse'?" *Skáldskaparmál* 3 (1994): 216–31.

– "Kveðskapur Egils Skallagrímssonar." *Gripla* 17 (2006): 7–35.

Kennedy, John. "The goðar in *Egils saga Skalla-Grímssonar*." In *Words and Wordsmiths: A Volume for H.L. Rogers*. Sydney: University of Sydney, 1989. 70–6.

Kjeldsen, Axel Speed, and Michael Chesnutt. "De ældste pergamentfragmenter af Egils saga, efter forarbejder af Jón Helgason." *Opuscula* 12 (2005): 51–227. Bibliotheca Arnamagnæana 44.

Knirk, James E. "Runes from Trondheim and a Stanza by Egill Skalla-Grímsson." *Studien zum Altgermanischen: Festschrift für Heinrich Beck*. Ed. Heiko Uecker. Berlin and New York: Walter de Gruyter, 1994. 411–19.

Koht, Halvdan. "Egil Skallagrímsson – diktaren." *Menn i historia*. Oslo: Aschehoug, 1963. 1–13.

Koch, Ludovica. "Le Bouclier et la corne à bière. Étude sur la conception de la poésie et du poète chez Bragi Boddason et Egill Skallagrimsson." *Studi Nederlandesi-Studi Nordici* 22 (1979): 125–63.

Kress, Helga. "Karnivalið í kirkjugarðinum." In *Sturlaðar sögur sagðar Úlfari Bragasyni sextugum 22. apríl 2009*. Reykjavík: Menningar- og minningarsjóður Mette Magnussen, 2009. 54–6.

Kries, Susanne, and Thomas Krömmelbein. "'From the Hull of Laughter': Egill Skalla-Grímsson's 'Höfuðlausn' and its Epodium in Context." *Scandinavian Studies* 74 (2002): 111–36.

Krijn, Sophia A. "Nogle bemærkninger om Egils stil." *Edda* 27 (1927): 462–85.

Krömmelbein, Thomas, and Susanne Kries. "Context and Composition: Language as Art in Egill's *Hǫfuðlausn*." *Preprints of the 10th International Saga Conference, Trondheim, August 3–9, 1997*. Trondheim: Senter for Middelalderstudier, 1997. 369–79.

Larrington, Carolyne. "Egill's Longer Poems: *Arinbjarnarkviða* and *Sonatorrek*." Ed. John Hines and Desmond Slay. London: Viking Society for Northern Research, 1992. 49–63.

Laxness, Halldór. "Egill Skallagrímsson og sjónvarpið." In *Upphaf mannúðarstefnu. Ritgerðir*. Reykjavík: Helgafell, 1965. 116–21.

Lárusson, Ólafur. *Ætt Egils Halldórssonar og Egils saga*. Studia Islandica 2. Reykjavík: Sigurður Nordal, 1937.

Lie, Hallvard. "Egil Skallagrimsson's livsaften. Et semifilologisk kåseri." *Festskrift til Finn Hødnebø 29. desember 1989*. Oslo: Novus Forlag, 1989. 180–92.

– "Jorvikferden. Et vendepunkt i Egil Skallagrimssons liv." *Edda* 33 (1946): 145–248.

– "Skaldestil-studier." *Maal og minne* 1952: 1–92.

Louis-Jensen, Jonna. "Egill Skallagrimssons sidste strofe." *Strengleikar: slegnir Robert Cook 25. nóvember 1994*. Reykjavík: Menningar- og minningarsjóður Mette Magnussen, 1994. 40–2.

– "Heimskringla og Egils saga – samme forfatter." In *Studier i Nordisk 2006–2007*. Copenhagen: University of Copenhagen, Selskab for Nordisk filologi, 2009. 103–11.

Males, Mikael. "Egill och Kormákr – tradering och nydiktning." *Maal og minne* 2011 (1): 115–46.

Maurer, Konrad von. "Zwei Rechtsfälle in der Eigla." *Sitzungsber. d. philos. philol. u. hist. Cl. der k. b. Akad. der Wissensch.* Munich: Druck der Akademischen Buchdruckerei von F. Straub, 1895.

McDougall, Ian. "Discretion and Deceit: A Re-examination of a Military Stratagem in *Egils saga*." In *The Middle Ages in the North-West*. Ed. Tom Scott and Pat Starkey. Oxford: Leopard's Head Press in conjunction with Liverpool Centre for Medieval Studies, 1995. 109–42.

McTurk, Rory. "Lot's Wife, Agni Dagsson and Egill Skalla-Grímsson." In *Þjóðlíf og þjóðtrú: ritgerðir helgaðar Jóni Hnefli Aðalsteinssyni*. Reykjavík: Þjóðsaga, 1998. 215–31.

Meier, Marina. "Om et nyt forsøg på at løse Eigla-gåden." *Maal og minne* 1963 (3–4): 94–101.

Meulengracht-Sørensen, Preben. "Høvdingen fra Mammen og *Egill Skalla-Grímssons saga*. Nogle bemærkninger om arkæologi og sagaer." In *At fortælle Historien: Telling History. Studier i den gamle nordiske litteratur: Studies in Norse literature*. Udgivet i samarbejde med Sofie Meulengracht Sørensen. Trieste: Edizioni Parnaso, 2001. 169–78.

– "Starkaðr, Loki, and Egill Skallagrímsson." In *At fortælle Historien: Telling History. Studier i den gamle nordiske litteratur: Studies in Norse literature*. Udgivet i samarbejde med Sofie Meulengracht-Sørensen. Trieste: Edizioni Parnaso, 2001. 27–35.

– "Starkarðr, Loki og Egill Skallagrímsson." In *Sjötíu ritgerðir helgaðar Jakobi Benediktssyni 20. júlí 1977. Síðari hluti*. Reykjavík: Stofnun Árna Magnússonar, 1977. 759–68.

Misch, Georg. "Egill Skallagrimsson. Die Selbstdarstellung des Skalden." *Deutsche Vierteljahrsschrift für Literaturwissenschaft und Geistesgeschichte* 6 (1928): 199–241.

Mitchell, P.M. "*Höfuðlausn*: Erik's izzat." *Mediaeval Scandinavia* 5 (1972): 45–8.

Neckel, Gustav. "Anmälan. A. Bley: Eigla-studien. Gent 1909." *Arkiv för nordisk filologi* 27 (1911): 209–14.

– "Egill und der angelsächische einfluss." *Beiträge zur Eddaforschung mit Exkursen zur Heldensage*. Ed. Gustav Neckel. Dortmund: F.W. Ruhfus, 1908. 367–89.

Niedner, Felix. "Egils Hauptlösung." *Zeitschrift für Deutsches Altertum und Deutsche Literatur* 57 (1920): 97–122.

– "Egils Sonatorrek." *Zeitschrift für Deutsches Altertum und Deutsche Literatur* 59 (1922): 217–35.

Nordal, Guðrún. "*Ars metrica* and the Composition of *Egils saga*." In *Scandinavia and Christian Europe in the Middle Ages. Papers of the 12th International Saga Conference Bonn/Germany, 28th July – 2nd August 2003*. Ed. Rudolf Simek and Judith Meurer. Bonn: Universität Bonn, 2003. 179–86.

– "Egill, Snorri og höfundurinn." *Lesbók Morgunblaðsins* 21 Dec. 2002: 8–9.

Nordal, Sigurður. "Átrúnaður Egils Skallagrímssonar." *Skírnir* 98 (1924): 145–65.

– "Egils saga og Skáldatal." In *Afmæliskveðja til próf. dr. phil. Alexanders Jóhannessonar háskólarektors 15. júlí 1953*. Reykjavík: Helgafell, 1953. 180–3.

Nordland, Odd. *Höfuðlausn i Egils saga. Ein tradisjonskritisk studie*. Oslo: Det norske samlaget, 1956.

North, Richard. "The Pagan Inheritance of Egill's *Sonatorrek*." In *Atti del 12 Congresso Internazionale di Studi sull'Alto Medioevo, Spoleto 4–10 settembre 1988*. Spoleto: Presso la Sede del Centro Studi, 1990. 147–67.

Olsen, Magnus. "Bemerkninger til Egils större digte." *Arkiv för nordisk filologi* 35 (1919): 137–42.

– *Egils lausavísur, Höfuðlausn og Sonatorrek. Edda- og skaldekvad: forarbeider til kommentar.* Vol. 4. Oslo: Aschehoug, 1962.

– "Egils viser om Eirik Blodøks og Dronning Gunnhild." *Maal og minne* 1944 (3–4): 180–200.

Ó[la], Á[rni]. "Hvar fól Egill silfur Aðalsteins konungs?" *Lesbók Morgunblaðsins* 19 June 1932: 183–4.

Ólafsson, Karl Óskar. "Á þúsund ára fresti." In *Varði reistur Guðvarði Má Gunnlaugssyni fimmtugum 16. september 2006*. Reykjavík: Menningar- og minningarsjóður Mette Magnussen, 2006. 69–70.

Ólafsson, Ólafur M.. "Sonatorrek." *Andvari*. Nýr flokkur 10 (1968): 133–200.

Ólason, Vésteinn. "Er Snorri höfundur Egils sögu?" *Skírnir* 142 (1968): 48–67.

– "Jorvik Revisited – With Egil Skalla-Grimsson." *Northern Studies* 27 (1990): 64–76.

– "Jórvíkurför í Egils sögu: Búandmanni telft gegn konungi." *Andvari*. Nýr flokkur 33 (1991): 46–59.

Ólason, Vésteinn, and Örnólfur Thorsson. "Snorri og Egils saga – Um höfunda fornsagna." *Lesbók Morgunblaðsins* 1 Feb. 2003: 6–7.

Ólsen, Björn M. "Er Snorri Sturluson höfundur Egilssögu?" *Skírnir* 79 (1905): 363–8.

– "Kvæði Egils Skallagrímssonar gegn Egilssögu." *Tímarit Hins íslenzka bókmenntafélags* 18 (1897): 87–99.

– "Landnáma og Egils saga." *Aarbog for nord[isk] Oldkyndi[ghed] og Hist[orie]* (1904): 167–247.

– "Til versene i Egils saga." *Arkiv för nordisk filologi* 19 (1903): 99–133.

Óskarsson, Þórir. "Kollgáta í Eglu." In *Sólhvarfasumbl: saman borið handa Þorleifi Haukssyni fimmtugum*. Reykjavík: Menningar- og minningarsjóður Mette Magnussen, 1992. 71–2.

Pain, Stephanie. "Egil the Enigmatic." *New Scientist* 187.2517 (2005): 48–9.

Pálsson, Árni. "Sonatorrek." *Skírnir* 100 (1926): 153.
Pálsson, Einar. *Egils saga og Úlfar tveir.* Rætur íslenzkrar menningar 9. Reykjavík: Mímir, 1990.
Pálsson, Heimir. "Óðinn, Þór og Egill." *Skírnir* 181.1 (2007): 96–121.
Pálsson, Hermann. "Bitið á barka." *Lesbók Morgunblaðsins* 16 May 1992: 11.
– "The Borg Connexion: Notes on *Bjarnar saga, Egla, Gunnlaugs saga,* and *Laxdœla.*" *Leeds Studies in English* New Series 20 (1989): 47–64.
– "Egils saga og fornir járnhausar." *Lesbók Morgunblaðsins* 17 June 1995: 9.
– "Fornfræði Egils sögu." *Skírnir* 168.1 (1994): 37–72.
– "Um kærleikann í Egils sögu." In *Afmælisrit til dr. phil. Steingríms J. Þorsteinssonar prófessors 2. júlí 1971 frá nemendum hans.* Ed. Aðalgeir Kristjánsson, Bjarni Guðnason, Jón Samsonarson, Ólafur Pálmason and Sveinn Skorri Höskuldsson. Reykjavík: Leiftur, 1971. 59–62.
– "Ættarmót með Eglu og öðrum skrám." In *Sagnaþing helgað Jónasi Kristjánssyni sjötugum 10. apríl 1994. Síðari hluti.* Ed. Gísli Sigurðsson, Guðrún Kvaran, and Sigurgeir Steingrímsson. Reykjavík: Hið íslenska bókmenntafélag, 1994. 423–32.
– "Tveir þættir um Egils sögu." *Andvari.* Nýr flokkur 21 (1979): 80–4.
– "Egils saga Skallagrímssonar." *Dictionary of the Middle Ages.* Vol. 4. Ed. Joseph R. Strayer. New York: Charles Scribner's Sons, 1984. 402–3.
Perkins, R.M. "Egils saga Skalla-Grímssonar." *Reallexikon der Germanischen Altertumskunde.* Vol. 6. Berlin: Walter de Gruyter, 1986. 469–75.
Poole, Russell. "Variants and Variability in the Text of Egill's *Höfuðlausn.*" In *The Politics of Editing Medieval Texts. Papers Given at the Twenty-Seventh Annual Conference on Editorial Problems University of Toronto 1–2 November 1991.* Ed. Roberta Frank. New York: AMS Press, 1993. 65–105.
– "'Non enim possum plorare nec lamenta fundere': *Sonatorrek* in a Tenth-Century Context." In *Laments for the Lost: Medieval Mourning and Elegy.* Ed. Jane Tolmie and Jane Toswell. Turnhout: Brepols, 2010. 173–200.
Ralph, Bo. "Om tilkomsten av Sonatorrek." *Arkiv för nordisk filologi* 91 (1976): 153–65.
Reichardt, Konstantin. "Die Entstehungsgeschichte von Egils Höfuðlausn." *Zeitschrift für deutsches Altertum und deutsche Literatur* 66 (1929): 267–72.
Salberger, Evert. "Egils *sǫl*-replik före Sonatorrek." *Gardar* 18 (1987): 19–23.
– "Metriskt till Egils *sǫl*-replik." *Gardar* 29 (1998): 33–6.
Sattler, E. "Das Märchen vom 'Retter in der Not' in Chrestien's 'Yvain' und in der Egilssaga." *Germanisch-Romanische Monatsschrift* 3 (1911): 669–71.
Sayers, William. "Poetry and Social Agency in *Egils saga Skalla-Grímssonar.*" *Scripta Islandica* 46 (1995): 29–62.
Sigurðsson, Gísli. "Æskuvísa Egils á vappi í Vesturheimi." In *Strengleikar slegnir Robert Cook 25. nóvember 1994.* Reykjavík: Menningar- og minningarsjóður Mette Magnussen, 1994. 20–1.

Sigurðsson, Jón. "'Nú er hér kominn Egill. Hefir hann ekki leitað brotthlaups.' Tilraun til að greina meginstef í *Egilssögu*." *Skírnir* 174.2 (2000): 321–48.

Sigurjónsson, Arnór. "Arghyrnu lát árna." *Andvari*. Nýr flokkur 4.3 (1962): 340–7.

– "Trolldómur Egils Skallagrímssonar." *Andvari*. Nýr flokkur 9.2 (1967): 234–9.

Storm, Gustav. "Kylvingerne i Egilssaga." In *Akademiske afhandlinger til Professor dr. Sophus Bugge ved hans 25aars jubilæum den 2den mai 1889*. Kristiania: ALB Cammermeyer, 1889: 73–9.

Sørensen, Jan Sand. "Komposition og værdiunivers i Egils saga." *Gripla* 4 (1980): 260–72.

Taylor, Marvin. "Rúmr inngangs, en þrǫngr brottfarar." *Arkiv för nordisk filologi* 112 (1997): 67–95.

Thorlacius, Örnólfur. "Hjálmaklettur Egils." *Náttúrufræðingurinn* 66.3–4 (1997): 133–8.

Toorn, M.C. van den. "Egils Sonatorrek als dichterische Leistung." *Zeitschrift für deutsche Philologie* 77 (1958): 46–59.

– *Zur Verfasserfrage der Egilssaga Skallagrímssonar.* Cologne: Böhlau, 1959.

Tómasson, Sverrir. "Á konungs vörnum." In *Dagamunur: gerður Árna Björnssyni sextugum 16. janúar 1992*. Reykjavík: Menningar- og minningarsjóður Mette Magnussen. 103–5.

– "Bezta var kvæðit fram flutt." In *Steffánsfærsla: fengin Stefáni Karlssyni fimmtugum.* Reykjavík: [Árnastofnun], 1978. 68–9.

Tulinius, Torfi H. "An Attempt at Application: Interpreting *Egils saga*." In *The Matter of the North. The Rise of Literary Fiction in Thirteenth Century Iceland.* Trans. Randi C. Eldevik. The Viking Collection. Studies in Nothern Civilization. Odense: Odense University Press. 2002. 234–88.

– "The Conversion of Sonatorrek." In *Analecta Septentrionalia: Beiträge zur nordgermanischen Kultur- und Literaturgeschichte*. Ed. W. Heizmann, K. Böldl, and H. Beck. Ergänzungsbände zum Reallexikon der Germanischen Altertumskundi 65. Berlin: Walter de Gruyter, 2009. 707–14.

– "Dularfullir Katlar eða Hví var katli sökkt í Krumskeldu?" In *Bókahnútur brugðinn Ólöfu Benediktsdóttur fimmtugri 4. febrúar 1997*. Ed. Rósa Þorsteinsdóttir and Sigurgeir Steingrímsson. Reykjavík: Menningar- og minningarsjóður Mette Magnussen, 1997. 103–6.

– "Egla og Biblían." In *Milli himins og jarðar. Maður, guð og menning í hnotskurn hugvísinda. Erindi flutt á hugvísindaþingi guðfræðideildar og heimspekideildar 18. og 19. okt. 1996*. Ed. Anna Agnarsdóttir, Pétur Pétursson, and Torfi H. Tulinius. Reykjavík: Háskólaútgáfan, 1997. 125–36.

– "'*Egils saga*' and the Novel." In *Snorri Sturluson and the roots of Nordic literature: Papers of the International Conference held at "St. Kliment Ohridski" University of Sofia (October 14–16, 2002)*. Sofia: University of Sofia, 2004. 117–28.

– "'... Er þess eigi getið ...' Um stílbragð hjá Snorra Sturlusyni, Egluhöfundi og tveimur til viðbótar." In *Vöruvoð ofin Helga Þorlákssyni fimmtugum 8. ágúst 1995*. Ed. Sigurgeir Steingrímsson. Reykjavík: Menningar- og minningarsjóður Mette Magnussen, 1995. 84–7.

– "Framliðnir feður: Um forneskju og frásagnarlist í Eyrbyggju, Eglu og Grettlu." In *Heiðin minni. Greinar um fornar bókmenntir*. Ed. Haraldur Bessason and Baldur Hafstað. Reykjavík: Heimskringla, Háskólaforlag Máls og menningar, 1999. 283–316.

– "Hjálpræði frá Egilsdætrum." In *Þorlákstíðir sungnar Ásdísi Egilsdóttur fimmtugri 26. október 1996*. Ed. Guðvarður Már Gunnlaugsson and Margrét Eggertsdóttir. Reykjavík: Menningar- og minningarsjóður Mette Magnussen, 1996. 68–71.

– "'Mun konungi eg þykja ekki orðsnjallur.' Um margræðni, textatengsl og dulda merkingu í Egils sögu." *Skírnir* 168.1 (1994): 109–33.

– "Political Exegesis or Personal Expression? The Problem of *Egils saga*." In *Neue Ansätze in der Mittelalterphilologie – Nye veier i middelalderfilologien: Akten der skandinavistischen Arbeitstagung in Münster vom 24. bis 26. Oktober 2002*. Ed. Susanne Kramarz-Bein. Frankfurt am Main: Peter Lang, 2005. 131–40.

– "La saga d'Egill et l'histoire du roman." *L'Atelier du roman* 3 (1994): 141–53.

– "Le statut théologique d'Egill Skalla-Grímsson." In *Hugur: Mélanges d'histoire, de littérature et de mythologie offerts à Régis Boyer pour son soixante-cinquième anniversaire*. Ed. Claude Lecouteux and d'Olivier Gouchet. Paris: Presses de l'Université de Paris-Sorbonne, 1997. 279–88.

– *Skáldið í skriftinni. Snorri Sturluson og Egils saga*. Reykjavík: Hið íslenska bókmenntafélag, ReykjavíkurAkademían, 2004.

– "Tentative d'application: une interpretation d'Egils saga." In *La Matière du Nord: Sagas Legendaires et fiction dans la litterature islandaise en prose du XIIIe siècle*. Paris: Presses de l'Université de Paris-Sorbonne, 1995. 211–59.

– "The Purloined Shield or *Egils saga Skalla-Grímssonar* as a Contemporary Saga." In *Samtíðarsögur. Níunda alþjóðlega fornsagnaþingið. Akureyri 31.7. til 6.8. 1994*. Akureyri: n.p., 1994. 2, 758–69.

– "'*Thykir mér gódh sonareign í thér.*' Pères, revenants et fantastique dans trois sagas islandaises." *Revue des langues romanes. Merveilleux et fantastique au maoyen age* 2 (1997): 145–62.

– "Towards a Poetics of the Sagas of Icelanders: The Examples of *Hallfreðar saga*, *Egils saga*, and *Grettis saga*." In *Arbeiten zur Skandinavistik 14. Arbeitstagung der deutschsprachigen Skandinavistik, 1.-5.9.1999 in München*. Ed. Annegret Heitmann. New York: P. Lang, 2001. 45–59.

Turville-Petre, Gabriel. "The Sonatorrek." In *Iceland and the Mediaeval World: Studies in Honour of Ian Maxwell*. Ed. G. Turville-Petre and J.S. Martin. Clayton: Organising Committee for Publishing a Volume in Honour of Professor Maxwell, 1974. 33–55.

Unwerth, Wolf von. "Excurs III. Zu Egills Sonatorrek." *Untersuchungen über Totenkult und Óđinnverehrung bei Nordgermanen und Lappen.* Breslau: Verlag von M. & H. Marcus, 1911. 173–5.

Vogt, Walther Heinrich. "Egils Hauptelösung." *Zeitschrift für deutsches Altertum und deutsche Literatur* 51 (1909): 379–415.

– "Von Bragi zu Egil. Ein Versuch zur Geschichte des skaldischen Preisliedes." *Deutche Islandsforschung* 1 (1930): 170–209.

– *Zur Komposition der Egils saga. Kpp. I–LXVI.* Götlitz: Hoffmann & Reiber, 1909.

Vries, Jan de. "Der chronologie der Egils saga." *De Wikingen in de Lage Landen bij de Zee.* Haarlem: H.D. Tjeenk Willink & Zoon, 1923. 359–64.

Wadstein, Elis. "Bidrag till tolkning ock belysning av skalde- ock edda-dikter. IV. Till Hǫfođlausn." *Arkiv för nordisk filologi* 13.9 (1897): 14–29.

Weinstein, P. "Palaeopathology by Proxy: the case of Egil's Bones." *Journal of Archaeological Science* 32 (2005): 1077–82.

West, Ralph. "Snorri Sturluson and *Egils saga*: Statistics of Style." *Scandinavian Studies* 52 (1980): 163–93.

Whistler, Charles Watts. "Brunanburh and Vinheith in Ingulf's Chronicle and Egil's Saga." *Saga-Book of the Viking Society for Northern Research* 6 (1908–9): 59–67.

Whiting, Bartlett Jere. "Óhthere (Óttar) and Egils saga." *Philological Quarterly* 24 (1945): 218–26.

Wieselgren, Per. "Die Höfuðlausn als Aðalsteinsdrápa." *Zeitschrift für deutsches Altertum und deutsche Literatur* 67 (1930): 122–7.

– *Författarskapet till Eigla.* Lund: Carl Blom, 1927.

Wood, Cecil. "The Skald's Bid for a Hearing." *Journal of English and German Philology* 59.2 (1960): 240–54.

Yershova, Yelena Sesselja Helgadóttir. "Egill Skalla-Grímsson: A Viking Poet as a Child and an Old Man." In *Youth and Age in the Medieval North.* Ed. Shannon Lewis-Simpson. Leiden: Brill, 2008. 285–304.

Þorvaldsson, Eysteinn. "Hugleiðingar um ástarsögu Egils." *Mímir* 7.2 (1968): 20–4.

Þórarinsdóttir, Brynhildur. "Hirðin og hallærisplanið. Forgelgjur og unglingar í Eglu." In *Miðaldabörn.* Ed. Ármann Jakobsson and Torfi H. Tulinius. Reykjavík: Hugvísindastofnun Háskóla Íslands, 2005. 113–36.

Þórðarson, Matthías. "Um dauða Skalla-Gríms og hversu hann var heygður." In *Sagastudier: Af festskrift til Finnur Jónsson den 29. maj 1928.* Copenhagen: Levin & Munksgaard, 1928. 95–112.

Contributors

Jane Appleton is a writer, translator, and editor. She has published travel writing and translations of contemporary Icelandic fiction and poetry, and is editor for the Fish Industry Center at Marel, Iceland.

Margaret Clunies Ross is an Emeritus Professor of English at the University of Sydney and Honorary Research Associate of the Department of Anglo-Saxon, Norse and Celtic at the University of Cambridge. She is one of the General Editors of the project Skaldic Poetry of the Scandinavian Middle Ages (for which she is editing the poetry attributed to Egill Skallagrímsson) and editor of the Research and Reception strand of the project Pre-Christian Religions of the North. Her main research interests are in Old Norse poetry, poetics, mythology, and saga literature.

Laurence de Looze is a Professor of Comparative Literature at the University of Western Ontario. He publishes on a wide range of medieval and more modern literatures in English, Icelandic, French, and Spanish. His books include: *Pseudo-Autobiography in the Fourteenth Century: Juan Ruiz, Guillaume de Machaut, Jean Froissart, and Geoffrey Chaucer* (1997); *Manuscript Diversity, Meaning, and Variance in Juan Manuel's El conde Lucanor* (2006); and *The Letter and the Cosmos: How the Alphabet Has Shaped the Western View of the World* (forthcoming).

Oren Falk is Associate Professor of History and Medieval Studies at Cornell University. He studies medieval cultural history, particularly as revealed through Icelandic sagas, and has published on the history of violence, medieval political imaginaries, and various absences – of wives, volcanoes, beards, heirs apparent, and more – in medieval texts. He is the author, most recently, of *The Bare Sarked Warrior: A Brief Cultural History of Battlefield Exposure* (2015).

Alison Finlay is Professor of Medieval English and Icelandic Literature at Birkbeck, University of London. She writes on poets' sagas, kings' sagas, and skaldic verse, and has just finished, with Anthony Faulkes, a new translation of *Heimskringla*, two volumes of which have already been published (2011 and 2014). In 2013 she gave the Dorothea Coke Memorial Lecture entitled "History and Fiction in the Kings' Sagas: The Case of Haraldr harðráði," which will be published in *Saga-Book* in 2015.

Jón Karl Helgason is a professor in the Department of Icelandic and Comparative Cultural Studies at the University of Iceland. His books include *Hetjan og höfundurinn* (1998), *The Rewriting of Njáls Saga* (1999), *Mynd af Ragnari í Smára* (2010), and *Ódáinsakur: Helgifesta þjóðardýrlinga* (2013).

Ármann Jakobsson is professor in Early Icelandic Literature at the University of Iceland. He has authored *Í leit að konungi* (1997), *Staður í nýjum heimi* (2002), *Tolkien og Hringurinn* (2003), *Illa fenginn mjöður* (2009), *Nine Saga Studies* (2013), *Íslendingaþættir: saga hugmyndar* (2014), and *A Sense of Belonging* (2014), edited Morkinskinna for the Ízlenzk fornrit series (23 and 24) (2011), and is the author of three novels (*Vonarstræti*, 2008, *Glæsir*, 2011, and *Síðasti galdrameistarinn*, 2014).

Guðrún Nordal is the director of the Árni Magnússon Institute for Icelandic Studies and a professor in the Department of Icelandic and Comparative Cultural Studies at the University of Iceland. Her books include *Ethics and Action in Thirteenth-century Iceland* (1998) and *Tools of Literacy: The Role of Skaldic Verse in Icelandic Textual Culture of the 12th and 13th Centuries* (2000). She is one of the editors of Skaldic Poetry of the Scandinavian Middle Ages (2007–).

Svanhildur Óskarsdóttir is Associate Research Professor and Head of the Manuscript department at the Árni Magnússon Institute for Icelandic studies in Reykjavík, Iceland. Her published work includes articles on medieval Bible translations and the development of universal history in Iceland, as well as philological studies and textual criticism, and she is the co-editor of *66 Manuscripts from the Arnamagnæan Collection* (2015).

Katelin Marit Parsons is currently completing a PhD in Icelandic Literature at the University of Iceland. She holds a Master's degree in Translation Studies from the same university.

Russell Poole is a Distinguished University Professor emeritus of The University of Western Ontario and a Fellow of the Royal Society of Canada and the

Royal Society of New Zealand. His books include *Viking Poems on War and Peace* (1991), *Old English Wisdom Poetry* (1998), *Skaldsagas: Text, Vocation, and Desire in the Icelandic Sagas of Poets* (edited, 2000), and, with Antonina Harbus, *Verbal Encounters: Anglo-Saxon and Old Norse Studies for Roberta Frank* (co-edited, 2004). He is currently Editor in Chief of the journal *Viking and Medieval Scandinavia.*

Timothy R. Tangherlini is a professor in the Scandinavian Section at UCLA. His work currently focuses on developing computational methods for addressing problems in the study of folklore and Old Norse–Icelandic literature. Recent books include *Danish Folktales, Legends, and Other Stories* (2013), *Interpreting Legend* (2015), and the edited collections *Nordic Mythologies* (2015) and *News from Other Worlds: Studies in Nordic Folklore, Mythology and Culture* (2012).

Torfi H. Tulinius is a professor in the Department of Icelandic and Comparative Cultural Studies at the University of Iceland. His books include *The Matter of the North: The Rise of Literary Fiction in 13th Century Iceland* (2002) and *The Enigma of Egill: The Saga, the Viking Poet, and Snorri Sturluson* (2014).

Álfdís Þorleifsdóttir has a BA from the University of Iceland. She has been taking courses for a Master's degree at the same university and the University of Uppsala and is currently working at the Embassy of Iceland in Stockholm.

Index

Toronto Old Norse and Icelandic Series

General Editor
Andy Orchard

Editorial Board
Robert E. Bjork
Roberta Frank

1 *Einarr Skulason's* Geisli*: A Critical Edition* edited and translated by Martin Chase
2 *Anglo-Saxon England in Icelandic Medieval Texts* by Magnus Fjalldal
3 *Sanctity in the North: Saints, Lives, and Cults in Medieval Scandinavia* edited by Thomas DuBois
4 *Snorri Sturluson and the* Edda*: The Conversion of Cultural Capital in Medieval Scandinavia* by Kevin J. Wanner
5 *Myths, Legends, and Heroes: Essays on Old Norse and Old English Literature in Honour of John McKinnell* edited by Daniel Anlezark
6 *The Legends of the Saints in Old Norse–Icelandic Prose* by Kirsten Wolf
7 *Essays on Eddic Poetry* by John McKinnell
8 *Into the Ocean: Vikings, Irish, and Environmental Change in Iceland and the North* by Kristjan Ahronson
9 *Egil, the Viking Poet: New Approaches to* Egil's Saga edited by Laurence de Looze, Jón Karl Helgason, Russell Poole, and Torfi H. Tulinius